A Student's Writing Guide

Are you struggling to meet your coursework deadlines? Finding it hard to get to grips with your essay topics? Does your writing sometimes lack structure and style? Would you like to improve your grades? This text covers everything a student needs to know about writing essays and papers in the humanities and social sciences. Starting from the common difficulties students face, it gives practical examples of all the stages necessary to produce a good piece of academic work:

- interpreting assignment topics
- drawing on your own experience and background
- reading analytically and taking efficient notes
- developing your argument through introductions, middles and conclusions
- evaluating and using online resources
- understanding the conventions of academic culture
- honing your ideas into clear, vigorous English.

This book will provide you with all the tools and insights you need to write confident, convincing essays and coursework papers.

GORDON TAYLOR is Honorary Research Associate at Monash University; before his retirement he was Associate Professor and Director of the Language and Learning Unit in the Faculty of Arts there. He was a pioneer in the development of content- and discipline-specific writing programmes for students in higher education. His many publications include *The Student's Writing Guide for the Arts and Social Sciences* (1989).

A Student's Writing Guide

How to Plan and Write Successful Essays

GORDON TAYLOR

CAMBRIDGE
UNIVERSITY PRESS

CAMBRIDGE UNIVERSITY PRESS
Cambridge, New York, Melbourne, Madrid, Cape Town, Singapore, São Paulo, Delhi

Cambridge University Press
The Edinburgh Building, Cambridge CB2 8RU, UK

Published in the United States of America by Cambridge University Press, New York

www.cambridge.org
Information on this title: www.cambridge.org/9780521729796

The Student's Writing Guide for the Arts and Social Sciences by Gordon Taylor was originally published in 1989 and was reprinted six times.
A Student's Writing Guide: How to Plan and Write Successful Essays by Gordon Taylor succeeds and replaces the above work.

First published 2009

Printed in the United Kingdom at the University Press, Cambridge

A catalogue record for this publication is available from the British Library

Library of Congress Cataloguing in Publication data

Taylor, Gordon, 1941–
A Student's Writing Guide: how to plan and write successful essays / Gordon Taylor.
    p. cm.
Rev. ed. of: The student's writing guide for the arts and social sciences, 1989.
Includes bibliographical references and index.
ISBN 978-0-521-72979-6 (alk. paper)
1. English language – Rhetoric – Handbooks, manuals, etc.   2. Report writing – Handbooks, manuals, etc.   I. Taylor, Gordon. Student's writing guide for the arts and social sciences.   II. Title.
PE1478.T37   2009
808′.042071 – dc22   2008055940

ISBN 978-0-521-72979-6 paperback

For Kasonde, Susan *and* Jeremy

Contents

Preface

When the first edition of this book was published I believed that it could and should have a fairly limited life. This belief was founded on the idea that, such is the closeness of language, thought and subject matter, the future of such books would be based on the disciplines of knowledge in the humanities and social sciences and that, consequently, the best people to write such a text were those who knew the rhetoric of their own disciplines more intimately than a generalist ever could. The teaching of a discipline, I have long held, should include as an inalienable component the teaching of how to write in that discipline, just as the Roman scholar–statesman Cicero had inveighed in his *De Oratore* against 'that absurd, needless and deplorable conception, that one set of persons should teach us to think, and another teach us to speak'.

To some extent this has come to pass – but only to some extent. There are now student manuals on how to write in some disciplines, particularly history, English literature, psychology, philosophy and sociology. What I did not foresee is the extent to which many of the old disciplinary boundaries have begun to blur, and the extent to which new inter-disciplinary 'studies' subjects have come to characterise the offerings of arts and social science faculties. Much in the climate of thought (and rhetoric) has changed. As a result, there still seems to be a good case for a general book such as this one, in which I have taken the opportunity to engage with these new developments.

Moreover, many other things have moved on. The kinds of essay topic now being set are often rather different from those that used to be the staple in many courses; the kinds of tasks have changed – particularly the opportunity now being given to undergraduate and course-work graduate students to devise and write research papers; and, of course, there are many new problems as well as advantages posed by the ubiquitous use of the computer/word-processor and the internet.

Even so, there would probably have been no second edition had it not been for a few terriers at my heels. Andrew Winnard of Cambridge University Press was a terrier with longer staying power than is usually found, ably abetted by colleagues at Monash University, Tim Moore and David Garrioch, whose encouragement and continuing assistance have been crucial. In getting up to speed with the more recent kinds of essay topics and many other things, I would have languished without the immense assistance of Steve Price, Matthew Piscioneri, Andrew Johnson and Jim Hlavac. To those many academics whose essay topics I have used for illustrative purposes I wish here to record my indebtedness. There are many books on the history of Jews, Muslims and Christians in mediaeval Spain (see chapter 3), but it was Constant Mews who pointed me to and lent me a more suitable text for my purpose, Maurice Glick on *Convivencia*. To Keith Allan, Marko Pavlyshyn and the School of Languages, Cultures and Linguistics at Monash University I owe a great debt for smoothing my path. Finally, Kate Brett, commissioning editor at Cambridge University Press, has been my constant guide for the life of this project.

Much of the emphasis in this book (as it was in the first edition) is on what writers (both you the student and the writers of the sources you use) DO with their language. Your attention is drawn to this throughout the text by the use of SMALL CAPITALS.

Preface to the original 1989 edition of *The Student's Writing Guide for the Arts and Social Sciences*

This book has grown out of a writing course I have taught for some years to students of the arts and social sciences. In both I have tried to emphasise the close connections between writing in these disciplines and grappling with the problems of knowledge and understanding they present. Writing is not merely a skill we employ to record our knowledge, but the very moment at which we confront what learning and understanding are all about. So, while the reader will surely find plenty of guidance on the practical issues that arise in writing an academic essay, a search in these pages for simplified techniques that side-step the very taxing work of coming to terms with knowledge and method in these disciplines will be fruitless. My project has been to clear paths, not to indicate short cuts.

It has been my experience that many students' writing problems arise from uncertainty about what it is they are trying to say and what it is they have to do. So far as is possible in a general work of this kind, I have attempted to establish, in a variety of representative disciplines, some of the connections between issues of content and the forms of language in which the content can be realised. I am conscious that there are arts and social science disciplines which have not received extended treatment in the examples. But I trust that in concentrating attention on some of the most important things that we *do* with language in academic studies I have been able to direct readers to the kind of thing to look for in the particular disciplines they are studying.

The book is divided into three parts. I suggest the chapters of Parts I and II be read through at least once in the order presented. In this way the student will get a general idea of how to approach the writing of an academic essay. Not everybody approaches writing and learning in quite the same fashion, so it is important that the suggestions in Parts I and II be interpreted in a way that works best for the individual reader. The chapters of Part III contain in many instances extensions of themes introduced earlier, but they can also be read as more or less self-contained introductions to particular problems in the use of language. For the most part, grammatical and other details of language use are dealt with not in the manner of the conventional guides to usage but as they arise in those contexts of meaning we concentrate on as we write. It will therefore be necessary to make good use of the index. Part III is not a comprehensive guide to the language of academic discourse. I have chosen to treat only those features of language which students often question me about, those which in my estimation cause most trouble, and those which (spelling apart) tutors most regularly draw attention to in their marking of essays.

The book has been some time in the gestation. To John Clanchy, Brigid Ballard and Elaine Barry I owe many thanks for their encouragement and for commenting on drafts which they have now probably forgotten. I. W. Mabbett helped me greatly to clarify my thinking on some of the material in chapter 3, and the readers of the Cambridge University Press have made this a better book than it would otherwise have been. My students have contributed much: not only have they let me use their work, they have pushed me to understand certain things about writing I would never have gleaned elsewhere. But it is on the person who, as the psalmist says, can 'alway keep judgement' and who has believed in this book when I didn't myself that I have depended most – my wife Angela.

Sources of extracts used in the text

Dwight Bolinger, *Language – the Loaded Weapon*. London and New York: Longman, 1980.

R. N. Campbell and R. J. Wales, 'Comparative structures in English'. *Journal of Linguistics*, 5:2 (1969), pp. 215–51.

E. H. Carr, *What is History?* Harmondsworth: Penguin, 1964.

Manning Clark, *A Discovery of Australia*. The Boyer Lectures. Sydney: Australian Broadcasting Corporation, 1976.

A. C. Ewing, *A Short Commentary on Kant's 'Critique of Pure Reason'*. Chicago: University of Chicago Press, 1938.

Thomas F. Glick, '*Convivencia*: an introductory note'. In Vivian B. Mann, Thomas F. Glick and Jerrilynn D. Dodds (eds.) *Convivencia: Jews, Muslims, and Christians in Medieval Spain*. New York: George Braziller Inc., 1992, 2007.

Sharon E. Hutchinson, *Nuer Dilemmas: Coping with Money, Wars and the State*. Berkeley and Los Angeles: University of California Press, 1996.

Immanuel Kant, *Critique of Pure Reason*, trans. Norman Kemp Smith. New York: St Martin's Press, 1965.

F. R. Karl and L. Davies (eds.) *The Collected Letters of Joseph Conrad*, vol. I. Cambridge: Cambridge University Press, 1983.

Norman Kemp Smith, *A Commentary to Kant's 'Critique of Pure Reason'*, 2nd edn. New York: Humanities Press, 1962.

F. R. Leavis, 'Two cultures? The significance of Lord Snow'. In *Nor Shall My Sword: Discourses on Pluralism, Compassion and Social Hope*. London: Chatto and Windus, 1972.

James Luchte, *Kant's Critique of Pure Reason: a Reader's Guide*. London and New York: Continuum, 2007.

Walter Nash, *Designs in Prose*. London: Longman, 1980.

A. R. Radcliffe-Brown and D. Forde (eds.) *African Systems of Kinship and Marriage*. London: Oxford University Press, 1950.

W. G. Runciman, 'What is structuralism?' In Alan Ryan (ed.) *The Philosophy of Social Explanation*. London: Oxford University Press, 1973.

George H. Sabine, *A History of Political Theory*, 3rd edn. London: George G. Harrap, 1963.

John B. Whittow, *The Penguin Dictionary of Physical Geography*. London: A. Lane, 1984.

John M. Wilding, *Perception, From Sense to Object*. London: Hutchinson, 1982.

Introduction

How do I know what I think till I see what I say.

E. M. Forster

How do I know what I'll say till I see what I think.

Anon.

This chapter is designed to help you think about how you fit in to the broad culture of academe and the kind of writing it asks for. It is about

- how to avoid procrastinating and how to discover a real desire or 'itch' to write

- how to gain a sense of confidence that you are making tangible progress with each piece of work you begin

- how to value your beliefs, prejudices, experiences and past learning as a springboard for producing considered, well-argued and adequately researched judgements

- how to relate in writing and in person with your audience – the tutors who examine your work, their expectations, academic traditions and foibles

- how, despite the difficulties, you can come to really enjoy using language to articulate your thoughts and ideas.

1   The main elements in academic writing

If we are to write well we need to know (as well as we can) what we are talking about. In order to find out what, precisely, we are talking about we need to write. Pushing ourselves to write will often reveal that we know more about a subject than we at first supposed; it should just as often reveal large gaps in our understanding of matters we thought ourselves fairly sure of. In writing we bring knowledge into being, we record and preserve it. Writing is the seed, the fruit and the pickle of our understanding.

Most people in the English-speaking world used to think that the student's and scholar's mind is an empty bucket to be filled by books, lectures and tutorials. Nowadays neuroscientists and psychologists tell us that the brain doesn't work in this passive, accepting manner. On the contrary, to learn and to write is, first, to make sense for ourselves of our new experience in terms of our old. So you need to be aware at the outset that, even to subjects you have never studied before, you can bring certain preconceptions, even prejudices, a certain amount of disjointed knowledge, and a certain facility with language – all of which can get you started. The most baffling of essay topics can soon yield some meaning if you take the initiative and begin to ASK QUESTIONS – of yourself, of the essay topic, of your books and lectures, of the school or department for whom you are writing the essay. To think of yourself as an active enquirer, rather than as a mere receptacle of ideas and knowledge or as a passive medium by which they are transmitted from your books to your essays, is essential to good essay-writing. Good academic writing actually *creates* new knowledge and new meaning.

Now there is no single *technique* by which this can be achieved. Rather, there seem to be four elements whose relationships with one another need to be balanced: the writer, the object of the analysis or discussion (the content), the reader, and the formal properties of the language itself. Not everybody will balance these elements in quite the same way; and this is as it should be, since there is no such thing as a uniform, ideal academic English. Getting the balance right will depend partly on how you, the writer, respond in particular circumstances and partly on those traditions of expression and scholarship which grow up within certain disciplines, schools of thought within disciplines, and within particular college and university departments.

These four elements of the writing situation – writer, subject matter, reader and the forms of language – are reflected in four main characteristics of a piece of written language itself. They must all be handled together in the act of writing. Their competing claims to attention are resolved in the choice of one word in preference to another, in the structuring of a sentence, in the placing of an emphasis in the paragraph, in the confidence with which you argue your case, and so on. The four characteristics are these:

- Your own point of view must emerge, not as a mere opinion but as a *justified judgement*.

- You need to treat your subject matter as comprehensively and as precisely as the essay topic demands. From the range of information and ideas found in your reading you need to create a unified view. You must read carefully and do your best to make your language clarify the information and ideas you find in your books.

- You must present your work in the appropriate fashion for academic readers. This means that you will have to learn certain *conventions* of academic writing which are, at times, quite different from those you may be used to, or those you will find in non-academic contexts.

- Finally, the text of your essay needs to forge a coherent unity from the many diverse elements of language and thought that go to make it. It is in many of the details of your text that your purpose is realised. An essay is not merely a vehicle for ideas, but is itself (whatever the discipline) a piece of literature.

It is best to conceive of essay-writing as entering into a debate. You need to work out what your own answer to the essay question might be. You need to debate it with the books and other sources of information and ideas you use. And then you need to convey the results of this engagement clearly to your reader, bearing in mind that the reader – because of what he or she already knows – needs to be convinced that your own answer is a reasonable one. Fundamental to this whole process is your use of language. This is the main evidence your tutors have to go on in making their assessment of your essay – just as you have mainly the evidence of language in your books to judge the usefulness and value of their authors' work to you.

The aim of this book is to show you how to fit together the elements introduced above, and to help you participate successfully in written academic debate. But first we shall examine each of our elements separately in a little more detail, beginning with that bane of all writers' lives – 'writer's block'.

2   You and your writing task

For most people writing is an extremely difficult task if they are trying to grapple in their language with new ideas and new ways of looking at them. Sitting down to write can be an agonising experience, which doesn't necessarily get easier with the passage of time and the accumulation of experience. For this reason you need to reflect upon and analyse your own reactions to the task of writing. That is to say, the task will become more manageable if you learn how to cope with your own particular ways of avoiding or putting off the moment when you start writing.

First of all, it is as well to be aware that this fear of writing is very widespread, and not only amongst students. The novelist Joseph Conrad describes his fear and lack of confidence in quite harrowing terms:

> I am not more vile than my neighbours but this disbelief in oneself is like a taint that spreads on everything one comes in contact with; on men, on things – on the very air one breathes. That's why one sometimes wishes to be a stone-breaker. There's no doubt about breaking a stone. But there's doubt, fear – a black horror, in every page one writes.

Just as the fear of writing is widely shared, even amongst successful writers, so are the frustrations of confronting the writing pad or computer screen. Bertrand Russell, one of the most accomplished and prolific of scholars and writers, has described in his autobiography how he would sit for days on end staring at his paper when he was working on the *Principia Mathematica*: 'it seemed quite likely that the whole of the rest of my life might be consumed in looking at that blank sheet of paper'. Russell had no 'method' to which he could turn to get him started.

If we could hazard a generalisation, it is this. Some degree of routine, of regular writing times alone by oneself, seems to be one ingredient that many writers find necessary. Even if nothing happens, it might be a good idea to sit out an allotted period before the pad or screen rather than go rushing off to the internet, the library or your friends in search of inspiration. Most books on study skills recommend drawing up some kind of timetable for your work, and even the most arbitrary of rules (like 500 words a day, even if all 500 have later to be scrapped or re-written) can serve a useful purpose. Many writers work like this. Others have more specific routines. The economist John Maynard Keynes worked in bed until lunchtime. By contrast, the novelist Graham Greene would get up each morning and start to write straightaway, before shaving, dressing or breakfasting. The solutions are as endless as the personalities, the family circumstances, the opportunities and the 'lifestyles' of the writers themselves. Only you can work these things out, with the help (as the acknowledgements pages of great numbers of books testify) of the people you live with.

Having said this, I hope I shall not be thought too inconsistent if I direct your attention to the historian E. H. Carr's excellent description of the way he works:

> Laymen – that is to say, non-academic friends or friends from other academic disciplines – sometimes ask me how the historian goes to work when he writes history. The commonest assumption appears to be that the historian divides his work into two sharply distinguishable phases or periods. First, he spends a long preliminary period reading his sources and filling his notebooks with facts: then, when this is over, he puts away

his sources, takes out his notebooks and writes his books from beginning to end. This is to me an unconvincing and unplausible picture. For myself, as soon as I have got going on a few of what I take to be the capital sources, the itch becomes too strong and I begin to write – not necessarily the beginning, but somewhere, anywhere. Thereafter, reading and writing go on simultaneously. The writing is added to, subtracted from, reshaped, cancelled, as I go on reading. The reading is guided and directed and made fruitful by the writing: the more I write, the more I know what I am looking for, the better I understand the significance and relevance of what I find. Some historians probably do all this preliminary writing in their heads without using pen, paper or typewriter, just as some people play chess in their heads without recourse to board and chessmen: this is a talent which I envy, but cannot emulate. But I am convinced that, for any historian worth the name, the two processes of what economists call 'input' and 'output' go on simultaneously and are, in practice, parts of a single process.

It seems to me that the procedure Carr describes – reading a bit, writing when the itch comes, reading further and then re-writing – is worth taking seriously because it changes the nature of the problem from one concerned vaguely and generally with the act of writing to the more manageable one of writing *something*. The critical phase of the Carr cycle is getting the 'itch' to write, and for this there is indeed no generally applicable nettle. It is, I suppose, dependent in the first instance on becoming *interested* in what you are reading. And becoming interested in that, as we shall see in chapter 2, is partly dependent on how well you ask your questions and on that part of you that you bring to choosing the essay topic in the first place.

Think, then, of the times when something in a book has caught your attention sufficiently to make you insert an asterisk or underline the words. You may have been stimulated to make a marginal note or a note on a sheet of paper. This is the important moment. Here is the first faint itch. Instead of covering it over with salve and a book mark, begin to sharpen your ideas on it immediately. Even half a page which manages to deal in some way with the point and take in a few snatches of your other reading will suffice for a nucleus to be worked on later.

(This, to my mind, is the single greatest benefit of word-processing programs.) Writing begets writing. As Goethe writes in the Prelude to *Faust*:

> **Only engage, and then the mind grows heated –**
> **Begin it, and the work will be completed!**

If you do this from time to time, your mind will be working constructively on the essay (even in periods off duty) and your attention will be shifted from the act to the matter when you come to write the essay as a whole. You will also have spread the load of facing that empty computer screen over many smaller, and more easily handled, instances.

There is, too, the role of discussion. Discussion is an essential part of academic work both as an informal preparation for writing and as writing's final justification. The coffee shop and the seminar room, while quite distinct, are essential to the architecture of academe. But although the autocrats of the coffee table do not necessarily deserve a good hearing in the seminar room, they are at least preparing themselves for one asset of the business of writing – trying out and building up confidence in the phrases and arguments that will later be written down. If you feel you lack confidence you might be tempted to shirk these discussions in favour of solitary thinking. It is better not to. Informal discussion with friends, fellow students and others on the internet is an important preparation and a foil for the necessarily individual and solitary business of writing.

3   You and your subject matter

Whilst nearly everybody suffers to some degree from 'writer's block', we tend to vary in our ability to handle the four major elements of the writing process itself. We have seen that a good piece of academic writing needs to achieve a certain balance between these elements. So what you need to do in order to help you achieve this balance is to decide which of the elements you need to work at most. You might need to give most attention to establishing your own point of view on the topic – or finding your 'voice' – and feeling able to hold to it with some degree of confidence. Or you might find manipulating your language to get it to say something sensible without too many hits on the delete key is the big problem. It could be that you find the main difficulty to be in structuring the essay in a coherent fashion out of the wads of notes you have taken, in being able to develop your ideas to 'fill up' the 2,000 or 3,000 words required or, conversely, to cut down your 4,000 words to the required length. And then you might be so worried about 'what they [the tutors] want' that you devote enormous amounts of energy to pleasing the reader and being unnecessarily meticulous in the conventional presentation of your work.

This list of common difficulties does not exhaust the possibilities. Furthermore, overcoming one of them might also require attention to one or two of the others. So, while the list does oversimplify somewhat, it is a good idea at this early stage to decide which of the writing problems apply most particularly to you. By identifying as well as you can your own strengths and weaknesses, you will be in a position to make the best use of this book.

We turn now to the problems of coming to terms with the subject matter in such a way that you will be able to develop confidence in establishing your own answer to the essay question.

The first, and perhaps most important, thing to bear in mind is that your tutor is not expecting in your essay the 'right' or the 'correct' answer to the question. It might be the case that there is a 'right' answer, but it is not likely that all of your tutors are going to be in complete agreement among themselves on what it is. Hence your job is not to find the right answer in the books, nor to find out what your tutor thinks is the right answer, but rather to use books and tutors to help you establish *your best answer*. This demands that you learn to exercise your faculty of judgement and to be as clear and explicit as you can about how you form your own judgements.

It is the manner in which we exercise this faculty of judgement that distinguishes academic enquiry at its best from much of the everyday writing we see around us. Much of your learning so far will have required you to produce accurate and coherent descriptions of things you have observed, things you have read and things you have been taught about. The questions, for the most part, have been raised by your teachers and your books. Now, these aspects of learning remain important in colleges and universities. But what may be new to you is the increasing responsibility thrust upon you to ask your own questions and to ANALYSE or DISCUSS (rather than just to describe) the objects of your enquiries and the statements that may be made about them. We begin to discover, for example, that what we had taken to be well-accepted facts about the world have an aura of uncertainty about them; they may turn out to be theories, interpretations or widely held beliefs rather than rock-solid 'facts'. We may discover, too, that facts about which there may be no serious debate can nevertheless have their importance valued or weighted differently by different authors or as a result of asking different questions. Such situations call for analysis and discussion, in which your own evaluations will become increasingly explicit, and in which descriptions, though present, play only a part. Two of the more common comments written by tutors on students' essays are 'Too descriptive' and 'Needs more analysis'.

Now, it is important to be quite clear about the nature of this process of judgement. It is not uncommon to see a student write 'In my opinion . . .', and a tutor write beside it 'We don't want your opinion.' Although this might seem to contradict what was said above about the importance of your own judgement, it does not. What the tutor is objecting to is 'opinion' unsupported by reason and evidence.

In chapter 2 we shall examine closely how, when you are first coming to grips with an essay topic, it is quite necessary to decide what your provisional opinion might be. Your opinion at this early stage of your work does not need to be justified at all. It can, as the philosopher Sir Karl Popper says, be no more than a 'prejudice' or a 'conjecture'. You *must* bring your prejudices and opinions to bear on your provisional answer to the question. But, by the time your reading and your writing are finished, prejudice and opinion must have been converted into a reasoned judgement, which might be significantly different from your initial reaction to the essay topic. We can see how initial prejudice and opinion are transformed into judgement on a broad scale in this memoir by the Australian historian Manning Clark:

> I happened to have the good fortune to experience in childhood all the conflicts which were central to the human situation in Australia. My mother came from the old patrician, landed magnificoes in Australia; my father from the working class first of London, then of Sydney. So, years later when I read those words by Karl Marx, 'The history of all hitherto existing society is the history of class struggles', childhood memories made me say 'and that's true, too' just as years of reading and observation later were to fill in the details for that proposition about human society and raise doubts about what it leaves out.

Clark announces his prejudice in favour of Marx's dictum, a point of view governed by his own childhood experience and not by any academic method. That prejudice is absolutely necessary to Clark's history, but by itself it is not enough. It must be complemented by 'reading and observation' expressed in a critical academic discourse which analyses the 'details' and comes to terms with the 'doubts'.

In beginning with our prejudices and opinions and then gradually converting them through reading and writing into considered judgements, we are committing a great deal of our own selves to the answer we give. We must be prepared to mean what we say. But we must also be able to feel a certain *confidence* in our judgements. This confidence does not come so much from 'within' us as from the success with which our language formulates the judgement and backs it up. If you find it extremely difficult to get words onto the page, then what is probably at fault is your understanding of what you are trying to say or an insufficiently worked-out argument to support it. This can only be overcome by going back to your books or by forcing yourself to clarify your point of view by writing a short summary of it.

We have noticed above the need to take care that we mean what we say. But we must similarly take care, as the March Hare and the 'Mad' Hatter crossly pointed out to Alice, to say what we mean. There can be a yawning gulf between the two into which most of us can easily fall. When we have put our thoughts and judgements into words, we need to look at what is on the paper to find out whether what is there does indeed say what we meant to say.

Some academic writers rarely feel that they have got their language to say just what they intended, and a kind of secondary 'writer's block' sets in: the words are amended, deleted, amended again and finally sent to the bin – the whole process to be gone through again. If you spend inordinate amounts of time agonising over choices of word and sentence structure, it may well be that you are aiming for a kind of perfection and precision which is more than you can handle at the time. Perfection and precision for their own sakes are false goals in academic enquiry and writing (despite what some books say). You should cut and change only where you have decided that the meaning and structure of your argument is going to be significantly improved. A tendency to perfectionism, especially in relatively superficial aspects of writing, is often a sign of a lack of confidence. Confidence cannot be built up by presenting a perfectly grammatical exterior to your reader, but rather by trying out your ideas in the language that you can best muster on the occasion. If you feel that there is something wrong with that language, scrutinise first the idea you are trying to express.

If, on the other hand, you are the kind of writer who rarely changes anything and who, once the draft essay is completed, gladly forgets about it, you need to begin thinking very seriously about what writing an academic essay entails. As we have noted, the word-processor takes more of the pain out of revising drafts than used to be the case with pen or typewriter, so you must make use of this facility. It is only when you read over your own work, well after it has been composed, that you will be able to see its shortcomings. This means that it is absolutely necessary to construct a timetable which provides that you finish the first draft of any essay well before it is due to be handed in. Some authorities recommend that you leave forty-eight hours between completing your first draft and going through it to prepare your second. This seems to me useful advice. Chapter 2 of this book is explicitly devoted to showing you how to approach your work so that you do not fall into the common pattern of finishing a first draft the night before the essay is due. Some people can produce excellence in a first draft; but they are probably the kinds of people referred to by E. H. Carr who can also play chess in their heads. If you do have difficulty in managing to say what you mean, you should pay particular attention to Part III of this book.

If you decide that clarifying the relationship between you, your subject matter and your language is a significant problem, then it would be a good idea to study closely what E. H. Carr says about how he approaches the writing of history (pp. 5–6 above). The implication is that your knowledge and understanding are formulated *in* your language, not merely 'communicated' *by means of* language. In choosing our language we are choosing and establishing our point of view on the subject matter and our answer to the question raised by the essay topic. Each time you go round the cycle of reading, writing and thinking, you are gradually improving your understanding of the subject matter and your expression of that understanding in English. You are getting away from that Mephistophelian voice in you which says 'I understand this, but I just can't express it.' If you can't express it, the presumption must be that you don't sufficiently understand it.

4   You and your reader

While grappling with the problems of understanding and knowing the material, you have another matter to attend to. This is the interpersonal or communicative function of your writing. Writing is not *wholly* a problem in communication, as we have just seen; but now we must look at those aspects of writing which are governed by the need to present your ideas and your argument in a way that will help to 'get them across'. In some senses communicating successfully involves little more than learning and exploiting certain conventions of writing and presentation. In this respect the aim to be achieved is to present your work in such a way that the medium (paper, fonts, setting-out, etc.) does not draw the reader's attention away from the argument you are making: you are not writing advertising copy, putting together a newsletter or making a Powerpoint 'presentation'. There is, however, one problem of communicating which will not go away quite so easily.

This problem is that of deciding whom you are writing for and whom you are writing to. The academic essay is in some respects an artificial task. Though you are ostensibly writing *to* a relatively depersonalised 'academic establishment', you are in effect writing *for* yourself. This is what assessment is about. The conflict thus engendered about the nature of your audience – department, tutor and self – makes the common injunction to writers, 'Know your audience', only a partly helpful truism. To make matters worse you are sometimes told to write as if a fellow student were going to read the essay, sometimes to write for the 'educated layman', and sometimes to write for academics in a different but related discipline. In desperation, or as a short cut, you may try to write *to* your tutor.

There are, however, very real dangers if you allow your tutor to dominate too much of your writing. (And be suspicious of writing handbooks which promise you techniques for impressing your tutors with a few tricks and little effort.) Most of the dangers stem quite simply from the conventions of the teacher–student situation: writing in order to 'pass'. You may be tempted into plagiarising others' work if you believe the tutor will not recognise the source. (But bear in mind there are computer programs the tutor can use to check these sources if he or she becomes suspicious.) This is no way to learn to write. More importantly, it constitutes a violation of your own selfhood as much as it does of the rights of the original author. It is a violation of yourself because your attempts to understand the substance of what you read are also attempts to understand yourself a little bit better each time you try to interpret in your own words what another person is saying. In a very real sense, your essays actually write you – they become part of your own developing conception of yourself, your own life story – if you will allow them to. You are a changed person. It does take time, so try to be patient.

Similarly, you might begin to ape the superficialities of the jargon of a discipline before you have really grasped the meaning of the language. By thus displaying a certain familiarity with this 'in-language', many believe the tutor will be taken in (which, of course, he or she can be). Many disciplines in the humanities and social sciences make use of a language not commonly found elsewhere: for example 'the Other', 'intertextuality', 'posthuman', 'totalising discourse'. To string together such words and phrases in order to create the illusion of control and understanding is relatively easy with a bit of practice. To understand them, to make judgements on them, to make (or not to make) them part of your own story or 'discourse' of yourself requires time and work. Dazzling the tutor is incidental to this more important task.

The third temptation in keeping tutors too much in mind is to toady to their theoretical predilections and opinions in the belief that this will earn you a higher grade. It must first of all be acknowledged that, as any number of studies have shown, tutors can be quite unreliable in their assessments of written work. (Many departments recognise this and use various techniques for improving reliability.) Different tutors can vary significantly in the grade they allow to a given essay. This fact might encourage you to believe that the best way to get high grades is to flatter your tutor's opinions. It appears, however, that even an individual tutor may vary quite considerably in the value he or she attaches to the same piece of work from one time to another. It is also the case that some tutors are flattered by having you attack their own work, since in order to attack it you will need to have read it with care and attention. In my own experience the genuine conflicts about the substance of an opinion occur mostly over the work of graduate students. With undergraduates many such difficulties turn out to arise from misunderstandings not so much about the substance of a particular opinion as about its *relevance* to the essay question or about the quality of the student's analysis of supporting evidence. So before you assume a tutor is biased against you, do as much as you can to put into practice the concerns of this book, which seek to initiate you into the rites and conventions of academic debate.

But where there is considerable disparity between your own assessment of the value of your essay and the assessment the tutor makes, the best recourse is to argue it out with the tutor in question. Any good tutor should be prepared to give particular comments, to defend his or her judgement and to revise it if warranted. It is this matter of detailed comment that you should ask for, whether the examiner seems biased in favour or against. Marginal comment, a defence of the overall assessment, and some help with what you need to do to improve, is what you should seek first. Only then should you begin to worry about the tutor who does not like your opinions. If, however, you do arrive at this point, most university departments and schools have procedures in place which enable you to appeal against the decision of your tutor.

One matter on which you should always submit to the wishes of your tutor concerns the conventions of presentation: the preferred *forms* of footnoting and referencing, and of headings, margins and type of paper, fonts or typefaces, line spacing, the quality of your proofreading and so on. Good communication is obtained in part by reducing to a minimum what engineers call 'noise' in the channel – anything that will distract the reader from the object of concentration. It is customary for writing handbooks like this one to justify these matters in terms of courtesy to the reader. But there is also a simple psychological factor. If your reader's attention is constantly distracted by attention-seeking or indifferent presentation, there will be less processing capacity in his or her brain to devote to the substance of your essay. Like so many of the things we discuss in connection with writing, successful communication is a matter of achieving an optimal balance in a given situation. It is even possible to make your presentation too perfect. If your cultural background has placed great emphasis on courtesy and convention, it is quite possible that you will expend a disproportionate amount of effort on parading immaculately labelled headings, brightly polished setting-out and crisply pressed footnotes. The excellence of the presentation may make it rather too clear that you have neglected more important aspects of your writing.

5   Your language: form and structure

So far, we have seen how aspects of language enter into such problems as how you establish your point of view on a topic, how you come to understand and express your subject matter, and how you establish a 'line of communication' with your reader. Now we look at some problems of writing which arise out of the nature of language itself. To make language work for you, it is a good idea to learn something of its forms and structures, just as cabinet-makers need to understand the properties of their timbers. The forms we are concerned with operate on two levels – that of the sentence and that of larger units of discourse like the paragraph and the essay as a whole. There are ways in which we use words, grammar and discourse to organise our diverse ideas into a coherent unity. Every piece of academic writing should strive for this unity.

A well-organised piece of writing reveals that the writer has established a pattern of relationships between the individual parts and between the parts and the whole composition. When we read, we are often dimly aware that the author of our book has achieved this formal balance without our being able to say exactly how. When we write, we are often uncomfortably aware that we haven't achieved it. Sometimes we begin to realise that our thinking and writing are just 'going round in circles'. We start to repeat ourselves unnecessarily, contradict ourselves or fail to show the connections between ideas. We become aware that, whenever we arrive at the end of a section of the essay, or of a paragraph or even of a sentence, we do not know where to turn next or how to establish a connection between what is written and what is to be written. We become more and more unable to decide between what should be included in the essay and what should be left out. Paragraphs become very, very long or very, very short. Sentences become long and convoluted, such that the end has quite forgotten the beginning. More or less random mistakes in some aspects of grammar begin to creep in. Overall, we get that feeling that our writing does not 'flow', that some aspect of its structure has collapsed.

The first difficulty we face is in learning to recognise when these symptoms are present. Sometimes they are not particularly apparent to us while we are writing, only revealing themselves when we read the piece over later. Sometimes our own sense of form is not sufficiently developed to enable us to see aspects of our problem at all. We learn these things by having our writing criticised by others, and by absorbing gradually from our reading a sense of what good writing 'feels' like. It is therefore often only a vague sense of discomfort, in the first instance, that alerts us to the situation in our own writing.

When this discomfort is felt, we may be able to go back over our work and describe in some detail what is going wrong – perhaps by identifying such particular symptoms as are listed above. For example, an almost invariable sign that something is wrong is a series of either very long or very short paragraphs – and this condition is easy to spot. But being able to locate and identify the symptom is often not enough, since local tinkering with, say, paragraph boundaries (running short ones together or chopping long ones into parts) does not always get at the heart of the problem. This is the point at which we often have to decide to cross out the whole passage and start again.

Far from seeking to improve the form for its own sake, our re-writing gives us a chance to improve our understanding of the *subject* we are writing about. There are aesthetes who fiddle with the form of their work to gain purely formal satisfactions, and there should indeed be something of the aesthete in all writers. But the chance to re-write is the chance to conceive afresh what it is we are trying to say. And that means searching for an idea which becomes the new focus of attention, a new unifying vision of the subject, around which the parts which once seemed so intractable will now cluster more or less easily. In short, to heed the formal signals of distress gives us the opportunity to think of a better answer to the question. The satisfactions of this are great.

Nobody, however, will deny the desire to get things more or less right the first time. If good structure depends, as we have seen, so critically on finding that elusive unifying idea, good structure therefore has its origins in your very first confrontation with the essay topic. There are, of course, many questions which can only be faced and resolved as the occasion arises. But that central issue of the overall organisation of your essay and its major parts is not something that can be added in as you 'write up' a draft. If you do recognise in yourself the 'scissors-and-paste' syndrome and the other symptoms of poor structure in your essay-writing, you may well need to pay especial attention to the way in which you come to terms with the essay topic.

Form and structure enter into most aspects of writing. Even so, this book, it should be clear, is about much more than getting the right words and grammatical forms into the right places. To write well you will also need progressively to learn about yourself and the way your own mind works, about the ways in which you attain to knowledge, and about the academic culture in which you and your readers live. Dealing adequately with all these claims to the attention demands that you gradually work out for yourself a set of procedures and conditions that will not only improve your efficiency but also open up new, more interesting and more subtle ways of approaching your work. You will find in this book various hints and recommendations about what you might take account of in trying to reach that happy state where you can even enjoy the taxing process of writing. The particular synthesis you make of the issues treated here is, however, your own responsibility. The success with which all these matters are resolved will be apparent in the artefact that emerges: every piece of your writing you preserve will always remain an articulate testimony to your state of mind when you wrote it. This is what makes writing – even if 'only' another academic essay – an attempt to deal not only with a 'topic' but with knowledge itself, with other people and with yourself.

Part I

Reflection and Research

2

Reflection: asking questions and proposing answers

I have always preferred to reflect upon a problem before reading on it.

Jean Piaget

This chapter

- encourages you to develop the confidence and ability to SPECULATE early about possible answers to your topic, and avoid getting bogged down in unproductive, time-consuming reading and notes.

It does this by

- emphasising the importance of your interest in and enthusiasm for the topics you choose to write on (as opposed to more utilitarian reasons)

- showing you the meanings of the question words and instructions used in essay topics, how to interpret them and how to ask your own questions

- providing a logical approach to speculating about the shape of possible answers, drawing mostly on your existing knowledge

- illustrating how you can come up with a draft paragraph which will help guide your later thinking and more detailed reading.

1   Speculative thinking and writing

This is a chapter about thinking and reflection. It comes first in our consideration of writing because it is the first of the many activities in writing an essay that you should engage in. Many, if not most, students leave the really hard thinking until after they have done the reading or research. They do this in the belief that one can't think constructively until all the information is gathered and the writing of the final draft is due to begin. This is not so, as the quotation above from the philosopher and psychologist Jean Piaget suggests.

One of the most important abilities needed to master essay-writing in the humanities and social sciences is the ability to ASK QUESTIONS of the essay topic itself as well as of the books you will read. If you can develop a facility in asking questions and in reflecting on likely answers to those questions, it is possible for a general shape for your essay (though not its precise content) to become evident to you even before you have begun on any detailed reading. The procedure is something like this:

1 Choose an essay topic because it interests you. Such a topic is more likely to be one about which you might already have a few questions or ideas.

2 Ask questions of the topic: try to work out what it is driving at, what is meant by various words or phrases in it, and what kinds of connection there may be between the various issues it raises. Do no more reading (or better, 'consulting' of a few very basic source books) than is necessary to suggest possible answers to your questions.

3 Propose to yourself a few likely answers to the question raised by the topic and write them down in no more than a sentence or two. Then choose which seems to be the best. Discussing the topic with friends is very useful at this stage.

4 Develop this answer into a paragraph which, so far as you can, lists the reasons for choosing the answer you did or some of the facts and ideas that you think might support it.

5 Regard this paragraph as no more than a hypothesis about, a proposal for, or a forecast of, your eventual answer. It might well lay the foundations of the opening paragraph of your essay, but it will need to be tested out (and probably changed) by your detailed reading – which should not begin until now.

The aim of this chapter is to show you how to do these things. You need to be aware at the outset that you may not find it easy to master and apply these techniques of reflective questioning and exploratory writing. You may well be strongly tempted to scurry back to the apparent security of your books and the deceptive sense of being 'busy' in the library, leaving the hard thinking until a night or two before the essay is due. There are two main reasons why you should resist this temptation.

The first is that hard preliminary thinking and writing leads eventually to better essays. The second is that it makes you more efficient in your work, and consequently saves you important time.

It might seem that a procedure which asks you to produce a draft paragraph which almost certainly will have to be changed, and perhaps wholly scrapped, is academically worthless, not to say inefficient. This is not so. You will remember we saw in chapter 1 that writing and thinking beget more writing and thinking. Now if your thinking is not constrained by the need to write down what comes of it, it will usually be fairly undisciplined, not to say idle and disjointed. Writing is your best way of discovering whether you have actually captured a thought and whether it is any good. Improvement does not emerge from nothing, but by changing what exists. The single chief value of a speculative answer in a short paragraph is not just that it might become the foundation of the eventual answer but that it gives you something to change, something to improve on by further reading, thinking and writing. This is what leads to better essays.

Having a speculative answer leads to a more efficient use of time in a number of ways. Your reading becomes quicker and you don't lose concentration on a book so easily. Since you have a better idea of what is likely to be relevant, you spend less time taking mountains of notes that eventually turn out to be quite useless.

Thirdly, you do not spend valuable hours towards the end of the research period hunting desperately through the library in the vain Micawber-like hope that 'something will turn up' to show you how to write your answer. Finally, there is long-standing psychological evidence that once you have consciously articulated certain issues to be worked on, your subconscious mind will beaver away at them whilst you are doing other things, with the result that every now and again an answer or an improvement will pop to the surface. (The philosopher Bertrand Russell prepared himself for these happy occasions by carrying round a little notebook in which to write these ideas down.) In this way you save time because your subconscious can be working on one essay while your conscious attention is engaged on another.

The steps summarised above we shall now treat in more detail.

2   Choosing a topic

Your choice of a topic on which to write should be governed most importantly by your own personal interest and 'prejudice'. Your only guide in this matter is yourself. Some people think that if you are too committed to a subject you will write an essay which is too strongly influenced by your desire to entrench a particular point of view, irrespective of evidence. This should not worry you, provided that you draw an important distinction. This is a distinction between your interest in the subject as being worthy of study and a commitment to be as detached as you can when you eventually come to analyse the evidence which supports one or another answer to the question. The early stages of preparing an essay dealt with in this chapter are purely private. So choosing a topic, like your first reflections on it, can be governed by as much self-interest and prejudice as you care to allow. It would be much more a problem if you find that none of the topics on a list interests you. If that happens, you should try to work one out for yourself on some aspect of the course that does interest you and then gain your tutor's approval of it.

There are some subsidiary issues which might enter into your choice of topic, and which might influence you in favouring one over others of equal interest. The first of these issues are somewhat negative ones.

One consideration that might weigh heavily with you is the relevance of a topic to the syllabus as a whole and to end-of-course examinations in particular. The 'pragmatic' student might decide that to write on such a topic effectively kills two birds with one stone, a decision which justifies the argument 'What am I studying for if not to get my degree or diploma in the most efficient way possible?' There is nothing wrong with this argument provided that it is not allowed to override the importance of being interested in the subject itself. Some research into student performance in universities suggests that to be too 'syllabus-bound' eventually works against academic success. If you pursue your interests within the broad scope of the courses you are taking, you will ultimately perform better than if you keep your gaze too firmly fixed on the qualification at the end of it all. Bear it in mind that enthusiasm for a subject will be manifest in your writing, and will convey itself to a grateful reader.

For similar reasons you should not reject an interesting topic because it has not yet been covered in class. Nor, having chosen such a topic, should you postpone the beginning of your work until it is. Lecturers and tutors rarely address their comments to the precise question or questions raised by an essay topic. This is not necessarily neglect – and may be quite deliberate, since they do not wish to read many essays which uniformly echo the lectures. Hence nothing that they say is likely to be of any more initial benefit to you than what is contained in an introductory book on the subject. Even if the classes do address issues of direct relevance to a topic, you must realise that the lecturer is not giving you *the* answer to the question but his or her answer, which must be analysed in exactly the same way as you will analyse other answers in your written sources. Indeed, if you have done your preliminary work before the classes take the matter up, you will be in a much better position to assess the value, the relevance and the significance of what is said.

There are, in addition, certain other practical considerations to be taken into account. Other things being equal, in courses with many students unpopular topics may be worth a closer look. This is because competition for the available references in the library will be less fierce and because the essays written on them will bear a relative freshness to the reader. Another rule of thumb is that, for some students, topics worded in a very general way are often harder to write on well than topics in which the issues are set out more precisely. General or broad topics leave to you so much more of the questioning process itself and the evaluation of the best questions to ask. The more clearly the questions are focused, the easier it is to control the *relevance* of the answers. Against this, it must be said, topics which are very precise in their demands may not allow quite so much scope for you to develop your own point of view. The price of safety may be a certain constriction of freedom.

Devising your own topic for a research paper

If you are asked not to choose a topic from a prepared list but to devise one for yourself, you face, at bottom, much the same problems as those we have already discussed. They may, however, be considerably magnified; it is really much harder to ask good questions than it is to answer them. Your interest in the subject is still paramount. Even so, it has to be weighed against such practical and intellectual matters as the availability of sufficient evidence or data relative to the broadness of the topic, the extent to which it allows theoretical or methodological questions of interest to the discipline to be asked of it, the amount of time available and the projected length of the paper. Factors such as these need to be nicely balanced, so you must discuss them in some detail with your tutor before you finally settle on the wording of your topic. Nor should you be afraid to seek a change in the wording of the topic if your early investigations lead you into major problems.

You will probably first conceive a topic of your own in fairly general terms – more an indication of the subject area in which you are interested than a precise topic: for example Shakespeare's treatment of women in selected comedies, J. S. Mill's ideas on freedom, the partition of India at independence in 1947, class divisions in 21st-century England. To turn such general subjects into something manageable within a word limit and interesting as a piece of academic enquiry, they need to be narrowed down and a particular perspective adopted towards them. The best way to begin this process is to ask questions of the subject, just as your tutors often do when they set essay topics. To these kinds of question we now turn.

3   Kinds of question

An object, event, situation, concept or idea becomes an object of *enquiry* because someone has raised an interesting or significant question about it. The object does not have to be a 'new discovery'. It might have lain around for years or centuries as a 'fact' or as part of our accustomed intellectual furniture until the thought strikes a fresh mind that there is about it an unresolved question with interesting implications. Indeed, far from having to wait until a novel object is brought in for study – like a fossilised skeleton from some previously unknown dinosaur – it is by raising new questions about existing objects of knowledge that we often uncover new objects whose existence was unknown.

Academic enquiry, as we have seen, proceeds in the first instance by asking questions. Your essay topics are examples of these questions. Just as your tutors ask questions of you by the essay topics they set, so you must learn to ask questions both of the essay topic itself and of the various books you use in your reading for the essay. It is the answers to these questions which, when integrated in a coherent fashion, become an essay. Skill in asking good questions (a 'good' question is one which opens up a fruitful line of enquiry) is something that comes with practice, knowledge and experience in the disciplines you are studying. There is no method or formula for coming up with really good questions. It is possible, nevertheless, that by learning to ring the changes on the question words we use, various lines of thought will be opened up and – an important consideration for many of us – this will help overcome 'writer's block'. These question words are 'what', 'who', 'whom', 'where', 'when', 'how', 'why', 'to what extent', 'how far' and 'which'.

What

'What' has a number of functions. Typically it asks for clarification about some phenomenon that is being REFERRED to, for example 'What is expressionism?' This is a request to establish the connection between a name (a word) and an object or phenomenon 'in the world' which has been observed: we say the *name* refers to the *object*, as the names 'morning star' or 'Venus' refer to a particular point of light in the sky. Some 'what' requests may seek a DESCRIPTION of a *particular* object, process or idea in answer to them:

> What brings the United States and Europe together, and what divides them?

> What is Rawls's theory of justice?

Other 'what' questions look for more *generalised* or *universal* DEFINITIONS and THEORIES:

> What is justice? (this is the question Rawls asked)

> What is a dialect and what is a language? Can any universally applicable criteria be used to distinguish them?

Definitions are treated at length in chapter 9.

Who, whom

These two words are requests for an IDENTIFICATION of people or groups of people. 'Who' queries the identity of people who do things or who are the responsible *agents* for some event. 'Whom', by contrast, raises a question about the people *affected* by an action or event. A question about the one will very often raise a question about the other. Notice, too, that the range of a 'whom' question can be considerably widened by prefacing it with a preposition (e.g. to, for, by, with, amongst):

> Who was ultimately responsible for the deportation of Jews in Vichy France to the Nazi death camps?

To whom does religious fundamentalism in the United States particularly appeal?

Weblogging has fundamentally altered the ways in which information and knowledge are shared. Evaluate the accuracy of this statement, addressing 'how' and 'for whom' this statement might apply.

Where, when

'Where' and 'when' query aspects of the *location*, *time* and *duration* of objects and events. These questions do not commonly turn up in the essay topics undergraduate students are asked to write on. Nevertheless, they are invaluable questions to turn upon the topics you are set, since your answer may well depend critically on whether certain conditions of place, time and duration can be satisfied. If asked, for example, to assess whether the 'pacification' programme in the Vietnam War was a success, you might answer that it was, but only for a certain period and in certain parts of the country. Being able to specify times and places reliably may be just as important in answering some academic questions as it is in a criminal trial. Asking questions about 'where' and 'when' can also raise detailed issues of distribution, extent, frequency, regularity and other important topics in a variety of disciplines.

How

'How' can be interpreted in a number of ways. First it can be a request for a DESCRIPTION of a *process* (rather than of an object or phenomenon):

How did General Douglas MacArthur honour his promise to return to the Philippines during the Second World War?

How did Buddhism change as it travelled from India to Japan?

How does Shakespeare achieve the integration of plot and subplot in *King Lear*?

A second sense of 'how' can be paraphrased as 'in what respects'. This is more like the kind of description we considered when discussing 'what' – a request for various characteristics or features:

> How has the decipherment of Linear B tablets improved our understanding of the Mycenaean religion?
>
> How does the structure of society contribute to adolescent delinquency?

Finally 'how' may demand an EXPLANATION, and this sense of 'how' is often hardly distinguishable from 'why'. Physical scientists commonly say they make no distinction between 'how' and 'why' questions, or if they do, they limit themselves to 'how' questions, the answers to which are to be sought in the mechanisms of nature rather than human will, intention or motives. Humanities and social science students will therefore meet this sense of 'how' in those disciplines whose subject matter and methods of enquiry more closely approach those of natural science:

> How does the 'chunking' of information help to explain individual differences in short-term memory performance?
>
> How were the Himalayan mountains formed?
>
> How are certain aspects of social structure affected by the physical environment in which a society lives?

In the examples above it is possible to detect a shifting about in the meaning of 'how', even though each could be re-written as a 'why' question. In the first, 'how' could simply be replaced by 'why'. In the second, 'how' might initially appear to require merely a description of processes. But the answer to this question would need to examine why the Himalayas are formed as they are or, alternatively, what caused them to be formed as they are. The third illustrates another sense in which 'how' can be interpreted as 'why'. This question can be paraphrased 'Why do certain aspects of social structure reflect the physical environment in which a society lives?' An answer to this question would need to examine the underlying *relations* between social structure and the environment rather than anything that could properly be called a cause. (For another example of such an explanation, see (4) under the list of explanation types below.) All these uses of 'how' seek varying kinds of explanation.

Why

If the meaning of 'how' has seemed to be rather complex, that of 'why' is much more so. 'Why' is a request for an EXPLANATION, and, very often, a THEORY. One of the difficulties with explanations, however, is that there are quite a few different kinds. That is to say, there are various quite different ways of answering a 'why' question, depending on the disciplines that you are studying, and even on schools of thought within disciplines. An explanation in anthropology can be a very different thing from an explanation in history. And an approach to explanation which is acceptable to the department of linguistics in one university or college might be discouraged in the linguistics department of another. Some of the commoner types of explanation are the following.

1 Causal explanations – what were the causes of some event or phenomenon? For example, 'Why did a militant movement advocating votes for women emerge in England during the Edwardian era?'

2 Purposive explanations – what were the reasons, aims, purposes or intentions of those responsible for some action, event, phenomenon, etc? For example, 'Why have social anthropologists traditionally paid so much attention to the study of kinship?'

3 Functional explanations – what function does something have, or what role does it play, within a larger system of which it is a part? For example, 'Why does the tone of voice change so often and so dramatically in T. S. Eliot's *The Waste Land*?'

4 Structural explanations – what abstract and universal rules, codes or laws account for the relations between features of a

system, and which of these rules generate its structure?
For example, 'Why is the industrial wealth of the First
World inseparable from the rural poverty of the Third
World?'

5 Deductive explanations – what combinations of conditions
   or premisses allow us to infer a logical conclusion? For
   example, 'Why are utilitarians committed to opposing
   capital punishment?'

To what extent, how much, how far, how significant

There are many ways of asking questions that call for a JUDGEMENT,
ASSESSMENT or EVALUATION. These are some of them. The simplest
idea of evaluating is to rank a phenomenon on a scale – say, cold
to hot, useless to useful, bad to good – which gives some measure
of degree. Those questions that begin 'How . . . ' will give you the
criterion or scale on which the phenomenon has to be assessed, for
example quantity in the case of 'how much', temperature in the case
of 'how hot', significance in the case of 'how significant' and so on.
'To what extent' and 'how far' are questions that leave to you the
task of deciding the best criteria by which to evaluate the issue in
question:

> ' . . . Mill's open-mindedness was too large for the system he
> inherited' (A. D. Lindsay). To what extent did John Stuart
> Mill differ from early utilitarian attitudes to state
> intervention in social and economic affairs?

> To what extent do you believe the mass media play a key
> role in social control?

> How far is the rise in suicide rates during times of economic
> prosperity attributable to people's earlier experiences
> during economic recession?

> How important is the Porter to the main plot of
> Shakespeare's *Macbeth*? Is he just comic 'relief'?

In the first and last of these topics you are given a hint about the criterion to be examined – qualities of open-mindedness and comic 'relief'. But when you ask evaluative questions yourself, the most appropriate criteria must be supplied by you.

Which

'Which' is used to do two related things – to IDENTIFY and to compel one to DECIDE. Identifying is the counterpart of referring. Whereas with 'what' questions we have a name and we wish to know the object, identifying involves fitting a name to the object or description before us:

> Which of the attitudes to capital punishment is favoured by utilitarians?

Simple identification itself involves little more than pointing to the desired object in a line-up. Interesting 'which' questions are raised when it is not easy to make a decision:

> Which of the two common theories that attempt to account for the origins of cities is the more plausible?

Such a question asks one to COMPARE and CONTRAST the two theories and make a *choice* between them. Choosing requires one to establish appropriate criteria according to which the final decision is made: if I have to decide whether today is colder than yesterday, I look to the thermometer readings, which give me a measure according to the criterion of temperature, and perhaps also to other measurements which are criteria – such as the wind chill factor and humidity. DECIDING is therefore an EVALUATIVE activity, too, in which one is explicitly required to COMPARE and CONTRAST the criteria on which the evaluation is to be made. The criterion to be used in answering the question above is plausibility. The next problem is to work out how plausibility can be defined for the purpose of this essay.

Finally, some 'which' questions almost cry out for you to challenge the assumption on which they are based:

> Which do you see as the more important, economic growth
> or environmental sustainability? How are these issues seen
> and dealt with in less developed countries?

While it would certainly be possible to choose between economic growth and environmental sustainability, a more interesting approach would be to REJECT the 'either . . . or' and write an essay based on 'both . . . and'. You could, for example, argue that while, obviously, in the long term, economic growth is pointless without environmental sustainability, it is possible to have both if economic development is approached in a certain way, which you would then have to specify.

This completes our sketch of the typical question words. It is important to keep in mind the fact that, just as these sorts of question (except for 'where' and 'when') commonly appear in essay topics set by the tutor, they must, in turn, be used by you on the essay topic itself. Hence, in the topic on the origin of cities given above, the first question that needs to be asked of it is a 'what' question: 'What are these "two common theories"?'

An essay topic phrased not as a question but as a statement (or quotation) followed by an instruction to discuss, examine, analyse, comment on, consider, account for, assess, etc., is really no different. (The differences in meaning between these instructions are not especially significant – so do not take too seriously those books on study skills which try to make fine distinctions between them.) Such instructions are open invitations to the writer to formulate from the statement or quotation the most fruitful question to ask. Hence it is best to treat them as questions.

Some topics allow you considerable latitude to formulate your own question. For example, the widespread exercises in English and French literature in which you are given a text and asked to comment on it (do a 'practical criticism' or an 'explication de texte') are as much a test of your ability to ask fruitful and appropriate questions as they are to write answers to them: 'What does this text really mean?' 'What is its context?' 'Is it a satire or is it only pretending to be?' 'Why does so much of the imagery seem to be pulling in a different direction from the "argument"?' 'How is the conflict that seems to be going on resolved, and is this resolution successful?' 'Is this text a sentimental platitude?' Having formulated the most interesting question about the text by which to guide the essay, you can then ask lots of others which might help with the discussion and contribute to the answer.

We are now going to examine the procedures you might adopt in the systematic unpacking of an essay topic and the proposing of an answer. Remember that the immediate purpose of this kind of reflection is not to write an essay but to do as much as possible to *prepare* for the writing of an essay. Your aim is to allow a free play of your mind on the topic, trying to forecast as well as you can the general line an essay might take.

The premium at this stage of your work is to be put on thinking, on the analysis of likely possibilities, on 'bold conjectures', and on the knowledge, experience and motherwit you already possess. Only when some of these things have clearly failed should you yield to the temptation to open a book, and even then it should be a general book in which you search for just that information you need to get your thinking to bite. Thinking is, as we saw earlier in this chapter, a difficult thing to do, particularly if you find formal reasoning in something of a vacuum not your natural style. It can, however, be practised. Bear it in mind that your essay will be *your* 'best' answer, not an answer to be found pat in some book. Therefore, you might as well begin with yourself in confrontation with your chosen topic.

4 Coming to terms with an essay topic

4.1 Making up your mind

Your essay will be your *answer* to a question – not a general consideration of issues and facts that might pertain to some aspects of the topic. Answering a question means that you must be prepared to make a decision – no matter which question words are used. And any decision runs the risk of embarrassing the person who made it. You might show considerable care, discretion and caution about how far out on a limb you are prepared to go, but climb out on the limb you must. The earlier you try it out, the less painful and embarrassing it is to have it snap under you. The path to learning is littered with the bruised bodies of crestfallen scholars. Nobody but the scholar with the bruises and fallen crest takes much notice of that; but you owe it to yourself to make as many as you can of the mistakes from which you learn *before* you present your final draft for assessment. An 'essay', in one of its early meanings, is a trial.

With one kind of question, for example 'Did the White Australia policy become whiter between 1901 and 1921?', one has no option but to choose either 'yes' or 'no'. The answer can be hedged about with all sorts of qualifications, and that is expected. But to respond 'Maybe it did and maybe it didn't' is not to answer at all. The best thing to do is to try out an answer and see whether it holds up.

The same principle applies to any question, irrespective of whether it is framed in yes/no terms. The fact that many essay topics do not enforce such a clearcut decision should not delude you:

> Human nature may be the foundation of politics, but the
> state is the key unit of political organisation. Discuss the role
> of the state.

Here you are challenged to agree or disagree with the proposition contained in the first sentence. You might agree that it is necessary to separate 'foundation of politics' and 'unit of political organisation' and that the latter is more important. Or you might not: you might argue that the state can never be much more than the sum of the individual human natures that make it up. Such a decision has to be made.

Even the most innocent of questions that appear to ask for no more than a straightforward description can contain the seeds of a controversy on which you will have to make up your mind:

> How did General Douglas MacArthur honour his promise to
> return to the Philippines during the Second World War?

With a little bit of reflection you can propose a workmanlike description of the likely processes: MacArthur's strategic and tactical decisions; battles won and lost with politicians, other generals and the enemy; his method of working; his character; his effectiveness as a field commander; and so on. But the very fact that this list can grow so easily should warn you that some of these things deserve more EMPHASIS than others. That is to say, you must *decide* provisionally which of these factors – or which combination of them – *best* explain MacArthur's success, and which are less important.

One of the popular images of an academic or a scholar is that you can never get a straight answer to your question. He responds with an 'on the one hand' and an 'on the other'. This is a caricature with a certain element of truth. As one burrows more deeply into a question it becomes harder and harder to answer it simply and confidently. When England was wracked by the claims and counterclaims of Catholic and Protestant dogma during the early seventeenth century, it was said of one scholar, William Chillingworth, that he 'contracted such a habit of doubting that by degrees he grew confident of nothing'. While allowing that the answers to many questions may be very complicated, you must nevertheless resist succumbing to this state of mind.

4.2   Problems of meaning and knowledge

Most people find that, while it is easy enough to propose an immediate tentative answer to some questions, others raise knotty problems of meaning and interpretation that need to be dealt with first. This will happen particularly where the topic makes use of terms with which you are not familiar, where it is worded in a vague or ambiguous manner, and where you feel you have so little background knowledge of the issues it raises that to speculate about a likely answer is impossible. We shall treat each of these situations in turn.

Clarifying the meaning of terms

When you are considering the meanings of terms in your essay topics, a major decision you have to make is whether any of them have a special meaning or use in the discipline you are studying. This applies equally to what look like ordinary everyday words as it does to those recherché terms (e.g. 'recherché', 'moiety', 'phoneme', 'hermeneutic', 'deconstruction') that are rarely to be found in everyday language. Indeed, it is the more common words that pose a problem, simply because their special uses are more likely to be overlooked. 'Class', 'language', 'democracy', 'comedy', 'the market', 'structure', 'function', 'justice', 'representation' are examples of terms whose uses can vary considerably in different disciplines. Moreover, they are examples of terms for which there are no generally accepted or conclusive definitions.

From this distinction between terms that are of no particular significance to a given discipline and terms that are, there follows an important lesson to learn. If you do not know the meaning of a word in your essay topic, look it up first in an ordinary desk dictionary. If you have no reason to believe it is of special significance to the discipline, you need not pursue the matter any further. (In particular, you should never bother to define such words in the essay, since your reader does not want to know the common dictionary definition of an unproblematic word.) You have merely used the dictionary to help you interpret the meaning of the essay topic. If, on the other hand, you suspect the word does have some special significance, you must go to your textbooks or to specialised dictionaries to find out what the problems with defining the term might be; your interpretation of the meaning of the essay topic as a whole might depend critically on which definition or interpretation of the term you use.

We have seen already (p. 28) how some essay topics will almost solely demand discussion of the meaning of a term or set of terms:

> What is the difference between literary language and everyday language? Illustrate your discussion by close reference to a few selected texts.

Your questioning of the meaning of the two significant terms in this topic ('literary' and 'everyday') is pretty well the questioning of the meaning of the topic as a whole. In other topics some formidable problems of definition need to be approached *in the course of* dealing with other issues raised in the question:

> 'In Western countries the upper class is no longer a ruling class.' Discuss.

What is 'class'? What grounds are there for distinguishing 'upper class' from 'ruling class'? How does the distinction fit into any of the widely canvassed theories of class? Only by dealing with questions such as these can one say very much of significance about Western society: whether there ever was an 'upper class' in all Western countries, how it ruled, and whether and in what respects it has been replaced by a 'ruling class' which is significantly different. The limitations of dictionaries – even specialised ones – will be obvious in dealing with issues like these.

There are few less inspiring beginnings to an essay than 'Let us first define our terms', particularly if that definition is taken from a standard dictionary. If there is a major problem of definition or interpretation, it will have to be DISCUSSED, letting the issues emerge during the course of the discussion. More is said about this matter in chapter 4 (p. 96) and chapter 9.

The meaning of an essay topic as a whole

The meaning of an essay topic is not to be discovered simply by adding up, as it were, the meanings of the individual words that compose it. As we have noticed before, the important requirement is that you try to understand the tutor's intent behind the topic. You should learn to ask yourself 'What is the author of this topic driving at in asking this question?' (Remember that essay topics are not drawn from some sort of Bible, but are formulated by your teachers because they probably think that in them lies an interesting or debatable issue on which they want to read your judgement. They reflect your teachers' changing interests in what they think worthwhile questions to ask, and so the topics of today are often quite different from those of yesterday.) While it is useful and important to underline what appear to be the significant words in a topic, this by itself is not enough. The topic on the nature of the state, mentioned earlier, is a good enough example:

> Human nature may be the foundation of politics, but the state is the key unit of political organisation. Discuss the role of the state.

Here it is necessary to recognise the force of the word 'but' in assessing what the topic is driving at. The author of the proposition in the topic is suggesting that the problems of human nature, though fundamental to politics, can safely be set aside if we are to find out what 'political organisation' really is. Hence you have to work out for yourself whether the proposed contrast (signalled by the 'but') between 'politics' and 'political organisation' is one that you are prepared to defend. This leads, as we saw, to deciding whether politics is the sum of the individual human natures that make up the state, or whether there is an organisational or structural dimension to the state which transcends the demands of human nature. Reduced to its bare bones, you might interpret the question as asking whether you are a traditional liberal/conservative exponent of individualist views or whether you think the needs of the state must override those of the individuals in it. All this rather deep philosophising hinges on your understanding the force of 'but' and the contrast it marks between politics and political organisation. So it is just as important to underline the 'but' as it is to underline the more substantive terms.

You need also to look for the ambiguities in essay topics. Sometimes these are accidental (do not assume that every essay topic you see is well worded). But often they test your ability to pick up the ambiguity and to find the real issue beneath it. Here is an example:

> Why was President George W. Bush accused of attempting to undermine the United States constitution during his 'war on terror'?

The ambiguity here hinges on the question word 'Why'. There are two questions here, neither of which – it is important to realise – is 'Why did President Bush attempt to undermine the constitution?' It would be possible to choose one or the other or, perhaps more interestingly, to tackle both. On the one hand, the question could read 'What were his accusers' reasons for saying he had tried to undermine the constitution?' On the other, it could be 'What (if anything) did President Bush actually do to try to undermine the constitution?' The first looks the more fruitful interpretation; but by combining both we shall be able to examine the gap that opens between any attempt he might have made to undermine the constitution and the strength of his accusers' denunciations of him. The use of the passive voice ('was accused') creates an indeterminacy. *Who* accused him? Was it only those with their own political motives, or has this chorus been joined by other more detached observers?

If, after plenty of the kind of consideration of the topic we are discussing in this chapter, you cannot decide between a few reasonable interpretations, you should consult your tutor. Do not forget, nevertheless, that such a consultation is not a substitute for saying in the essay itself *how* you have chosen to interpret the topic and, if you can, *why* this seems the more fruitful interpretation (see chapter 4).

Essay topics that contain a number of questions

Some essay topics are constructed in such a way that they ask you to answer a number of related questions. The difficulty posed by such topics is that, although there are many questions, the tutor still expects you to come up with your own single unified answer, not a series of mini-essays which separately answer each of the questions. Here is one such topic from the philosophy of religion:

> 'Religious ideas . . . are illusions, fulfilments of the oldest, strongest and most urgent wishes of mankind.' Why does Freud say this? What does he mean by it? Is he right? Does this claim have any consequences for questions about the existence of God?

In order to give your initial reflections some focus, it is best to search the topic for what seems to be the main or overarching question into which the other questions can be integrated. Though certainly not always the case, a rough rule of thumb to guide you is to look first at the final question in the topic. This is the case in our example. The three initial questions are subsidiary to the one about whether Freud's proposition carries any consequences for arguments about the existence of God. So what you need to do is to try out a provisional answer to this question and then consider possible answers to the initial questions which are *relevant* to establishing this provisional guiding answer.

For example, you might decide to answer 'No' to the last question. You would then be able to answer the 'why' question by pointing out that Freud was trying to reinterpret religious ideas as a psycho-social phenomenon which accords with his own theory of personality, rather than as a metaphysical phenomenon; that what he means is that these 'wishes of mankind' must therefore be taken seriously even though they are 'illusions' which could gradually be stripped away by some kind of social psychotherapy; and that in some respects he is right if we accept the boundaries he himself places on the meaning of 'religious ideas'. These considerations bring us back to the main question: all this might be of significant anthropological or psychological interest, but none of it seriously affects metaphysical questions about the existence of God.

Background knowledge

Since each of us brings a partly idiosyncratic general knowledge and experience to a given topic, it is not possible to generalise about the point at which any one of us should open a book. But, in putting off any reading until we have worked out a few *particular* things we want to find out about, we can create mental space for the kind of *formal* analysis of the topic we shall study in the next section. Postponing detailed reading also gives us the chance to articulate whatever general knowledge and experience we are able to bring to the issue in question. The list of suggestions I put forward on p. 36 to account for how General MacArthur honoured his promise to return to the Philippines owes nothing to reading I have done on MacArthur. I have never read any book on MacArthur. But I have read books on, and memoirs by, other generals from Cromwell to Eisenhower. I have seen (as most of us have) many TV movies about modern war, and read newspaper articles. It is in such very general storehouses of the mind that we can look for a few tentative ideas to get our thinking going. The richer and more articulate your initial 'personal response', the better your library research will be.

When we think of knowledge we do not only have in mind a store of information about a subject, though that is clearly part of it. Knowledge also includes knowing how to *approach* information.

All disciplines develop particular approaches to their material, and these approaches constitute part of the definition of a discipline. If you look back at the list of issues raised about MacArthur, you will see that it is made up of a number of approaches to, or *categories* of, the study of military general*ship*. There may be others (to be found in one's detailed reading), but that list is enough to get us going.

But the mere listing of categories may ignore the complexity of the relations between them. For example, strategic and tactical brilliance, effective political lobbying, ability to choose and devolve responsibility to subordinates, character, popularity with his troops and so on might all be useful categories under which to think of the success or otherwise of a military commander. To use them as a list of sub-headings to organise the essay on MacArthur, however, may distort the subject or miss the particular dynamic of their combination which explains this particular general's success. Even so, they can be part of the process by which you can get a purchase on the subject matter of the essay.

4.3 Formal meaning: the logical shape of possible answers

We shall now study the ways in which categories or classes of things can enter into various formal *relations* of meaning. There is much to be said for analysing essay topics formally since this kind of analysis can often throw up for consideration alternative answers which we might not otherwise think of.

By 'formal meaning' here we are thinking particularly of the meanings of a few logical expressions: the conjunctions 'and', 'or' and 'if'; the expression of negation 'not'; and the fundamental expressions of quantity (the so-called 'quantifiers') 'all' and 'some'. By applying these logical 'constants' to our essay topics and ringing the changes on their likely combinations, we can develop a number of useful ideas for an essay to explore. In what follows I wish to direct your attention particularly to what can be done with negation (not) and quantification (all, some). It can be very fruitful to ask of the topic, or some part of it, what is *not* the case, as well as what is. And we find, too, that what cannot easily be demonstrated to be universally true of all aspects of the case may be true of *all* aspects of it under *some* circumstances or conditions, of *some* aspects of it under *all* conditions, or of *some* aspects of it under *some* conditions.

An example

> What part did President Ronald Reagan's so-called 'hawkish' policies play in the fall of the Berlin Wall in 1989 and the end of the Cold War?

The one-line answer to the question may initially be phrased in such alternative terms as these:

1 Reagan's hawkish policies were solely responsible.

2 Reagan's hawkish policies played no (significant) part.

3 Reagan's hawkish policies played some part.

Now, these possibilities can be represented in terms of the relations between circles, a representation called 'Euler circles' after the eighteenth-century Swiss mathematician who devised them. The important first step in analysing the topic is to decide how many major terms (or subjects) there seem to be. In this example there seem at first to be three: Reagan's hawkish policies, fall of the Berlin Wall, and the end of the Cold War. But we can treat the last two as essentially the same, since by common consent the fall of the Berlin Wall symbolised the end of the Cold War. This leaves us with two – Reagan's hawkish policies and the end of the Cold War. Each of these terms is represented by a circle, which we shall label A and B respectively. Our first answer of the three above will be represented as in Figure 1: Reagan's hawkish policies and the end of the Cold War are coterminous ($A = B$). This means that *all* of Reagan's hawkish policies brought about the end of the Cold War *and that there were no other factors* responsible for the end of the Cold War. The extreme alternative (see Figure 2) is represented as two circles with nothing at all in common: Reagan's hawkish policies played *no part at all*, the end of the Cold War being wholly due to other factors. They are two quite separate issues, so the former can be expressed as a 'not-cause' of the end of the Cold War.

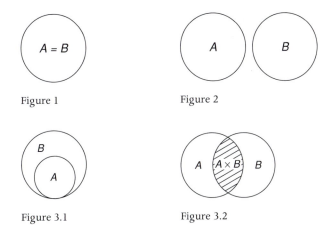

Figure 1

Figure 2

Figure 3.1

Figure 3.2

For the most part, in the humanities and social sciences, it is rarely the case that the propositions represented by Figures 1 and 2 can be successfully argued, however *logical* their basis might be.

The general answer that Reagan's hawkish policies played *some* part in the end of the Cold War can be represented in two quite logically distinct ways with two quite separate meanings. Figure 3.1 means that *all* of Reagan's hawkish policies played *some* part in the end of the Cold War, but that there were also other factors which had nothing to do with these policies (i.e. that these policies were a subset of causes). On the other hand, the overlapping circles of Figure 3.2 give us three quite separable but simultaneous propositions:

- that *some* of these policies played *some* part (the shaded area $A \times B$),

- but that *some* of these policies played *no* part (A),

- that there were factors other than these policies which also played *some* part (B).

Now we need to stop for a moment at this point and do a bit of practical thinking about how best to proceed from our logical analysis. Because our topic explicitly asks us to focus on the connection between Reagan's hawkish policies and the end of the Cold War ($A \times B$), that is where the emphasis throughout the answer we are preparing to give will need to fall. But we cannot adequately make a judgement about this without also taking into account causes of the end of the Cold War which are *not* related to those policies (*B*). Had the wording of the topic been more open, say, 'What brought about the end of the Cold War?', we could have treated all sorts of questions raised by *B*, if only to REJECT them. But since our topic is not quite so open, while we need to treat *B*, we will do so only insofar as this treatment is relevant to answering the question set.

A first attempt at an answer to our question might read something like this, in which the first three propositions are taken up in a sentence each (and in which my own initial prejudices or prejudgements are beginning to become apparent):

> **President Ronald Reagan's 'hawkish' policies certainly played some part in ending the Cold War and bringing down the Berlin Wall. However, some of these hawkish policies were quite counter-productive and might be said to have actually prolonged the process. Moreover, there were many other factors which contributed to the collapse of the Soviet Union, factors which turn out to be much more important than President Reagan's hawkish policies.**

This sketch for an answer has also taken another step: it implicitly assumes that there are what we might call 'degrees of someness'. These can be represented graphically as in Figures 3.2a, 3.2b and 3.2c, and in language in terms such as these:

> 3.2a Reagan's hawkish policies played an *overwhelming* part.

> 3.2b Reagan's hawkish policies played an *important* part.

> 3.2c Reagan's hawkish policies played a (relatively) *minor* part.

Figure 3.2a

Figure 3.2b

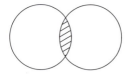

Figure 3.2c

We have more or less assumed so far that the two main terms in the essay topic – Reagan's hawkish policies and end of the Cold War – are simple terms. In fact terms consisting of a number of words can be quite complex. If we take the first, the adjective 'hawkish' limits or restricts 'policies', and implies that there may be, at least in theory, some *non-hawkish* policies of Reagan's (i.e. some more peaceable or conciliatory policies) which played a part and which we shall need to look out for when we begin our preliminary reading. Secondly, with respect to the end of the Cold War (and the fall of the Berlin Wall), we will need to be alert to other factors that might be relevant. There are a few fairly obvious candidates:

- developments in the Soviet Union and the policies of its president, Mikhail Gorbachev;

- developments in Europe, both eastern Europe and western Europe (the Berlin Wall symbolised the division of Europe by the iron curtain);

- developments elsewhere in the world, to the extent that the Cold War was global in its reach.

This list has one fairly obvious organising principle, namely these developments are regional or geographical in nature. Using the negating technique we employed above with respect to Reagan's non-hawkish policies, we could ask ourselves whether or not there might be factors which are *non-regional* or *non-geographical* in nature, but of some other kind.

Our formal analysis has now put us in a position to flesh out our first attempt at the shape of an answer. We can give it some substance by calling further on our general knowledge and by doing some preliminary reading of some sources on the reading list for this topic, as well as a few general internet sites, bearing in mind the questions our analysis has so far thrown up. My first results are these:

- Reagan's policies: some were definitely 'hawkish', especially in his first term as president, but a number of scholars suggest that in his second term he realised that such an approach might be pressing the wrong buttons in Moscow and became more conciliatory and diplomatic in his approach.

- Developments in the Soviet Union, especially the rise to power of Gorbachev: he perceived how the USSR was economically and militarily over-extended, unable to keep up with American arms spending.

- Developments in eastern Europe: Gorbachev gradually reduced the dependence, economic and strategic, of eastern European states on the Soviet Union and, unlike his predecessors, refused to guarantee Soviet intervention if these countries faced internal unrest, e.g. East Germany and Poland.

- Developments in western Europe: the growing economic strength and way of life of the then European Community (EC) provided a constant enticement to east Europeans, especially in Hungary and Poland, to once again become part of the European economy – which west European leaders actively encouraged. Another, quite different, western European factor was the British PM Margaret Thatcher's influence on both Gorbachev and Reagan.

- The rest of the world: the Soviet economy became incapable of supporting its client states in the rest of the world, e.g. Afghanistan, Cuba and parts of Africa were cut out from Moscow's spheres of interest. [Perhaps this is not especially relevant to the fall of the Berlin Wall and could be dropped.]

- Non-regional/geographic factors: the 'internal' decay of Communist ideology in the Soviet Union and a growing interest there in western Europe's 'social model'.

- Possible conclusion? When Reagan called on Gorbachev to 'tear down this wall' in 1987, it was mostly bellicose rhetoric for public consumption. Reagan was already, probably quite consciously, 'pushing at an open door' rather than engaging in 'hawkish' policies.

Well, there is a wealth of possibilities here, made available merely by a bit of general knowledge and a few hours of reading. There may already be too much to deal with, depending on the word limit of our essay. So this is going to have to be disciplined, at least a little bit.

The only way to discipline such musings is to try to write a draft paragraph in sentences that somehow have to start connecting with one another. This paragraph will probably be largely scrapped or re-written by the time the essay is finished; but it will give your later thinking and reading a guide. It is only one *proposal* for the *shape* of an answer out of the many that are possible. (As an exercise, if you are at all interested in this topic, you might try to use what we have done to draft a proposed shape of your own, before reading the one offered below.)

In matters of substance, as opposed to rhetoric designed for public consumption, President Reagan's policies towards the Soviet Union were at their most 'hawkish' in his first term of office from 1981 to 1985. In his second term, which was when progress really started to be made, as the State Department steadily eroded the influence of the hawkish Department of Defense, and as the influence of others such as the British prime minister Margaret Thatcher grew, Reagan became much more conciliatory and diplomatic in his approach. This was an approach which was to be continued by Reagan's successor George Bush, who had been president for almost a year when the Berlin Wall actually came down in November 1989. Moreover, as many historians think, Reagan was 'pushing at an open door' – nothing much would have happened if Mikhail Gorbachev had not been in power in Moscow from 1985. It was Gorbachev, not the Americans, who realised that the USSR was economically and militarily over-extended. It was Gorbachev who realised that the USSR could not forever prop up the internal security and the economies of client states in eastern Europe, a few of which (Hungary and Poland) were already developing closer economic ties with a prosperous and welcoming western Europe. We can add to all this a growing disenchantment in the Soviet Union itself with Communist ideology and an increasing receptivity towards the European 'social

> model' (rather than America's unconstrained economic neo-liberalism). The best that can be said for the idea that Reagan's hawkishness played a part in the ending of the Cold War is that it prepared some of the ground for these major developments that succeeded it.

Our formal analysis of this essay topic has enabled us to see that the question cannot be answered adequately by confining our attention to Reagan's hawkish policies. We have had to draw upon a much wider range of possible explanations. The analysis also helps us to see that had, say, 'the problems of the Soviet economy' replaced 'Reagan's so-called "hawkish" policies' in the topic, the answer would differ more in *emphasis* – including the space allotted to discussing the various possible explanations and the sequence in which we take them up – than in what is included or left out of the discussion.

To conclude this account of the way in which one can attempt a formal analysis of the possible answers and the shape of those answers, it must be said that this technique lends itself better to some essay topics than it does to others – at least as a way of examining relationships between terms whose relations are to be analysed, in the way that 'Reagan's hawkish policies' and 'the end of the Cold War' are placed before us in the topic above. In the topic on General MacArthur, for example, you would need to put forward a number of possible terms (such as we did on pp. 36–7) before you could begin to carry out the analysis of the possible relations between them. Some more sample analyses, including ones on topics of this latter kind, are briefly presented in Appendix 2.

4.4   Evaluative criteria

As soon as you begin to make choices about following one line of enquiry rather than another suggested by your analysis of the topic, you are implicitly making use of certain criteria according to which the choice is made. You saw me doing this in proposing an answer based upon Figure 3.2. No attempt was made at that point to examine *why* I should choose this proposal rather than another. The final stage in your preliminary reflection should therefore be directed towards a consideration of the terms in which your choice might provisionally be justified.

It is useful to begin by asking yourself what you mean by any of the very general evaluative terms thrown up by the formal analysis of relations. In the Cold War topic, for example, it is necessary to ask how terms like 'some part', 'overwhelming part', 'important part' and 'minor part' are to be understood. The proposed answer on pp. 49–50 above seems to be assuming that Reagan's hawkish policies were 'not an overwhelming' cause of the end of the Cold War simply because they were just one amongst many others. That is to say, the criterion operating here seems to be based on simple (perhaps simplistic) arithmetic. You will also notice that the major factors in that proposal were, judging by the space allotted to them, the other issues brought up, so that by comparison Reagan's hawkishness was of little if any importance. To do this, however, is only to shift the problem. By what criteria are the other factors to be judged as 'major'? What is meant by 'major' here? Such general 'quantitative' judgements are certainly necessary; but by themselves they are not sufficient.

Perhaps the most useful strategy in searching for ways of giving substance to such criteria is to try to derive, from either the wording of the topic or the few facts that you have so far assembled, an appropriate 'principle' or a metaphor of some kind. Many, if not most, explanations in academic writing (as well as more widely) are based on metaphors. The metaphor tentatively offered in the final sentence of the draft paragraph above is 'preparing the ground'. (Further reflection might be able to improve on this.) By paying attention to the kinds of explanatory principles and metaphors used in the disciplines you study, it is possible to build up almost by second nature a store of approaches to finding suitable criteria to use in your essays.

5   Summary

The most fruitful way of revealing to yourself how far your reflection has taken you is, as we have done, to try writing a provisional introduction to the essay as early as you can, even though there will be many gaps of information or analysis that you cannot fill. I think a draft opening paragraph or two is superior to jotting down rough notes, making outlines or (as many writing handbooks suggest) making concept maps in which you write down various ideas and then link them with lines to show that some of them are related. What none of these stratagems does is to push you to crystallise the precise *nature* of the relationships between the ideas in your head: only continuous prose can do that.

The whole process of reflection on your essay topic should yield these things:

- Some appreciation of the meanings of the terms used in the topic and the ideas or entities to which they refer, an interpretation of any vagueness or ambiguity in the meaning of the topic as a whole, and just sufficient background knowledge and a few basic categories in which to organise it to get you going (see section 4.4).

- A few proposals to examine, arising from the formal analysis of the possible relations between the terms (see section 4.3).

- A few suggestions as to which criterion or criteria might be appropriate to help you decide among the tentative proposals (see section 4.4).

- A decision whether you will answer 'yes' or 'no' to a yes/no question, whether you will agree or disagree with a stated or implied proposition in the topic, or which of the proposals that you have developed in answer to a more open-ended topic you will provisionally argue for (see section 4.1).

- An attempt at a provisional opening paragraph or two to help you clarify an argument which you can then put to the test in the wider and more detailed reading you are now ready to embark upon (see section 4.3).

3

Interpretation: reading and taking notes

But be ye doers of the word, and not hearers only, deceiving your own selves.

New Testament, James 1:22

If you think of reading and taking notes not so much as absorbing information as entering into a discussion with the authors of your sources, many common reading problems begin to solve themselves. This chapter helps you do this by

- showing you how to deal with different kinds of source material – primary source material, secondary discussions of evidence, and tertiary statements of authoritative opinion

- getting you to focus on what the authors of your sources are DOING as they themselves engage with other scholars, evidence and ideas; and how they structure their text into patterns which you need to be able to follow

- providing you with a vocabulary of terms with which to analyse what authors are doing – terms which become the basis for your note-taking and the essay or paper you are writing

- suggesting ways to bring your own knowledge and experience into reading and taking notes, so that you yourself can enter into the discussion taking place, even with very difficult sources.

1   The 'problem' of reading

1.1   Common difficulties

Your essay, we found in chapter 2, is your 'best' answer to a question. It is not an answer to be found in some book. Nor is it an answer to be found in some combination of books. It is not, on the other hand, an answer to be spun wholly out of yourself as a spider spins its web. The problem of reading for an academic essay is the problem of establishing the relationship between ourselves and our books on a reliable and firm footing. Many students pose the problem in words such as these: 'I know so little about the subject and those who write the books know so much. In addition, these authors express their ideas much better than I can. How, then, can I be expected to give my own answer in my own words when it is all in the books? Much of the time I have to struggle to merely understand what they say, far less give my own ideas.' Put this way the problem is misconceived, because such a student sees his or her role as being on the one hand to comprehend and reproduce what the books say while on the other to be 'original'. It is hard to reconcile such extremes. In this chapter the problem will be posed somewhat differently – as a problem not of comprehension, reproduction and 'originality', but as one of *interpretation*. Reading is an attempt by you to interpret what a book is saying from your own standpoint and from that of the essay question you are attempting to answer.

If reading is seen thus to be part of a process that includes thinking and writing, you should be able to approach the task in an active frame of mind. Interpreting a book is rather like taking part in a conversation. The reader and the author of the book converse on a subject in which they have mutual, though somewhat varying, interests. Some of the skills you might employ in any conversation which aims at resolving an issue can be brought into play: asking questions of the text, seeking clarification on a point you haven't fully understood, judging the relevance to your question of what the book says, looking for evidence of the author's mood or attitude to the subject, noticing whether and how one thing said squares up with what was said earlier or what was said by another author, and so on. The more thoroughly you have reflected on your essay topic (see chapter 2), the better prepared for interpreting the books you will be, if only because you will have a good stock of questions in your mind and on paper when you go to the library. It is this preparation, and the approaches to interpretation set out in this chapter, that should help to give you the independence you will need in order to avoid turning your essay into a pastiche of other people's work.

Such an approach should also help you to cope with some of the other problems of reading:

- How do you stop your mind wandering off on paths of its own, no matter how hard you try to concentrate? By concentrating less on trying to concentrate and giving your attention to your own part in the conversation.

- How do you take notes more efficiently, so that piles of unused paraphrases do not remain when your essay is complete? By constantly interpreting the *relevance* of what your sources say in the light of your developing argument for the essay.

- How do you read more quickly? By first of all slowing down and taking the time to build up a general interpretation of what an author is DOING with his text.

- How do you get away from the domination of the writer's language over your own? By putting her text away from you and thinking about what she says before you make your notes.

- When should you copy an author's words verbatim into your notes? Not so much when you find an idea very well expressed as when you find something about it that you might want to put under your interpretative microscope in the essay you are planning to write.

It will be the purpose of this chapter to elaborate on these snap answers to some common questions and to put before you some of the various dimensions of interpretation.

1.2   The importance of background reading

Many textbooks emphasise the 'skills' of reading. It is wrong to get the idea, however, that mastering these skills is all that you require to become a good reader. You will probably notice that you have many more initial difficulties with reading in those disciplines whose content or approach is new to you. Some recent research in reading tends to confirm the common-sense conclusion that the more you know about a subject the easier it is to read in it. The problem, though, is that we usually read academic works in order to learn about the content. There is no simple skill or technique that can easily be applied to the solving of this conflict. There is, however, a general programme that you can follow.

The programme is this. You need first to distinguish between the kind of close, critical reading you will need to engage in for your essay-writing and simply beguiling the time with a book because you have a general interest in the subject. Secondly, it is important to give as much time as you can to this general background reading of whole books, and not to confine your reading to poring slowly over the central texts in your course. Both kinds of reading are necessary because they help each other.

General background reading should be done by sitting in an armchair and letting the book wash over you, so to speak, without your stopping to clarify puzzling points, to enquire into the connections between the book and the syllabus, or to assess its relevance to any particular question. What is important in this kind of reading is to grasp the 'plot' and the general rhythm of the exposition, rather as we are commonly supposed to read a novel or watch a movie. If we look for anything in particular, it is only for the beginning, the middle and the end – which is why it is important to read whole books rather than (as our typical essays minimally require of us) just bits of books. A book read in this way can rightly be considered to be as disposable as a late-night television movie or a newspaper article. If there is anything that particularly engages your attention you can mark it or note it briefly on a scrap of paper for later critical attention.

Critical interpretation and evaluation such as we use for writing essays feeds on the half-formed images and experiences of general reading. Critical reading must respond to details. General reading gives to these details a context which, though difficult to specify or quantify, enriches them, and over time helps them to make sense. We saw earlier (p. 25) the particular dangers of becoming too 'syllabus-bound'. You can escape these dangers, whilst simultaneously helping your studies, by choosing background reading which is broadly relevant to your course of studies. Many disciplines are now well served by general books for the layman, autobiographies by, and biographies of, significant figures in the advancement of that branch of learning, and some textbooks that are as readable as they are informative. 'Preliminary reading' lists for certain courses are sometimes a guide, and should be treated in the manner suggested above rather than as laborious treatises to be learned. Many publishers have series of very short, inexpensive books on major figures and major topics in particular subject areas which make ideal background reading. And, of course, there is the internet. Speed, enjoyment, relative superficiality and satisfaction are the criteria which should govern this kind of reading. None of these criteria has of itself any public academic standing. The value of this reading appears only through a crystal lightly in the way you reflect on an essay topic and impart almost unconsciously a richer texture to your writing. Background reading is not time wasted.

2   Evidence, interpretation and fact

2.1   Primary, secondary and tertiary sources

Before we can bring tools of interpretation to bear on a text, we must first of all decide what kind of text it is and what we hope to gain from it. Some texts contain mostly data. Others contain discussions and interpretations of data, in which the author is arguing for a particular point of view. A third kind of text contains relatively little argument, much presentation of information and few references to the sources of that information.

We shall call these three kinds of text primary, secondary and tertiary sources. Primary sources consist in the object observed;

this has to be interpreted by you and by the writers of your secondary sources. They include the poem, novel or play studied by literature students, the documents studied by historians, the painting or the composer's score studied by art critics or musicologists, the 'raw figures' economists analyse, the survey data of the sociologist, the experimental results of the psychologist, and so on. Now, while this seems to be clear enough, the distinction between primary evidence and secondary interpretation does not work so easily in some disciplines. For instance, anthropology students must accept much of an anthropologist's ethnographic data on trust, since the act of recording aspects of a social structure or a custom is itself something of a secondary interpretation on the part of the field anthropologist. Interpretative statements can therefore look very much like statements of fact or pieces of evidence. Even so, it is useful to make the attempt to distinguish where you can.

Secondary sources are the monographs with which the library shelves are mostly filled, and the articles in academic journals and books of 'readings'. It is useful to distinguish two types of secondary source. The first, which we shall call 'theoretical', consists almost entirely of abstract argument which starts from certain premises and argues its way to a conclusion – somewhat like a mathematical proof. The second is 'empirical', and in this case the author takes care to base his or her arguments on carefully constructed interpretations of empirical data. Such works refer constantly to the primary sources so that readers can check them out themselves if they wish, though such works may also have a strong 'theoretical' component.

Tertiary sources, by contrast, are the typical course 'textbook', encyclopaedia, desk dictionary, handbook, etc., which might either be a practical 'how to' book (like this one) or a survey of generally held knowledge in the field. They tend to be based not on primary sources but on secondary sources, and present much of their information dogmatically as received opinion.

Like most boundaries, the borderlines between primary, secondary and tertiary sources can become blurred in certain works. For example, there are textbooks which are very broad in scope but which on some aspects of the subject matter may look very closely at primary evidence and argue for one interpretation of the evidence over others. Similarly, there are often sections in secondary monographs which present information very much in textbook style. In your reading you should watch out for transitions such as these, for reasons we shall go into below.

And again, the same text may fall into two categories, depending on the purpose with which the discipline treats it or on your own particular purpose. An example of this is the status of novels in literary studies and in history respectively. In a literature course, a novel will usually be treated as a primary text. But if the novel contained a portrayal of the life or politics of the times in which it was written, a historian might use it as a secondary source – one writer's interpretation of the times he or she lived in. Even so, if the historian were to switch his or her interest to the history of contemporary attitudes to the government or life of the day, the novel could then be regarded as a primary source. Plato's *Republic* may constitute a primary source for an essay on Plato, but a secondary source for an essay on theories of government. The issues of interpretation that arise from that same text may therefore vary considerably. This double life is led by many of the classic secondary sources in a discipline: books which were written in order to throw new light on a certain problem themselves become the primary evidence on which later interpretations of their authors' thought are based.

2.2   The consequences of this distinction for essay-writing

To be able to recognise whether, for the purposes of your essay, a source or part of a source is primary, secondary or tertiary will determine how you treat it in your essay. The important question you should always ask is 'Is this statement (or series of statements) a piece of primary evidence, an author's interpretation of the evidence in which the reasoning is shown, or is it authoritative opinion?' Two things follow from this distinction. First, in the unlikely event that all your essay topic requires is a DESCRIPTION (see pp. 8–9 above), then you can rest fairly content with tertiary sources; if you attempt to justify a point of view (to 'discuss' – as we said most topics require), then secondary and primary sources are critical. Put another way, most academic essays cannot be based upon the reading of textbooks

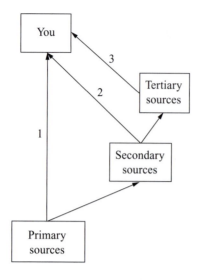

1 Evidence
2 Evidence + interpretations
3 Accepted 'fact' + interpretations

Figure 4

alone. Not only that, but your own essay-writing technique should, in general, be modelled more closely on the way evidence and interpretation are handled in secondary sources than on the style of tertiary texts.

Secondly – and this is of supreme importance because many students have difficulty with it – what is offered as (tertiary) authoritative opinion or as (secondary) interpretation in a book should not normally be used uncritically as evidence in an essay, unless, of course, you are writing about the interpretations and opinions of the scholars you are examining. Only primary evidence and well-established facts about which there seems to be no debate should be used in this way.* Something of these relationships between you and your sources can be seen in Figure 4.

---

* A fact should be distinguished from primary evidence, though both can be used to build an interpretation on. Facts are really the long-term outcomes of investigations into primary evidence. A fact can be defined pragmatically as a

The interpretations and opinions you read should be presented as such in your essay (Smith concludes that . . . , Smith believes that . . . , Smith interprets this to mean that . . . , In Smith's view . . . , etc.). A writer does not always signal clearly when he or she passes from the presentation of evidence to interpreting or giving an opinion, so you must learn to recognise the implicit signs yourself. Let us examine two short passages.

The first is from a popular book on the use of language written by a distinguished linguist, Dwight Bolinger:

> This chapter is about the nature of THINGS. About entities and pseudo-entities. About reality, and the sorcery of words.
>
> On 29 May 1976 the female employees at Carter's Semiconductors in Ipoh, Malaysia, left their workbenches and ran from the factory, terrified and shrieking that they had been molested by a ten-foot ghost without a head. The worried management called in a witch doctor who proceeded to sprinkle rice and water around the factory and sacrificed a goat to appease the spirits of the dead. The workers went back to their jobs and the ghost back to its limbo. Ghosts in Malaysia are a restless lot. Every so often one will show up at a school and frighten the daylights out of the pupils. There are clinical-minded people who claim that the youngsters are just hysterical from overwork, but that of course is pure speculation.

The second paragraph of the extract begins with the recounting of certain facts. Now, since this is not what might be called an 'academic' book, the author does not give the source of these facts, and so we must take it on trust that his version of the story is accurate (and note this in our reference). Everything down to the last sentence, except

statement (or theory) whose truth is agreed on by all or most authoritative opinion. Hence it must be distinguished from the authoritative opinion of just some scholars. Not everyone agrees with this definition of a fact, but it does help explain why some of yesterday's 'facts' are today's discarded theories: somebody successfully challenged uniform authoritative opinion. The only sure way to discover whether a statement is truly a fact is to compare several authorities. To take a short cut by relying on a single textbook can be dangerous.

the interpretative comment, 'Ghosts in Malaysia are a restless lot', will count as fact. The last sentence is, however, interpretative. The author reports other 'clinical-minded' people's interpretation of these events, and then offers his own whimsical and ironic interpretation of their interpretation. Hysteria from overwork is not fact or evidence but, as he says, 'speculation'. That naturalistic interpretation is no less an interpretation than positing the existence of ghosts is: the facts are that these people said they saw a ghost; one possible interpretation of this is that they did see a ghost.

The second extract is from a book on the psychology of perception. The author, John M. Wilding, is examining theories which attempt to explain how attention works. Psychologists conduct their enquiries by putting hypotheses through various kinds of experimental test. One kind of test designed to study how attention works is the 'dual-task experiment'. Wilding reports this in the first sentence, and we can take it on his authority that such tests are used 'quite widely'. He then goes on – in the way characteristic of disciplines which carry out experiments – to describe an experiment performed by Taylor and to summarise Taylor's results. This is the evidence. In the fourth sentence ('Taylor concluded . . . '), Wilding moves away from the evidence and presents Taylor's own interpretation of it. This interpretation is that judgements about whether two lines of digits are the same or different are not performed using the same kind of strategy: one is 'holistic', the other 'serial'. At this point Wilding signals his disagreement with Taylor's interpretation of his evidence, and then goes on to show why he disagrees, offering an alternative explanation:

Dual processing tasks have been used quite widely to study micro-attention. In an experiment by Taylor (1976) examining letter matching, same–different judgements were made of letters formed out of straight line segments (like those in digital watches and calculators). Same judgements were made equally quickly, regardless of how many segments had to be matched, but 'different' judgements were slower as the number of segments by which two letters differed decreased. Taylor concluded that same judgements were holistic and different judgements were carried out segment by segment. However, it does not follow that the segment analyses were necessarily carried out serially, since clearly if segments are analysed in parallel, completion of one difference signal is adequate to trigger a response. If the time to complete each comparison varies on different trials, then, the more such comparisons are being made, the more likely it is that one will finish quickly and trigger a response. Hence responses will be slower when letters differ by only one segment than when they differ by several. Obviously same judgements could not be explained in the same way, since time to complete analysis of all dimensions would increase as the number of segments to be handled increased, unless of course extra capacity is deployed for the more difficult task.

This is a good example of a secondary text. There are no assertions or generalisations which are not based on evidence and interpretation. The processes by which Wilding arrives at his own conclusion are spelled out in detail. In writing such as this, however, we are relying on the author to give an accurate summary of the primary evidence – Taylor's experimental procedures and results. We are not given the results in detail. But since there is no question raised about the methods or results, we should probably be justified in accepting Wilding's account. Students of psychology and similar subjects might usefully compare the way in which Wilding constructs this piece of writing with that in which the authors of many introductory texts present received knowledge in the discipline.

Looking thus at the interplay between evidence, interpretation and authoritative opinion in the kinds of source we consult is the beginning of good, critical reading and a necessary foundation for writing.

2.3   Authoritative opinion and the internet

Unlike most of the books, journals and other material you read for your essays and research papers, much of what is found on the internet has not been through a process of screening by publishers' editors and academic readers before it appears on a website. The internet is therefore a seductive medium for special-interest groups, propagandists and even tricksters to place their opinions before a large audience. (There are websites which in their layout and many of their details mimic 'official' websites so closely that it takes some experience and a shrewd eye to recognise them for the parodies they are.) With this in mind many tutors will provide a list of authoritative websites appropriate for the subjects you are studying, just as they give you reading lists for printed matter. This should not, however, prevent you from casting your net more widely, any more than you have to restrict your reading to books on the reading lists, as long as you are aware of the potential pitfalls.

Most commentators on how to approach websites appeal to a variant of what we have noticed above about distinguishing evidence, interpretation and authoritative opinion, and weighing these factors up. In this respect the critical reading of websites is much the same as that which you apply to printed matter. Are the sources made explicit, and the evidence both reported accurately and presented as objectively as possible within the terms of the argument being put forward? Do the interpretations or opinions flow from the evidence presented rather than being plucked out of thin air; and how well are other opinions engaged with and discussed? What clues to the authorship or sponsorship of a website can you glean by noting the domain in the address (e.g. .gov, .ac.uk, .edu, .org, .co, .com) or by clicking an 'about us' button on the website? Finally, as with a book or journal article, you want to know when the site was posted, when it has been maintained and updated and whether the information in it is still likely to be current. For a more complete introduction to how to analyse a website, the following two online tutorials have proved (at the time of writing) to be thorough, well maintained and durable:

E. Place *et al.* (2006), 'Internet detective: wise up to the web', 3rd edn, Intute Virtual Training Suite. www.vts.intute.ac.uk/detective.

Susan E. Beck (1997, 2008), 'The good, the bad & the ugly: or, why it's a good idea to evaluate web sources'. http://lib.nmsu.edu/instruction/evalcrit.html.

3   What an author does

There is a kind of note-taking commonly carried out with a finger of one hand on a line of text and the fingers of the other holding the pen on the notepad. The note-taking proceeds a few words at a time, with the eyes flicking from book to pad and back again. This kind of note-taking comes rather close to the 'automatic' response of the old-fashioned copy-typist, who could transfer symbols from one page to another, almost entirely short-circuiting the centres of the brain which process the meaning of the text. Such activity in the library often gives us the sense of being busy, of 'working'. In fact, the productivity of such work is not very high, since sooner or later we are going to have to go through these notes and interpret them. When we do get round to this, we sometimes find that our notes, notwithstanding their faithful rendition of parts of the text, are somewhat incoherent. We are then placed in the position of having to search out the book again.

Your notes should therefore attempt to be as intelligible an interpretation of the text as you can make them. This means getting away from simply processing the 'surface' of an author's language onto the notepad. You need to keep up your end of the conversation and to question the text for its meanings. One way of testing whether you have come up with an interpretation of the passage is to put the book from you while you make your note. Unless you have tried (even subconsciously) to memorise the text, most of the words and sentence structures that come to your pen should be your own. If they do not come, either in part or at all, you will need to study the text further – not to memorise but to interpret.

Putting an author's words into your own is called 'paraphrasing', and if you simultaneously shorten the length of the author's text, you are 'summarising' or making a 'précis'. Now, it is important to be aware that, the moment you stop quoting or copying the author's words, you are paraphrasing, and that every paraphrase you make involves you in the interpretation of the author's meaning. Even in relatively slight changes, a bit of the author is lost and a bit of your interpretation is added. This is inescapable. So it is best to bite the bullet and to begin to see your reading and note-taking not so much as a faithful record of what the author wrote (for which quoting is the only solution) as your considered interpretation of what the author meant. To paraphrase is to make concrete what you think the author means.

If you lack confidence in your ability to interpret an author's meaning without greatly misrepresenting what he or she says, you might need to work quite hard at what is to be said in the rest of this chapter. But if you keep it in mind that your essay is to be your 'best' answer to the essay question, you will see it follows that your use of the sources must equally be your 'best' interpretation of what they mean. You should try – so far as you can – to make your notes preliminary sketches for some part of the finished essay, just as an artist sometimes makes pencil or charcoal 'studies' of the subject before composing it in paint.

The usual way of representing what the author means is, as we have seen, to paraphrase his or her words in your own. What paraphrasing does is to give your account of what the author is SAYING. The focus is entirely on the content of the author's 'message'. Though necessary, to concentrate exclusively on what the author is saying – on the content – is to miss most of the really important clues that enable you to establish your own 'best' interpretation.

Another way of approaching the question 'What does the author mean?' is to ask what the author is DOING with his or her language. Academic writing (you will remember from chapter I) does a great deal more than simply try to represent the truth about the subject under scrutiny: a point of view has to be established, the evidence must be assembled and turned into a coherent argument, meanings must be clarified, the reader must be addressed, and the writings of others taken into account. Academic authors will usually be quite explicit about their major aims in the introductory chapter of a book or in the opening paragraphs of a chapter; but not many stop and tell you constantly what they are up to – partly because they themselves are not fully conscious of what they are doing. Good writers (and don't forget that not all academics are good writers) will often litter their text with clues and signposts, but the reader must be able to find and interpret them. Hence it becomes quite necessary to puzzle out what the authors of your books are trying to DO.

You are already familiar with this practice from everyday language. Statements which appear on the surface to be rather similar we easily interpret as DOING different things. When you see an advertisement

> **Buy now, pay later**

you will have no difficulty in recognising this to be ENCOURAGING or EXHORTING. When you see a rather similar piece of language, say on the notice board outside a church or mosque,

> **Sin now, pay later**

you interpret its function to be quite different – WARNING rather than exhorting. You use your experience of the two contexts and your knowledge of language in the word-play on 'pay' to ascribe differing functions to these statements.

Similarly, two statements set side by side may in certain circumstances be easily interpreted:

> **He fell into the river. He got wet.**

The first statement EXPLAINS why he got wet, and this causes no difficulty. In

> **The winter of 1788–9 was a very harsh one in France, inflicting untold misery on the peasants. The Revolution broke out in July 1789.**

we might similarly interpret the first statement to be explaining the second, ASCRIBING A CAUSE of the Revolution. But were this to have been written

> The winter of 1788–9 was a very harsh one in France, inflicting untold misery on the peasants. Nevertheless, the Revolution broke out in July 1789.

we are immediately faced with a puzzle. Far from ascribing a cause, the first statement is now CONCEDED to be a *countercondition* for the outbreak of revolution: perhaps the implication is that miserable peasants turn in on themselves and their problems and are not expected to be found fomenting revolution on the streets. The signal of the change in function from 'ascribing a cause' to 'conceding a countercondition' is contained wholly in the linking adverbial 'nevertheless'. You may speculate what other changes of function and meaning would be signalled by 'coincidentally', 'be that as it may' or 'indeed'.

There are three main kinds of motive and intention you need to be able to recognise in order to begin to interpret what an author is doing. The first concerns the author's relationship to other writers; the second the author's ways of analysing the subject matter; and the third the structuring of the subject matter into a coherent sequence of ideas. We shall put them in terms of questions you can ask the text. They are these:

- What is the author's main aim or motive in writing the work (or the part of it in which you are interested), with respect to what others have previously written on the subject?

- What modes of discourse does the writer employ to analyse the subject matter itself, and how is this carried out?

- What does the writer do to structure his or her analyses into a coherent sequence of ideas? How are the parts fitted together in order to compose the whole?

The next three sections of this chapter will examine each of these in turn.

4   An author's major motives

An academic author has to have some overriding reason for writing and publishing his or her work. Some of these reasons will be personal, but they need not concern us. More importantly, the author hopes to make a contribution to an ongoing debate in his or her discipline, and so the work produced must be seen as part of that debate. The major aims of the work will usually be defined in terms of what is already known and thought about the subject and what the writer wishes to add to the work of others. If you look at the foreword or preface to your books, you will sometimes find a writer apologising for producing yet another book on the subject, but this apology will quickly be followed by a justification for 'yet another book'.

This justification will usually be worked out in more detail in the first chapter (or, if the work is a journal article, in the opening paragraphs). For this reason, your first task on opening a book is to study the preface and the opening chapter. Only then should you make use of the index and the table of contents to hunt down those parts of the work that might be especially relevant to your essay. The author's major aims provide the context which enables you to make sense of the detail in the body of the book, and provide the first clues as to how you will begin to interpret the substance of what is said. Such discussions, it is true, are often very general, abstract and theoretical. You might therefore find them difficult to follow. But some slow, careful reading here will produce enormous dividends in the speed and success with which you will be able to read and interpret other parts of the book. And by the same token, your reading of the detail will help you understand more clearly those general and abstract points over which you initially puzzled. (If this sounds circular, it is. But it is not a vicious circle: the general and the abstract help you see the significance of the particular and the concrete, and vice versa.) All academic work demands attention to both.

The most common motives which govern academic writing are these:

- AGREEING WITH, ACCEDING TO, DEFENDING or CONFIRMING a particular point of view;

- PROPOSING a new point of view;

- CONCEDING that an existing point of view has certain merits but that it needs to be QUALIFIED in certain important respects;

- REFORMULATING an existing point of view or statement of it, such that the new version makes a better explanation;

- DISMISSING a point of view or another person's work on account of its inadequacy, irrelevance, incoherence or by recourse to other appropriate criteria;

- REJECTING, REBUTTING or REFUTING another's argument on various reasoned grounds;

- RECONCILING two positions which may seem at variance by appeal to some 'higher' or 'deeper' principle;

- RETRACTING or RECANTING a previous position of one's own in the face of new arguments or evidence.

These major motives are not mutually exclusive: they can be combined in various ways. We shall find out how this can be done by examining an essay by Thomas F. Glick entitled '*Convivencia*: an introductory note' (1992, 2007), which for reasons of space I have had to abridge. The essay discusses different interpretations of the interactions between Muslims, Christians and Jews in mediaeval Spain. *Convivencia* is usually translated as 'living together' and some historians have seen this period as a 'golden age'; others more sceptically have called it 'co-existence'.

(The chronological background is briefly this: communities of Jews had started to settle in Spain in the first and second centuries AD, while Christianity took hold among the rest of the population between the fourth and the sixth centuries. The country was invaded in 711 by Muslims from North Africa who established a flourishing multicultural and multi-religious civilisation in southern and central Spain (al-Andalus), for a time stretching as far north as Saragossa. In the middle of the eleventh century, the Christian states of Leon-Castile and Navarre in the far north of the country began their counter-attack (*reconquista*), had retaken Toledo in central Spain by 1085, and gradually whittled away the Muslim states until the last of them, Granada, capitulated to the Christian monarchs four centuries later in 1492 (the year Columbus set off on the voyage that led to his landfall in the Americas). It was also in this same year that Jews who would not convert to Christianity were expelled from Spain. Most Muslims were expelled some 120 years later.

Glick concentrates on the latter part of this period as Christian influence begins to dominate. He starts off by describing how a mid-twentieth-century historian, Américo Castro, who popularised the label *convivencia*, made it carry many idealistic overtones and how others have disagreed. Glick then announces his over-arching motives for the essay: to DEFEND ('retrieve') Castro from his critics by REFORMULATING the nature of the argument 'in sociological terms'. We shall trace his other motives after presenting Glick's text. (Endnote reference numbers are reproduced, but not the endnotes themselves; the paragraphs have been numbered for ease of reference; and a few clarifying notes have been added in square brackets.)

After a longish peroration on the historical background of the notion *convivencia*, Glick gets to the heart of the matter on page 2, where we pick him up:

(1) ... recent historians of ethnic relations in medieval Spain have preferred the term 'coexistence,' rather than *convivencia*. They have rejected Castro's view of intergroup relations as idealised, romanticised, and idyllic, presenting only the positive aspects of cultural contact and underrating the negative ones.

(2) Here I would like to state how that social dynamic is presently perceived in post-Castro historiography, and then attempt to retrieve Castro's social psychological component and restate it in sociological terms.

II

(3) To reformulate these questions, we must inquire to what extent, and how, social distance configures the nature of cultural interchange. Any answer to this question must take full account of the complexities of the social dynamics of cultural interaction, and of the fact that the relationship between cultural and social processes changes over time and according to specific contexts. It is also well to bear in mind Mark Meyerson's distinction between assimilation and integration. To the extent that both Jews and Muslims were expelled, they were never assimilated by Christian society, and hence it is easy to argue that they were never acculturated either. But if they were not assimilated, they were indeed integrated; and integration, a process of normalization of day-to-day interactions, provides the immediate social context for cultural change.

(4) *Convivencia*, under any kind of operational definition, must encompass the ability of persons of different ethnic groups to step out of their ethnically bound roles in order to interact on a par with members of competing groups. We admit, however, that many kinds of interactions are conditioned by ethnic role playing. Are there roles not ethnically bound? The ability of medieval peoples to assume them was limited, or rather interactions were sharply structured by both ethnic/religious ascription as well as by social class. Nevertheless, one person can play multiple roles, some of which are more ethnically bound than others.

(5) Elena Lourie, in her exploration of the differing roles that Jews and Mudejars (Muslims living under Christian rule) could successfully play in the medieval kingdom of Aragon, states that those Mudejars who had military skills were successful in playing the role of soldier in Christian units, regardless of ethnicity. But Jews she views as unable to play multiple roles except in very limited, mainly socially marginal contexts, as when Jewish and Christian criminals conspired without respect to ethnic identity, or in the specific case she describes, built on the ethnic connotations of moneylending in order to set up a clever confidence game.

(6) But what of less exceptional interactions? Lourie may be right in referring to St. Thomas [Aquinas'] admiring citation of Maimonides [a Jewish philosopher] as merely an instance of academic courtesy, but the same cannot be said of Jews and Christians who formed translation teams. As we shall see, [this reference is to another essay later in the book] in twelfth-and thirteenth-century Christian Spain, Christian translators were frequently subordinate to Jewish scholars whom they addressed as their 'masters.'

(7) One of Lourie's goals is to test the 'relative vulnerability' of Jews and Muslims to persecution in Christian Spain. One of her conclusions is that Mudejars ran less risk of mass assault (that is, pogroms) than Jews did, but greater risk of individual kidnapping and enslavement. What were the cultural concomitants of vulnerability? On the face of it there was an inverse relationship between vulnerability and cultural openness. As a group, Muslims were less vulnerable to persecution than Jews, yet their culture was more highly bounded and impervious to Christian pressures. Such a conclusion, while standing on its head the commonsense expectation that tolerance would encourage acculturation, has a certain kind of psychological logic arising from the dependence of the persecuted upon the persecutor. I raise the issue only to restate, in another form, that the relationship between cultural dynamics and social dynamics is a complicated one and cannot be left to insight or ideology.

(8) As Lourie also makes clear, the different social structures of Muslim and Jewish minority communities in Christian Spain affected differentially the reactions of each to the dominant caste. The Jewish community was internally stratified to a much greater degree than were the Mudejars. It is precisely in the pattern of class stratification that we can locate the ability of Jewish *maiores* [magnates] to interact with Christians, notably in the market-place and in the financial departments of royal administration, by stepping out of their ethnic roles. This in turn makes intelligible the conversion of Jewish magnates and intellectuals in the fifteenth century, for substantial acculturation must be assumed to have been characteristic of members of this group prior to their conversion. Indeed, the working out of the cultural concomitants of class

stratification among late medieval Jews will provide the necessary social grounding to strengthen and make more intelligible Castro's pioneering study of the Jewish presence in Spanish literature. Castro, incidentally, wisely observed that class stratification among Christians strongly affected the different relationships of members of that caste to the Jews.

(9) In assessing the variety and range of cultural elements exchanged, we must recognize that these did not merely include vocabulary, techniques, or manners of speech, dress or diet, and that acculturation involved conscious shifts of the most subtle and intimate nature. For example, in northern Europe, Jews living among Christians acquired from them a distinctive consciousness of self that distinguished both groups from their coreligionists in the Mediterranean world. Any notion that borrowing across cultural boundaries is merely superficial is wishful thinking. The image of a sealed, pristine, pure, and uncontaminated culture that ethnic groups typically ascribe to themselves (even if only to lament its loss) is contrary not only to all the evidence but to everyday experience. There are no cultural isolates, not in remote jungles, and much less in the cosmopolitan towns of medieval Spain.

(10) In both al-Andalus and Christian Spain the dominant caste wanted to isolate minorities religiously but not economically, creating an inevitable tension in intergroup relations. This tension, however, opened up avenues for cultural interchange by making the market a place where ethnic distinctions mattered less than in other walks of life. A similar tension is revealed in the ethnic exclusivity of [craftsmen's] guilds. Meyerson notes that Christian guilds in late medieval Valencia feared revealing their technological secrets to Muslim rivals, at least in periods when the rattle of war could be heard from the frontier. Muslims conveyed similar fears: thus ibn 'Abdūn, in his treatise on regulation of the market, warns Muslims against selling books of science to Jews or Christians. Such strictures, however, more than likely reflect the intensity of technical and scientific interchange that attracted the attention of religious zealots but was impossible to stop.

III

[Here Glick has a long paragraph describing in detail shifts in the relative dominance of Muslims, Jews and Christians over the period, with respect to the theory, practice and teaching of medicine, in order to demonstrate the complexity of the cultural interactions among the three groups.]

(11) The *dhimma* contract ['the peoples of the book': the injunction in the Qur'an which stipulates that Jews and Christians, as co-descendants with Muslims of the Abrahamic tradition, be tolerated and protected] in al-Andalus that regulated the social interaction between Muslims and the minority communities also ensured that in the normal course of events such relations would be less supercharged emotionally. Lourie's assertion that the caste hierarchy in Christian Spain was a 'mirror image' of Islamic law is not true as stated. The fact that the *dhimma* contract was a religious obligation upon Muslims provided those relationships with a solidity that the shifting sands of Christian administration and politics could in no way provide, although the *dhimma* model is clear. The Christians borrowed the model but implemented it as civil, not religious, law; therefore the borrowed version lacked the universal sanction of the original concept . . .

(12) Historians' views of cultural contact frequently conceal two ideological modes or sets of preconceptions: one that emphasizes conflict and one that, while recognizing the reality of conflict, stresses cultural congruence and creative interaction. In Jewish history, for example, the first view – the 'neo-lachrymose' view, as it has been called, is promoted as a corrective to an older school that is considered to have portrayed various 'golden ages' of the Jewish past in too idyllic and optimistic terms. In Spanish history a similar polarity characterized the polemic between Américo Castro and his detractors such as Claudio Sánchez Albornoz, who remarked that the symbiosis of the three castes as Castro depicted it was more nearly an 'antibiosis.' Such polemics are the result of inadequate theoretical grasp of the relationship between social relations and cultural interchange, between social distance and cultural distance.

> **(13)** Castro's *convivencia* survives. What we add to it is the admission that cultural interaction inevitably reflects a concrete and very complex dynamic. What we retain of it is the understanding that acculturation implies a process of internalization of the 'other' that is the mechanism by which we make foreign cultural traits our own.

We saw at the beginning that Glick's over-arching motive is to DEFEND Castro's notion of *convivencia* by REFORMULATING it in different terms, motives which he restates in his final paragraph. But just as there are these governing motives, there are others that crop up at appropriate moments throughout the text, most commonly when he is referring to the work of other historians. Thus in paragraph (3) he ACCEDES to Meyerson's 'distinction between assimilation and integration'. In (4) he CONCEDES ('admits') that ethnic role playing is a conditioning factor in social interactions, *but* that of the many roles people play not all are fully ethnically determined. In (5) to (7) Glick sets his sights on the work of Elena Lourie. In the first of these paragraphs he is content merely to report what Lourie says. The change is signalled by the 'but' which opens (6): he CONCEDES that Lourie may be right with respect to Aquinas and Maimonides but wrong in the case of the Jewish–Christian teams of translators, where the Jews were the leaders (because they were much more fluent in Arabic, from which they were translating, than the Christians).

In (7) the phrase 'on the face of it' signals that he will REJECT Lourie's interpretation of the nature of the relationship between 'vulnerability and cultural openness', going on to REFORMULATE it ('restate, in another form') to emphasise what he had been arguing earlier, whereas in (8) he ACCEDES to Lourie's argument, as he also does to a point of Castro's. In (9) he DISMISSES (since, though he mentions evidence, he neither reports it nor gives any references to it) the idea that any ethnic group can isolate itself from the culture around it. Again in (11) he returns to his pattern of REJECTING Lourie in order to REFORMULATE her identification of *dhimma* in Islamic law with what is found in Christian law. In the final sentence of (12) Glick PROPOSES that the whole problem that other historians have had with these questions is their lack of 'theoretical grasp'.

5   Modes of analysis

We turn now from how the author establishes his position in respect of various points of view to the modes in which he analyses the subject matter itself. The fundamental modes of analysis are these:

- OBSERVING and IDENTIFYING the objects to be analysed;

- DESCRIBING the characteristic features of what is being enquired into;

- DEFINING terms and concepts by NAMING them, REFERRING to objects, CLASSIFYING individuals into classes, and by DISTINGUISHING between and COMPARING similar classes by means of ASCRIBING CHARACTERISTICS to them;

- ILLUSTRATING or EXEMPLIFYING a general point in order to make its meaning or application clear;

- THEORISING about and EXPLAINING how or why things are as they are;

- CONJECTURING or SPECULATING about possible explanations – how things might be or might have been;

- EVALUATING the adequacy of our observations, descriptions, definitions, explanations and theories in the light of criteria appropriate to each.

The kinds of statement an author makes in order to analyse the material are the answers to the common kinds of question, set out in chapter 2 (pp. 27–34): 'what', 'which', 'who', 'how', 'why', 'to what extent', etc. The technique to develop for reading and taking notes is the ability first of all to be able to identify which of these analytical modes the author is operating in at any given point in the text and, secondly, to be able to say how the author goes about doing it. Identifying them is not always as easy as it might seem, since there are parts of explanations and definitions of general ideas or concepts that look very like descriptions of particular events or situations. To make judgements about how the author performs these kinds of analysis is a skill that takes some time to build up. It means gradually learning to expect what the main ingredients of, say, an explanation or definition are, and then to measure what the author does against it. This is one of the most important abilities to develop if you want to become a good, critical reader of academic work.

A number of the analytical modes listed above can be seen at work in the Glick text. First of all he IDENTIFIES Castro's approach to the question of *convivencia* as 'social psychological' and, as part of his attempt to reformulate the question, he DISTINGUISHES his own approach from Castro's as a sociological one. He then goes on in (3) to draw a sociological DISTINCTION between social processes and cultural processes, EXPLAINING that there is a complex relationship between 'social distance' and 'cultural interchange' which changes with time and with particular contexts. At this point I get into some difficulty because Glick does not clearly DEFINE what he means by these two terms, and when he says that the first 'configures' the second I am left wondering how he will CHARACTERISE the nature of this configuring. These are questions that I must hold in my head as I read on. What Glick does immediately is to draw yet another DISTINCTION, that between assimilation and integration, arguing that integration did occur between Jews, Muslims and Christians and that this provided the social foundations for cultural exchange. Paragraph (4) opens with a problem of DEFINING *convivencia*, ASCRIBING one necessary characteristic for the definition to work.

Rather than point to all the instances of modes of analysis in the body of Glick's essay, we shall instead take up those unresolved questions about the DEFINITION of 'social distance' and 'cultural interchange' and the connections between them. We get a brief hint in (4) that interaction is, as he says, 'sharply structured' (which is a bit clearer than the earlier 'configured') by two things – 'ethnic/religious ascription' and 'social class'. It is not until paragraph (7) that the latter of these is more fully developed: because Muslim culture was 'more highly bounded' or less pervious to Christian influence than was Jewish culture, Muslims as a group were less likely to suffer persecution. Perhaps this is one CHARACTERISTIC of 'social distance'.

But the major one seems to become clearer in (8). Here 'social distance' is DEFINED in terms of class stratification. The greater the degree of class stratification within the two minority groups, Jews and Muslims, the greater the chance of cultural interaction with Christians, i.e. higher-class members of the minority group interacted more, and since Jewish society was more stratified than Muslim society the cultural interaction between Jews and Christians was greater. This, then, seems to be the THEORISING that informs much of the rest of the essay – including a CONJECTURE ('more than likely') about strictures on the interchange of scientific knowledge in the final sentence of (10) – and which is restated at the end of (12).

From this kind of reading it should be clear to you that the various modes of analysis interact in quite complex ways, not only amongst themselves but also with the major motives examined in the previous section. What is also critical to realise is that the kind of language used above in dealing with an author's motives and analytical intentions is the kind of language, suitably modified, that should find its way into the essay you are preparing to write. That is to say, when you are taking notes, you should try to cast them in something like the form used above – in terms of what the authors of your sources are DOING.

6 An author's structural intentions

The structure of a book is studied by identifying its parts, clarifying the relations between those parts, and understanding the relations between the parts and the whole. The book, as we have seen, will have an overall controlling motive, which is broken down into parts which are usually expressed in chapters which relate to each other in various ways as well as to that overall motive. Similarly, the chapter will have a governing motive, to which its parts – sections, subsections and paragraphs – will contribute. Paragraphs, and even sentences, can also demonstrate these same principles of structure. One of the difficulties of reading any moderately complex work is that of holding together in your mind the very general points whilst simultaneously keeping straight the variety of its detail. Sometimes, there might be little point in worrying too much about the detail, for example when you are doing some background reading, as described on p. 56 above. In reading for an essay, however, you will usually need to fit all the pieces of a text together before you can decide what you need to concentrate on for the purpose of taking notes.

Structuring a text involves you, therefore, in deciding:

- where the author is GENERALISING and where he or she is PARTICULARISING;

- which statements or stretches of text belong together in the ITEMISING of points at any given level of particularity or generality;

- when the author is FORESHADOWING what is to come and REVISITING or REMINDING the reader about what has gone before;

- when the author is SUMMARISING or RECAPITULATING a previous argument or exposition;

- when the author is DIGRESSING from the main thrust of the argument or exposition.

Let us make this a little clearer by looking at the Glick text. In the conventional manner Glick FORESHADOWS his argument in paragraph (2). The next few paragraphs are all highly GENERALISED, and it is not until (5) and (6) that we get any clarifying PARTICULARS that provide some concrete substance to these generalisations. He ITEMISES four: Mudejars serving in Christian armies, co-operation between Jewish and Christian criminals, Aquinas' compliment to Maimonides, and Jews and Christians working in translation teams. The last of these is used as evidence to question Lourie's assertion that interaction took place only at the margins of society. (Notice, too, there is a brief FORESHADOWING here – 'as we shall see'.) Paragraph (7) returns to more GENERALISING, while (8), (9) and (10) display the more common structure in historical writing of supporting the generalisations with many more particular details and illustrations. Paragraph (8) concludes with a slight DIGRESSION ('incidentally'), inasmuch as this comment is about the effect of class stratification in Christian society on its interactions with Jews rather than the converse, which is the main subject of the paragraph.

The place of paragraph (11) in the structure of the whole is not at first easy to determine, and the author doesn't give the reader any clear orientation. It is not until we tumble to the fact that the whole focus has changed that we can begin to see what is going on: whereas most of the essay, as we have seen, is about social and cultural relations under Christian dominance in the late mediaeval period, Glick here focuses first on the earlier period in which the Muslims were dominant in al-Andalus and the Jews and Christians were the minorities. Only then does he return to the later period in order to make a comparison between Muslim and Christian practices surrounding *dhimma*. Even so, it remains difficult to see how this consideration fits into the structure of the argument about the 'structuring' role played by 'ethnic/religious ascription' and social class raised in paragraph (4).

The essay concludes, conventionally enough, not so much by RECAPITULATING the argument but by REVISITING the historiographical debates with which the essay opens from a somewhat different angle, before a final restatement of his thesis.

Summary

The account of an author's motives and intentions given in the last three sections is by no means exhaustive. First, we have said nothing of that aspect of an author's intentions which may be particularly directed at influencing the reader's judgement by means of various rhetorical devices. Nor have we examined the ways in which we can assess the author's own degree of confidence in his or her arguments. You might, for example, have noticed the considerable vigour with which Glick attacks the inadequacies of some other historians both at the beginning and at the end of the essay, all on the basis of their theoretical *naïveté*. We have considered in this chapter only those things which are basic to interpreting a text and taking notes on it.

Secondly, the terminology suggested to you for describing an author's motives and intentions is only a basic vocabulary which seeks to draw your attention to the main things to look for. There are many, many more such words that can be used to talk about what an author is doing. You can build up your vocabulary of such terms best by noticing how the authors of your books use them when they are discussing the work of other scholars. It is here that you will see these terms in action much better than in a textbook such as this. You will also be doing something of great importance: learning to pay attention to academics' language and the way they approach the business of writing academic work.

7   Interpreting a difficult text

The approach to reading and taking notes outlined above is suitable for most books. However, you will at times be faced with texts that you have to labour over in great detail if you are to understand them. These texts are sometimes the 'classics' in your discipline which, because of the quality of their thought, are given considerable attention in some courses. Because of their relative difficulty you might be tempted not to read the texts themselves, but to make do with others' commentaries on them. They can, however, be approached with a bit of work, the rewards of which are inestimable when you come to read the more straightforward works in your discipline. The techniques we have examined remain useful, but now we shall pay much closer attention to individual statements and to the author's use of words. In doing this we can see how, even with very difficult material, we can still bring an author to our own terms and can invest what he or she says with our own personal significance.

Kant's *Critique of Pure Reason* (1781, 1787) is generally reckoned to be one of the more important and, at the same time, one of the most difficult books in Western literature. Still, we can worry at the first three paragraphs of the second edition (1787) as a useful exercise in interpretation. My purpose here is to try to re-create a microcosm of the situation you face when you have difficulty understanding a text and turn to 'secondary' interpretations to help you out. The *Critique* is a 'theoretical' secondary source, as defined on p. 58 above, but one which is nevertheless a primary source for those who wish to understand Kant's thought. The translation used here is that by Norman Kemp Smith (1929, 1965: 41–3).

The Distinction Between Pure and Empirical Knowledge

There can be no doubt that all our knowledge begins with experience. For how should our faculty of knowledge be awakened into action did not objects affecting our senses partly of themselves produce representations, partly arouse the activity of our understanding to compare these representations, and, by combining or separating them, work up the raw material of the sensible impressions into that knowledge of objects which is entitled experience. In the order of time, therefore, we have no knowledge antecedent to experience, and with experience all our knowledge begins.

But though all our knowledge begins with experience, it does not follow that it arises out of experience. For it may well be that even our empirical knowledge is made up of what we receive through impressions and of what our own faculty of knowledge (sensible impressions serving merely as the occasion) supplies from itself. If our faculty of knowledge makes any such addition, it may be that we are not in a position to distinguish it from the raw material, until with long practice of attention we have become skilled in separating it.

This, then, is a question which at least calls for closer examination, and does not allow of any off-hand answer:– whether there is any knowledge that is thus independent of experience and even of all impressions of the senses. Such knowledge is entitled *a priori*, and distinguished from the *empirical*, which has its sources *a posteriori*, that is, in experience.

The essence of Kant's distinction between pure and empirical knowledge is summed up in the first sentence of the second paragraph (not, you will notice, from 'there can be no doubt' in the first paragraph, a phrase which almost invariably signals that the writer will heavily QUALIFY the statement later on). But what does Kant mean by the contrast between knowledge 'beginning with' experience and knowledge 'arising out of' it? All your note-taking should so far as possible be guided by a question of your own, and this is ours. Below are three quotations from commentaries on the *Critique*:

1. Kant here lays down his famous principle that all our knowledge begins with experience but does not all arise out of experience, i.e. there is no knowledge temporally before experience but it is not all either causally due to or logically based on experience.* Kant is here using experience to mean sense-experience. Towards the end of the second edition version of the section Kant distinguishes between relatively *a priori* and absolutely *a priori* knowledge, the latter being not merely 'independent of this or that experience but absolutely independent of all experience'.

   * 'Throughout the Introduction the term experience has (even at times in one and the same sentence) two quite distinct meanings, (1) as product of sense and understanding acting co-operatively, and (2) as the raw material (the impressions) of sense' (Kemp Smith, *Commentary*, p. 52).

   (Ewing 1938: 16–17)

2. The argument of Kant's Introduction . . . starts by defining the problem of metaphysical knowledge *a priori*, and through it leads up to the logical problem of the *a priori* synthetic judgement. In respect of time all knowledge begins with experience. But it does not therefore follow that it all arises from experience. Our experience may be a compound of that which we receive through impressions, and of that which pure reason supplies from itself.† The question as to whether or not any such *a priori* actually exists, is one that can be answered only after further enquiry.

   † This statement is first made in the Introduction to the second edition. It is really out of keeping with the argument of the Introduction in either edition.

   (Kemp Smith 1962: 27)

3. . . . Kant holds that while knowledge is occasioned by experience, it does not arise out of experience. Knowledge, especially that with an *a priori* character, is that which is before experience. In the case of causality, this notion is not derived from the facticity of experience through habitual association and inductive generalisation [as Hume argued], but is an *a priori* concept of active consciousness which is

> projected upon the transcendental object in such a way that the very
> event of experience arises in the consciousness of the subject for the
> very first time . . . In this way, the active consciousness of Kantian
> transcendental philosophy displaces any merely *receptive*
> characterisation of its theoretical activity to the extent that it is an
> *anticipatory* consciousness – and this is perhaps the best
> characterisation of the meaning of the *a priori* in knowledge.
>
> (Luchte 2007: 43)

Each of these three 'note-takers' or interpreters fixes on Kant's main point – the distinction between knowledge 'beginning with' and knowledge 'arising from' experience. All three note the issue of time in the drawing of this distinction, but whereas Ewing and Kemp Smith follow Kant in *asking* the question whether there is indeed an *a priori* knowledge, Luchte seems to take it as read that *a priori* knowledge is established. All three offer their own interpretative comments, whether in main text or footnote. Of the three I find Luchte the most helpful in the first instance because his paraphrase of the main distinction is different from the others:

Kant	begins with . . . does not arise out of
Ewing	begins with . . . does not arise out of
Kemp Smith	begins with . . . does not arise from
Luchte	is occasioned by . . . does not arise out of

Luchte's 'is occasioned by' (which he appropriates from Kemp Smith's translation) suggests to me more strongly than 'begins with' that *a priori* knowledge is already lurking there in stand-by mode, to use a modern metaphor, waiting upon passing experience to bring it into action, an interpretation that is later reinforced by Luchte's use of the term 'anticipatory'. 'Occasioned by' also makes a better contrast with 'arise' because it lacks the kind of common association between beginning and causing. Ewing also comments that knowledge is preceded by experience in time, but is neither caused by it nor logically based on it.

The next problem is the plethora of terms Kant uses. I cannot be sure about the relationship between knowledge and experience until I am clearer about the meanings of each. It seems from the first paragraph that 'faculty of knowledge', 'understanding' and 'pure knowledge' (in the subheading) are very similar in meaning, if not synonyms. None of the commentators helps here, though Kemp Smith uses the 'pure reason' of the book's title. The meaning of 'experience' is much harder to pin down. Throughout the extract Kant uses a variety of terms which seem to be equated with experience of one kind or another: 'objects affecting our senses', 'raw material of the sensible impressions', 'knowledge of objects', 'empirical knowledge', 'impressions of the senses'. Ewing is helpful. His footnote quotes a later page of Kemp Smith's *Commentary*, which reduces 'experience' to just two interpretations: 'the raw material (the impressions) of sense' and 'product of sense and understanding'. It is difficult to see, as Kemp Smith points out in his own footnote, how experience can be both. But at least we can understand that experience is associated with our sensation of the external world, whereas knowledge has a component ('pure knowledge') that it 'supplies from itself' or that, as Luchte says, resides 'in the consciousness of the subject'. I think I can now construe Kant's meaning. My own note on the passage may go thus:

> **Kant is attempting to clarify the relative contributions of our experience of objects in the world and a pure 'faculty of knowledge',**
> **uncontaminated (as it were) by experience, to our knowledge as a whole.**
> **Kant's assumption: we can't have knowledge without first having had experience to 'occasion' it or bring it to life.**
> **Kant's argument: but to say that e. precedes k. in time is not to say that e. causes k. to arise (Ewing), because e. itself may be partly supplied by the pure faculty of k. or 'understanding' within us. One part of e. – 'raw material' in the outside world acting on our senses – is the part that precedes knowledge. 'Empirical experience', by contrast, is the 'product' (Kemp Smith, quoted by Ewing) of our independent understanding (pure k.) acting on the raw material of sense impressions, and in this sense 'arises from' pure knowledge. The pure k. he calls**

a priori knowledge and empirical experience *a posteriori* knowledge.
Kant finishes by asking whether it can be shown that *a priori* k. exists.

Summary: a latent *a priori* knowledge exists on stand-by within our consciousness, and when occasioned and incited by raw material from outside acting on our senses, combines with it to produce empirical experience (*a posteriori* knowledge).

NB. This formulation looks somewhat like a chemical reaction, and Kemp Smith uses the word 'compound' (line 13). The *a priori* k. within us compounds with experience to produce something new; otherwise it remains inert. To try a more recent metaphor, an *a priori* operating program on a computer remains inert (on stand-by) until it is brought into action by contact with external experience (e.g. keystrokes) which produces new knowledge.

Well, you say, this is hardly a 'note', since it is about as long as the original text. But I think any student of literature who has had to write a 1,000-word essay on the 14 lines of a sonnet will sympathise. Where the text is complex, one has to expand before one can produce a summary. Moreover, this note, with appropriate tidying up, could itself be part of an essay. As to the final NB, I have used my more general reading of the Introduction of the *Critique* (the 'whole') to help me see one aspect of the significance of this part, and to justify my own metaphor of the chemical reaction; and, just as importantly, my own (perhaps inadequate) understanding of a quite different realm – modern computer technology – to make it understandable to me.

Finally, although I have had to make many judgements in producing this interpretation, I have not given any overall evaluation of Kant's argument – such as the one based on lack of coherence offered by Kemp Smith, itself the result of his wider and deeper reading of the *Critique*. The interpretative judgements I have made are largely, though not wholly, as we have just seen, by seeking new metaphors within the framework of the three paragraphs quoted. This has involved judgements of various kinds:

- how Kant structures his argument;

- how elements of the text function;

- how different parts of the text and the commentaries compare;

- what similarities there are between the meanings of different terms and statements, and what differences of meaning there are in the use of the same term;

- what is implied by certain statements (e.g. if pure knowledge is 'within us', sense impressions, by contrast, must come from outside us; if understanding is 'pure', then experience is perhaps 'contaminated' in some sense), and so on;

- what metaphors from my own experience I can bring to trying to understand and interpret what Kant is saying for the age in which I live.

This last point indicates that I do bring my own language from outside the text to help me interpret it. The language of my notes becomes, in effect, a 'compound' of Kant's, the three commentators' and my own – just as each commentator makes a new compound from the elements of his own language and Kant's. In this way one uses the techniques of interpretation to avoid merely paraphrasing the primary text or becoming dominated and confused by the secondary sources. My interpretation is, if not 'original', in important respects my own. That is what to aim for.

To progress to the highest level of reading by attempting an evaluation, say, of the justifiability of the distinction between *a priori* and *a posteriori* knowledge, as Kant draws it, would mean a lengthy discussion of the *Critique of Pure Reason* and of many other books which tackle not just Kant but the problem of knowledge itself. Such an enterprise we cannot embark on here, but you will see that it would involve similar processes of interpretation welded into the justification of a new argument. That really begins to take us away from the problems of reading proper and back to those of writing.

Part II

The Dynamics of an Essay

Introductions

A speech has two parts. You must state your case and you must prove it. You cannot either state your case and omit to prove it, or prove it without first having stated it; since any proof must be a proof of something and the only use of a preliminary statement is the proof that follows it.

Aristotle

The introduction is best seen as a microcosm of the essay as a whole (and usually needs the most re-writing) in which you must at the very least

- give your answer to the question or implied question raised by the topic

- give the reasons for your answer, or an indication of the criteria according to which your judgement has been made.

This chapter shows you how to accomplish these minimal tasks, and also goes on to ring some of the changes on how your introduction can take on extra depth and sophistication:

- how to integrate background material into the giving of your answer

- how to marshal all the many and varied factors and issues your research might throw up into the unified vision which is your answer

- how to decide on your own governing motive or motives which take account of differing viewpoints either contained in the essay topic or discovered in your reading

- how to model your introduction in such a way that it makes clear the sequence of issues to be taken up in the body of the essay without your having to say so explicitly

- how to structure the introduction to a research paper which is not an answer to a set question.

1   The constituents of an essay

What Aristotle has to say about a speech applies equally to a modern academic essay: the introduction states your proposition or answer, and the body of the essay justifies that answer. Our study in chapter 2 of the ways in which you can reflect on your essay topic has already prepared you for the writing of your introduction. In this chapter we shall say more about how you can establish your case. Chapter 5 will take up the problems of justifying or demonstrating that case. In chapter 6 we learn how to write that part of an essay which Aristotle thought only an optional element, the conclusion.

We shall think of an essay, therefore, as a structure with an introduction, a middle and an end. The introduction states your case, the middle justifies it and the end reflects on the beginning and the middle. Within this broad structure there are quite a few elements which also have to be taken into account, fitted together and turned into a coherent unity.

These elements are set out below. As you study them, bear in mind particularly that this list is not a sequence of stages in the setting-out of an essay. Nor is it an ordered formula which you can apply in a uniform manner to every essay you write. The discipline in which you are writing, the essay topic itself and the nature of the answer you decide to give will all affect which of the elements you emphasise, how you will treat them and where in the essay some of them will be introduced. The relations between the elements in this list can be quite complex, so do not try to oversimplify them:

- an interpretation of the question if you find it ambiguous, vague in some respect or rather open-ended; and, where relevant, such introductory material as a clarification of the meaning and significance of any important terms or 'background' necessary to establishing your proposition;

- a proposition (or a series of propositions) with whatever qualifications and conditions you deem necessary to defend it, which formulates your 'best' answer in language as clear, precise and economical as you can muster;

- an account of the evidence and interpretations on which you have chosen to base your proposition: evidence may consist of facts, primary data, descriptions or generally accepted definitions; interpretations will consist of the connections (explanations, theories) to be made between them;

- an account of the evidence which 'best' tells against some aspect or aspects of your argument, CONCEDING its force where necessary, CRITICISING it where you can, and INTERPRETING it in such a way that your original proposition is left substantially intact;

- an evaluation of the strengths of your argument and evidence (and the counterarguments and counterevidence) by reference to appropriate criteria;

- a demonstration of how your chosen approach has been *relevant* to the question with which you began – for the essay as a whole, for some section of it, or for some paragraph;

- a concluding reflection on some aspect of your answer.

If all this is going to work well, we shall need to pay particular attention to the writing of our introduction since it is there that the 'golden thread' which makes our argument *relevant* and *coherent* is crafted. So we shall now take up the first and second of the elements above.

2 The constituents of an introduction

For many students an introduction suggests a discourse on the background to a topic, a definition of terms, a setting of the scene, or attention to some other set of preliminaries to the essay proper. An introduction may well include a number of these things, but not at the expense of coming to grips with the essay topic itself: stating your case is the fundamental function of your beginning, not only because readers tend to look for such a statement but also because it is here that the relevance of your answer to the question and the coherence of your argument are first established. A relevant and coherent beginning is perhaps your best single guarantee that the essay as a whole will achieve its object. That is why your introduction – of all parts of the essay – needs the most careful consideration and the most frequent re-writing.

The only necessary constituent of an introduction is, as we have seen, a statement of your case. This statement will typically take the form of an *answer* to the question (or implied question) contained in the topic. But once an answer is given, it tends to beg another question: what are the reasons for your answer, or (which may often amount to the same thing) what are the criteria according to which you have made your judgement? This, in turn, may suggest yet another constituent of an introduction. If you make a judgement, the implication is that you have decided in favour of one answer (your 'best' answer) over alternative answers – you have made a *choice*. Consequently, your introduction will need either to indicate the nature of that choice or convey in some way the confidence you place in the adequacy of your answer (or, when your topic asks you to discuss another writer's viewpoint, the adequacy of that viewpoint). In other words the introduction should express your 'motive', as this term was developed in the previous chapter (see pp. 69–70). It can say

- what point of view you are PROPOSING or ACCEDING TO;

- what point of view you are CONCEDING subject to certain QUALIFICATIONS, CONDITIONS or EMPHASES you wish to highlight;

- how you will REFORMULATE a point of view to make it more acceptable;

- how you will RECONCILE two apparently conflicting points of view;

- what in a point of view you are REJECTING, REBUTTING or REFUTING entirely.

Only RECANTING is inappropriate in a student's essay, since a recantation implies that you have written and published on the subject before.

Finally, once you have decided on the major motive or motives that will govern your answer, your introduction will go on to indicate the lines on which the main body of the argument is to be conducted.

Our plan will be, so far as is practicable, to build up a series of introductions which take somewhat differing approaches to the same topic. This is not to say that later versions of our introduction are necessarily a cumulation of all the virtues of the earlier ones. In taking one tack we often lose some of the advantages of another. In opting for a more complex introduction, we sometimes have to sacrifice some of the virtues of simplicity. I have composed all the examples for the present purpose.

We shall begin by examining the misuse of introductory material. Then we shall go on to see how an introduction can be built up.

3   The use and misuse of introductory material

Having reviewed the circumstances in which various kinds of 'introduction' are appropriate, Aristotle observes:

> Introductions are popular with those whose case is weak, or looks weak; it pays them to dwell on anything rather than the actual facts of it. That is why slaves, instead of answering the questions put to them, make indirect replies with long preambles.

The usual function of an introduction in academic writing is to tell the reader what issue is being raised and what justifies the writer in raising it. You will see this kind of introduction in the articles to be found in academic journals and in the preface or introduction to a book; and we shall examine it later in this chapter, where we discuss how to write an introduction to a research paper (section 5, p. 107). For the most part it is not appropriate to an essay in answer to a question set by your tutor, since you need not offer the reader an excuse or a reason for taking up the matter.

This is not to say, however, that no material which might be considered introductory to the main argument should be included in your introduction. It may, just so long as it does not *replace* the essential feature of that introduction, a statement of your case. There is often good cause to indicate *how* you will tackle your case. Some essay topics, as we have seen in chapter 2 (pp. 39–41), are either ambiguous in meaning or very general in scope, such that you need to say how you have interpreted the topic, and, further, to say *why* this interpretation is a fruitful one. It might be that you suspect the answer will not be as obvious as it appears on the surface, that it has implications beyond the immediate problem, that you are aware of significant new evidence which might suggest a revised interpretation of the problem, that it throws up an interesting methodological issue, and so on. In such situations you need to inform your reader how you have interpreted the topic, what it is you find interesting in your question, and what needs to be concentrated on to answer it.

Any such introductory material should, as far as possible, be thus integrated into some aspect of your statement of the case. The criterion to be employed in choosing and integrating this material is its *relevance* to your case. There is no point in 'defining your terms' unless your case is going to hinge in part upon the definition (or interpretation) you give of a term. 'Background material' (historical, biographical, geographical, sociological, cultural, etc.) must similarly be selected for its relevance, or passed over so quickly as not to disturb the reader's concentration on the case you are putting. For example, the facts that the nineteenth-century German composer Richard Wagner would wear nothing but silk or satin next to his skin, and that in private moments, it seems, he liked to wear women's clothes, might be a trivial distraction to one essay introduction. In another, it might be a succinct way of making concrete and objective a case about some qualities of his music. Introductory observations are thus not so much a means by which you ease your way into the main issues of the essay. Rather, they are a necessary or arresting adjunct to the formulation of your point of view on the topic, or an indication of the scope within which the discussion of the issues will take place.

But first we shall exemplify an introduction which has no place in an academic essay. The topic we shall take in all the examples that follow in this section is this:

> Speaking in 2006, the then British prime minister Tony Blair said that the struggle against global terrorism 'is not a clash between civilisations. It is a clash about civilisation.' Examine the meaning of this statement in the context of Samuel Huntington's thesis about the clash of civilisations. Can Blair and Huntington be reconciled?

1

In 1993 Samuel Huntington put forward his hypothesis that future international tensions and conflicts would develop less between individual nation states than along the 'fault lines' between civilisations. 'Civilisations', he said, can be defined both objectively in such terms as language, history, customs, institutions and, especially, religion, as well as subjectively in terms of how people identify themselves. He tries to show that many peoples in the world outside the West define themselves and their civilisation as non-Western or anti-Western, and wish to modernise without adopting many Western, particularly secular, values, which they refuse to see as universal. The West, argues Huntington, will have to learn to recognise this and to learn how to coexist with these other civilisations. For Tony Blair, by contrast, modern terrorism against the West means all this is dangerous relativism which undermines what he sees as the truly global values of 'liberty, democracy, tolerance and justice'. This is what 'civilisation' means, or should mean, to everybody in the world. Both have arguments in their favour.

This preamble makes no case, it barely glances at the question underlying the topic, particularly that part of the topic which relates to global terrorism, and it ignores the final question whether Blair and Huntington can be reconciled. The information here might be necessary background to making a case, but is wholly insufficient as an introduction.

4   Setting out your case

We shall now begin to build up a few introductions that do set out a case. At first sight Introduction 2 looks as if it is answering the question, but in fact what we have here is really only the raw material on which an answer could be based. There is no emphasis, nor any indication of a controlled interpretation of the differences between Blair and Huntington. Nor is there any attempt to relate the matters listed to the war on terror.

2

Having examined Tony Blair's and Samuel Huntington's differing views on civilisation and terror I conclude that they cannot be reconciled. This is because (a) they are talking about two different things – 'civilisation' and 'civilisations'. (b) Blair talks about the values of 'liberty, democracy, tolerance and justice', whereas Huntington emphasises the importance of language, history, customs, institutions and, especially, religion. (c) Blair thinks that the values he states are truly global or universal, whereas Huntington says there are 'fault lines' between civilisations which make for different views on values. (d) Blair makes no mention of different peoples' or civilisations' conceptions of their own identity, while Huntington thinks this is very important. (e) Blair seems to think that the West's failure to stand up for its own values makes it an easy target for terrorists who have their own dogmatic values, while Huntington believes that the values in all civilisations are equally entrenched. (f) Blair argues that economic globalisation produces interdependence so powerful that it will eventually compel everyone to adopt the same value system, whereas

---

Huntington believes that economic globalisation is only one amongst a number of forces, the most important of which is religion, which he calls 'perhaps the central force that motivates and mobilises people'.

Finally, (g) whereas Huntington's thesis is a theory of what he thinks is most likely to happen, Blair is calling for what he thinks *ought* to happen.

When they are analysing factors, reasons, causes and so on, most academics feel what E. H. Carr (1964: 89–90) calls a 'professional compulsion' to try to decide which of these or which grouping of them 'should be regarded "in the last resort" or "in the final analysis" . . . as the ultimate cause, the cause of all causes'. Not everybody nowadays agrees with Carr in this matter, inasmuch as there are many post-structuralist authors who resist it in principle, if not always in practice. Moreover, there are some methodological approaches, such as factor analysis in psychology or accounting for variable speech habits that linguists study, which preclude it. But it is undeniable that the desire to tie heterogeneous things up in a 'unified vision' has exerted a powerful influence on the academic imagination.

So, even though you are not able to establish 'in the final analysis' a wholly unifying interpretation, you should still feel a 'compulsion' to reduce the list of issues, factors, reasons, causes, 'aspects', variables, categories or whatever they may be, as far as you can. The number that suggests itself to me is three or four. While it does not constitute a reason for fixing on these limits, the fact that in English we routinely say 'firstly', 'secondly' and 'thirdly', rarely 'fourthly', and never 'fifthly' unless we are having a joke, might be taken as informal corroboration. There will be exceptions, such as those noted above, but I recommend that you think very carefully before allowing the factors underlying the organisation of your answer to multiply beyond three or four.

With this in mind, Introduction 2 can be rescued. First, there is the problem of how to group these disparate factors. A little reorganisation of the items in this shapeless list will reduce these factors to a few major ones for which we need to find suitable categorising labels, for example:

(i) differing conceptions of civilisation, now and in the future (a, g)

(ii) differing conceptions of values and how they function in society (b, c, e)

(iii) differing views on the nature of the historical forces which will affect the outcome (d, f)

In re-writing the paragraph we do a little bit more than just categorise these differences. We must add to the organising principle of conjunction ((a) *and* (b) *and* (c), etc.) something that will show more interesting relationships between the factors in the list. In the introduction below, this is done by *ranking* the three groupings (i), (ii) and (iii) above in order of importance. (This is done in the usual way, you will notice, in ascending order, reserving the most important until last.) Thus the differing conceptions of values (ii) is said to 'lie behind' the differences over conceptions of civilisation itself (i). The third (iii) is made the linchpin that holds it all together. Blair's and Huntington's attitudes to the war on terror are interpreted in terms of their views on the nature of historical and social forces: to put it another way, Blair is something of an economic determinist; Huntington is not.

Most of the information in Introduction 2 has been retained.

3

There is little likelihood of any reconciliation between Tony Blair's and Samuel Huntington's views on how to handle global terrorism for three main reasons. In the first place they have quite contradictory notions of the nature of 'civilisation'. Blair sees civilisation as a moral and universal absolute which must be aspired to in the future, whereas Huntington views it as a product of the very different histories of the world's major cultural groupings. Hence the latter's emphasis on the plural 'civilisations'. Lying behind this difference is the second reason why they cannot find common ground. This is that the sets of values they think are most important cannot properly be compared with each other. Blair's are specific and prescriptive – liberty, democracy, tolerance and justice. By contrast Huntington's are more diffuse and descriptive – such things as language communities, mores, shared institutions and, especially, religions, all of which are already very deeply rooted in all civilisations, and show few signs of changing except in superficial ways. Thirdly, and most importantly, their analyses of the historical forces which are shaping the present and the future display very different emphases. To Blair global economic developments (trade, financial markets, communications) almost alone produce interdependence among peoples so powerful that, for this world market to work, common values will become a necessity. Huntington is more circumspect and inclusive: economic globalisation is only one force among many, particularly, as I have mentioned, religion. 'Modernisation', he says, 'does not equal Westernisation', and peoples like to preserve their traditional identities. Thus we can see that for Blair active political and, where necessary, military intervention against global terrorism is justifiable. For the sceptical Huntington, the West's political, economic and military leverage on other civilisations is now declining. Terrorism is an expression of this, but little is going to be achieved by attempting to force what are essentially Western values on other civilisations at gunpoint.

The core of a 'discussion': debating your answer

The kind of answer exemplified in Introduction 3 is certainly adequate for many purposes. It is reasonably well *unified* and it embodies a JUDGEMENT – it puts forward a case, as Aristotle says it should. But what it lacks is a sense of self-awareness, an awareness that comes from the recognition that this may not be the only answer, and that, even if it is the 'best' answer, there might be some important considerations that have been neglected or pushed aside in its desire to be forceful.

If you look at that introduction carefully you will see that it does not explicitly advance any *reasons* for the interpretation it offers. It does, of course, advance reasons for why Blair and Huntington are unlikely to be reconciled, but that is a different matter. What we are looking for now is a reason why the *proposition* that they cannot be reconciled should be accepted. Introduction 3 only gives plenty of *support* to the proposition announced in the first sentence.

For the introduction to be self-aware it needs to be aware of other interpretations or, at least, of certain shortcomings in itself which might raise the possibility of other interpretations or judgements. A judgement, in the words of the literary critic F. R. Leavis (1972: 62), implies more than just the statement of a (private) proposition:

> the implicit form of a judgement is: This is so, isn't it? The question is an appeal for confirmation that the thing *is* so; implicitly that, though expecting, characteristically, an answer in the form, 'yes, but–' the 'but' standing for qualifications, reserves, corrections.

The answer to Leavis's question might equally be 'no, but–', in which the respondent disagrees with the proposition while finding certain things in it to be commended or CONCEDED. Our fourth introduction will try to convey this sense of a discussion.

4

The differences between Tony Blair and Samuel Huntington on how to handle terrorism in the age of globalisation are very stark and at first glance irreconcilable. Blair is engaged in a struggle against terrorism because he believes that it undermines the core universal values of a unitary 'civilisation' of all peoples. Huntington believes there is no such thing as a single civilisation, but rather groupings of civilisations with what he calls 'fault lines' between them. Secondly, Blair's values are specific and apparently prescriptive ideals – liberty, democracy, tolerance and justice. Huntington's are more diffuse and descriptive – language communities, mores, shared institutions and religions – all of which are deeply rooted in the histories of these civilisations and unlikely ever to conform to Western secular humanistic values other than in fairly superficial ways. Thirdly, whereas Blair is convinced that economic globalisation (trade, financial markets, communications) is now so 'mature' that it is in everybody's self-interest to develop common political values in order for the markets to work properly, Huntington sees things differently. For him economic globalisation is only one force to be reckoned with among the various others, particularly religion. Such entrenched forces, combined with the re-emergence of senses of self-identity distinctively non-Western, mean that the West must learn to co-exist with these civilisations, that military responses to suppress them are counter-productive and will be increasingly unsuccessful. Blair thinks the values he espouses can and should be defended by military action.

Even so, it would be a mistake to characterise Blair as a gung-ho unilateral militarist who responds to all global threats to 'civilisation' with force. There have been few statesmen anywhere in the world in recent times who have devoted more energy to peaceful multilateral approaches to global problems in such forums as the United Nations and the Group of 8 (not to speak of his undoubted success in peacefully nullifying terrorism in Northern Ireland), and to tackling the sources of terrorism in poverty, lack of education and so on. He knows there are other cultures and civilisations which have to be listened to. For his part, Huntington knows that the 'fault lines' between civilisations are not 'sharp' – they 'blend and overlap', which implies the possibility of a multilateral dialogue between the West and other civilisations. Huntington could hardly disagree that Blair's list of values are not *only* Western values; and neither could Blair, however much he himself might see them as the legacy of the Western Enlightenment. These values might well be universal, since it is unlikely that they or similar values do not exist in one form or another in most of the world's civilisations, however imperfectly practised. What both Blair and Huntington, or their advocates, need to address is that while the *interpretation* of Blair's values is quite clearly not universally agreed on, they do provide some common ground with which to begin. They are certainly not absolutes that can be imposed; but neither can Huntington's pragmatic relativism by itself solve the problems raised by global terrorism.

In this introduction most aspects of the answer contained in Introduction 3 are accepted, but found to be insufficient. It CONCEDES that differing attitudes to civilisation, values and historical forces are vital factors. The awareness that this is not the whole story turns on the 'even so' beginning the second paragraph, a foretaste being signalled by 'at first glance' in the very first sentence of the introduction. Hence, running through this introduction is a dichotomy between an initial impression and a more deep-seated interpretation which MODULATES that impression.

'But', 'however' and 'yet' are the workaday signals of QUALIFICATION, along with the stronger 'nevertheless', 'even so', 'notwithstanding', 'despite this', 'in spite of this', and so on. As we saw in chapter 3 when discussing an author's major motives, the proposition or preliminary statement makes the point to be CONCEDED, and the linking terms above introduce the qualification. (With 'although' and 'even though' the reverse applies: these conjunctions introduce not the qualification but the point to be conceded – for example, 'Although there are stark differences between Blair and Huntington, we can find sufficient common ground to begin the process of reconciling them.') Here are some examples of the ways in which these phrases can be used:

This description characterises the situation in certain societies well, but it does less than justice to what is observed in society *X* and society *Y*.

The programme was a success, but only insofar as it achieved a limited set of goals.

The considerable support we find for this interpretation notwithstanding, it is still necessary to point out that . . .

It can hardly be denied that *X* is . . . Even so, this does not account completely for the fact that . . .

Notice how many of these examples are thick with functional terms referring to what scholars (or their writings) DO: characterise, observe, support, find, interpret, point out, deny, account for. The use of such language is a correlate of that 'self-awareness' of a good introduction (or much good academic discussion) we spoke of earlier.

Closely related to concession and qualification, though serving a slightly different function, is the imposition of certain *conditions* upon your acceptance of a proposition. The problem with conditions is that there is a danger the whole question will be begged. For example, when asked to say whether marriage is a universal human custom, we might decide that it is, *provided that* our definition of marriage dispenses with criteria which prevent it from encompassing certain difficult cases. To accept woman-to-woman 'marriage' among the Nuer in southern Sudan or same-sex 'unions' in the West as marriage would be to impose the condition that marriage need not be heterosexual. To accept the customs traditionally followed by the Nayar of southern India or by certain societies in the Amazon basin of Brazil, which allow a woman many sexual partners, would be to impose the condition that marriage is not necessarily an institutional means of establishing the legitimacy of children. The obvious retort to such arguments is that the set of criteria we adopt to define marriage is precisely the point that needs to be discussed in the body of the essay. To set conditions such as these may be to avoid discussing it. Nevertheless, where a discipline conventionally adopts certain conditions (such as the *ceteris paribus* clause – 'other things being equal' – sometimes found in economics), we can with care formulate cases such as these:

This is true provided that we confine our attention to . . .

The reasons are . . . only if we accept that . . .

Here is an attempt at one conditional approach to the question on Blair, Huntington and terrorism which tries to skirt these objections.

5

The stark differences between Blair and Huntington over how best to respond to terrorism can be reconciled, but only on the condition that we heavily discount their own estimates of the nature of the arguments which divide them – the meaning of 'civilisation', their conceptions of 'values' and their differing takes on the driving forces of history. In short, these things have to be redefined or re-conceptualised before any common ground can be established. There is, in the first instance, no necessary dichotomy between Blair's unitary conception of 'civilisation' and Huntington's pluralistic 'civilisations'. Civilisation (even in the localised Western Enlightenment tradition) cannot be defined in a way which includes certain essential characteristics (essences) and excludes everything else; just as there is no way in which the characteristics of differing civilisations the world over, which Huntington canvasses, are hermetically sealed off from one another with little or nothing in common. Much the same goes for values. There is no 'one size fits all' definition of Blair's values – liberty, democracy, tolerance and justice. This can be demonstrated, for example, by the West's intolerance of some countries' restrictions on liberty or democracy and its benign tolerance of others' (which can lead to quite baffling attempts to define who is a terrorist and who a legitimate fighter for freedom). Nor can Huntington deny that many of those in civilisations who hold to his values of language ties, community mores, institutions and religion have nevertheless shown considerable ingenuity in accommodating them to new, cosmopolitan challenges, and are themselves hostile to terrorism. Finally, Blair's faith that globalisation will bring everybody to a common view of civilisation and its values, his economic determinism, is as naïve and inadequate as Huntington's view that economics plays a minor part. If the conditions I outline can be accepted, there is a clear theoretical – if not an immediately obvious practical – solution to understanding the disjunction between civilised behaviour, anywhere in the world, and terrorism.

So we must begin by examining the nature of definitions of civilisation and values and of the conditions that attach to them . . .

It will be left to you to decide on how well both the content and the method of treatment of this introduction compare with the earlier ones and whether it is a suitable model for your own writing. It is obviously more abstract, it is very free – almost cavalier – in its criticisms of Blair's and Huntington's positions, and it does take a certain amount of knowledge contained in the earlier introductions for granted. Indeed, it would not have been possible to write it *without* having done the work that went into the earlier ones. But in challenging the very *grounds* of the debate, it does open up many new and interesting avenues of discussion.

We shall close this section with one observation. None of the beginnings illustrated above has explicitly told the reader how the argument in the main body of the essay will be organised. There are no statements to the effect that 'we shall first investigate such and such and then turn our attention to this and then that'. For the most part, an essay (unlike a longer work) can eschew such explicit guidance to the reader in its introduction, if the introduction is composed in such a way that it models both the argument and the sequence of issues to be taken up in the middle. If an introduction is thus a microcosm of the essay as a whole, there should be no need to address your reader directly about the order in which you propose to deal with your material.

5   Writing an introduction to a research paper

We saw earlier (p. 95) that Aristotle's slaves are expected to answer the question put to them without preamble. But when you are writing a research paper, the advice to get straight to the answer to a question no longer applies. This is simply because in a research paper it is *you* who is asking the question, not one of your tutors (even though he or she might have helped you to formulate it). There are, consequently, a few things you need to do before you get to the point where you state your answer. This involves setting a *context* for the work you are carrying out, a context which alerts the reader to the broad issue you are examining and what makes it interesting, one which gives an indication of what others have said about it beforehand, and one which points to any deficiencies in what has been said. Only then are you in a position to say what you are going to do, what answer you are going to give.

The guide below is a rough point-by-point skeleton of these 'moves' that you need to make. Different disciplines often tend to vary the emphasis given to each of these moves, expanding some into a relatively full discussion and contracting others to a brief mention. For example, some disciplines in the social sciences might require you to consider the constraints imposed on your study by the method you choose to adopt; while others (such as history) might require you to mention the availability of particular kinds of primary source material or your familiarity with the languages in which they are written. The best way to get a sense of the range of practices in your field of study is to observe the structure of introductions in the journal articles you read, using them to help you flesh out the skeleton below.

The moves are these:

1 A statement of the issue you propose to examine focusing on its importance, relevance or significance in the context of the field of study in which you are working. This amounts to a preliminary justification of what it is about the issue your research paper will address that makes it worth taking up.

2 A statement of what is known, understood or argued with respect to the issue you are taking up. This can be a fairly brief indication of what is sometimes called 'the state of the art', making reference to the kinds of conclusions that have been drawn, the theories or viewpoints that obtain, with perhaps a few references to major statements in the literature.

3 An indication of any gaps, silences, shortcomings, problems, unresolved disagreements, misunderstandings – whatever is appropriate to your topic – in what is being said by others. This move typically begins with a 'but', 'yet', 'however', etc.

4 A statement of what you propose to DO in your paper to fill the gaps, make something else heard, solve the problems, resolve the disagreements, correct the misunderstandings, etc. etc. This will usually take the form of setting out the argument you will be putting forward and indicating the kind of conclusion to which you will come.

5 An explanation of how your paper will go about achieving (4) – often (as we noted above) an indication of the method or approach you will be taking, together with any constraints on it or assumptions that need to be made. This move is often optional: if there are no significant methodological

matters, constraints or assumptions, then there is no point in raising them. Even so, it might be worth exploring whether there is something worth mentioning here, in order to set the boundaries within which your conclusions need to be interpreted – a matter to which many papers return as part of the Conclusion to the whole study (see chapter 6).

The amount of space devoted to the introduction as a whole and the various moves within it will in large part be determined by the overall length of the paper (a lengthy paper can afford to have a longer introduction) and the importance for the subject matter of each of the moves. For a short paper, all of this might be achieved in two or three paragraphs; for a longer paper you might need two or three paragraphs to deal with just one of these moves, depending upon its importance and complexity within the scope of the paper as a whole.

Here is an example of an introduction to what would be a shortish paper, in which the first three moves are given a paragraph each and the fourth and fifth combined into one.

The Concept of Patriarchy: a Historical Approach

Modern feminist theory, for better or worse, revolves around many disputes over ideologies, theories and terms. It would appear on the surface that there is little or no agreement on how to tackle these problems. Almost every theorist of feminism has a quite idiosyncratic view of the reasons behind women's oppression and the ways to put an end to that oppression. Moreover, each tends to begin her analysis by criticising all other feminist theories, emphasising their differences and giving scant attention to finding common ground. The longstanding debate concerning the concept of patriarchy is no different.

While it is true that the German sociologist Max Weber had introduced the idea of patriarchy in the early twentieth century (Walby 1989: 214), and, according to Veronica Beechy (1979: 66), the term had been used occasionally in the 'first wave' of feminist thinking, it was only with the revival of the feminist movement in the 1960s and 1970s that patriarchy began to be debated seriously as a theoretical construct. But this was to be relatively short-lived. By the mid to late 1980s, doubts about its adequacy as a theoretical term began to be raised. Lisa Tuttle in *The Encyclopedia of Feminism* (1987: 243) states that 'not all feminists find the term "patriarchy" useful; some alternatives which have been used for the same basic concept include "sex–gender system" (Gayle Rubin), the "Planetary Men's Association" (Mary Daly), [and others] "phallocracy" or simply "sexism" '. Joan Acker (1989: 236) argued that 'patriarchy could not be turned into a generally useful analytic concept'. These views rapidly became the norm.

More recently, however, there has been a trend back towards the use of patriarchy, led by Marxist feminists and by Sylvia Walby. This trend examines the concept not as an isolated theoretical term that tries to explain everything, which is what had happened in the past, but as part of a constellation of issues that include gender, class, work and sexuality. It is only by teasing out the complex inter-relationships between these things that the concept of patriarchy can be made useful and understandable, not just to theorists of feminism but to society as a whole.

This I shall do by analysing these relationships not as a purely theoretical exercise but by examining them in the work of just one group of feminists, namely feminist historians. The advantage of such an approach is that it is in the concrete application of the concepts of patriarchy, gender, class, work and sexuality in actual historical situations that the nature of these relationships can be clarified and the position of patriarchy established. The scope of this paper confines me to a very limited number of such historical situations, which can only be illustrative. But, as Beechy (1979: 79) pointed out long ago, it is only by tracing the development of patriarchy within its historical context that we can deconstruct its nature and demonstrate its continued usefulness to feminist studies.

5

Middles

His knowledge is extensive, various, and profound. His mind is equally distinguished by the amplitude of its grasp, and by the delicacy of its tact.

Macaulay, of Hallam's *Constitutional History of England*

This chapter provides solutions to some of the practical problems that often arise in the writing of the middle:

- changing your mind about the answer, grinding to a halt having lost the thread of ideas, going too far over or falling too far short of the word limit, and the uses of outlines.

It then shows you how to EXPAND the case you have set out in your draft introduction:

- EXTENDING your answer by asking what more needs to be examined to establish a point, what exceptions there might be, and whether there are alternative accounts of the material that need treating

- ELABORATING a point by CLARIFYING its meaning or significance, SUBSTANTIATING a generalisation with evidence, or ILLUSTRATING it with concrete examples

- ENHANCING the value of what you have said by restricting the range of situations to which it usefully or truthfully applies.

Achieving a balance between these competing requirements is the art of writing a middle.

The middle of your essay is the introduction writ large. Its under-lying constituents will therefore be quite similar to those studied in the previous chapter. But there is in the middle a major shift of emphasis away from bald propositions and conclusions towards the careful working-out of arguments and the balancing of interpretations with the evidence you call upon to support them. To justify the case presented in your introduction is to develop arguments, to deploy evidence, to evaluate the strength of counterarguments and apparent counterevidence, and to demonstrate their relevance to the question with which you began. In all this your aim is to show not so much that the answer you have decided on is the right answer, but that it is a reasonable point of view to hold.

If the process of writing always went ideally according to plan, then the crafting of a good introduction should forestall most (though not all) of the difficulties one might otherwise encounter in writing middles. But just as you need to get an introduction of some sort written to help guide the argument of your middle, so you might often find that problems encountered in the writing of the middle lead you back to a reconsideration of your introduction. The introduction should never be regarded as finished and out of the way until you are satisfied that you cannot fundamentally improve the argument of your middle and that your middle justifies the case put forward in the introduction as well as you can make it do so. If you get stuck at some point in the writing of the middle, it is often, therefore, a good idea to hunt for the source of the difficulty in the introduction itself or in the analysis you carried out in preparation for drafting it (see chapter 2).

1   Some common problems

1.1   Changing your mind about the answer

There are times when even the most careful preparation might seem to be mocked when you discover half-way through the writing of the middle that you have quite changed your mind about the case set out in your introduction. This can happen because it is only in the grappling with details of argument and evidence necessary to a middle that the full significance of something strikes you. (Remember that it is often in the act of writing itself that new knowledge and new interpretations of evidence are created.) When this happens the first thing to keep in mind is that it is no disaster – unless you have left the writing until a minute or two to the twelfth hour. First, you must convince yourself that you really have changed your mind, and not just come to doubt the degree of your commitment to the case you have been making. If this doubt is not too great, it might be possible to accommodate it in the conclusion to your essay (see pp. 137–8 below). Secondly, having decided to change your case, you must accept that revisions to your previous work will have to be made, since it is not acceptable to submit an essay that changes its argument half-way through. This does not mean, however, that you must begin all your work from scratch. It means that you will have to go through what you have written, reinterpreting the facts you have assembled in the new light and modifying the point of view on the arguments set forth. This might involve no more than, for example, elevating what previously seemed a minor point to major status or CONCEDING that what seemed before to be a major argument is now only a QUALIFICATION to another argument. But before making any changes to the earlier parts of your middle, always try re-writing the introduction to test whether you have got your new argument sufficiently straight in your head.

1.2   Grinding to a halt

Many academic writers find that, no matter how carefully they have prepared the ground in advance, they sometimes come to a stop, and there sets in a 'writer's block' that owes less to doubts about what they are writing than to the elusiveness of an argument or thought that is being developed. The thread that was being followed or grasped at is lost.

- Sometimes this block can be overcome by re-reading from the beginning of the section on which you are working in order to catch the drift of your ideas.

- At other times you may need to scrutinise the main point of the section quite closely: the problem might lie in the way the initial point was formulated either in the introduction or in the section of the essay that takes it up. There might be an unintended emphasis, an ambiguity, a confusion, or some other problem in your expression of the point, which led you astray.

- If you find nothing of this kind, it sometimes helps to go into something like a trance, in which you try to recapture the essence of what you were trying to say (a kind of mental correlate of attempting to grasp a word on the tip of your tongue).

- If these strategies fail, it is often a good idea to leave your desk for a while and do something quite different: the resolution of the difficulty has often been known to spring to mind in the most unlikely circumstances.

- Sometimes writing comes to a halt because one cannot find the right word to use. It might be on the tip of the pen, so to speak, but won't flow off. The best way of dealing with this kind of block rather depends on the nature of the elusive word and what you perceive to be its importance in the development of your argument or exposition. If the word is a fairly common or simple one, which you know you know but just can't quite dredge up from your mental dictionary, and if you can manage to carry on without it, it is often best just to leave a blank and wait for the word to come to you later. There are, however, times when the word you want is so necessary that the idea can't be quite grasped until the word is found. If, under these circumstances, you hurry on, leaving a blank or making do with a substitute, it can happen that your thought can easily begin to drift off course, even if it does not cause you to get quite lost. A major lexical block is often sufficient warning in itself that you are not as clear about what you want to say as you might have thought; so while a thesaurus may be able to help you out, you might also need to reflect more carefully on the argument of the whole paragraph or section of the essay.

1.3 Writing too much

If you are the kind of student who finds the word limits of essays an irritating restriction on your freedom to elaborate your point of view, it is well to bear in mind that there are good reasons for setting word limits. Part of the task of learning to write is to learn to select your material from the large amount of it often available and to deal with it as concisely and economically as you can. Space – whether in a journal, newspaper, book or report – is always at a premium, as is the time your readers can devote to what you write. The French polymath Blaise Pascal once apologised for having written a long letter, giving as his excuse the fact that he hadn't had the leisure to make it shorter. This is the attitude you should cultivate.

Writing too much is often the result of not having examined closely enough the *relevance* of what you say to the essay question or to the answer you are developing. Hence it is a good idea to begin to tackle the problem by going back to your introduction to make sure that it does address the question as directly as possible. A tightly defined case in the introduction leads to a more tightly argued, relevant middle. Having satisfied yourself that the introduction cannot be substantially improved, scrutinise what you have written in the middle to see whether all passages contribute something substantially new to the argument – that you have not been making the same point in a number of different ways, some of which are not strictly necessary. The decision to cut such passages is often one of the hardest to make in writing, because when we are in full flight the words will flow quickly and what looks like our finest writing will sometimes result. It is only later that we begin to realise that the flow of words has seduced us away from our main object. It is important to be ruthless in paring away any material that can be done without, no matter how well written.

Finding a balance between the amount of information we use and the depth with which we analyse it is a major subject of section 3 below.

1.4   Writing too little

Not having enough to say is perhaps a commoner problem. If you have this difficulty, the first question to ask yourself is whether you have done sufficient reading for your essay. Tutors will expect an essay to be reasonably (but not exhaustively) *comprehensive* in its treatment of the topic, and this can only come from sufficiently wide reading. But there is no way in which we can say what 'sufficiently wide' will mean here in terms of the number of works you should consult. Lecturers and tutors in particular courses will sometimes give you an indication, but just as often they will not.

This is because the comprehensiveness with which you cover the available material needs to be balanced against the depth and perceptiveness with which you analyse it. An encyclopaedic store of information is of little use if you merely skate across its surface without analysing its significance to your answer. It is (as we saw in chapter 3) by developing the ability to analyse and interpret your sources in the light of your questions that you will best overcome any problem you might have in finding enough to say. In this you must learn to find your own level as early as you can, and then gradually to increase the amount of information (the number of books) your analytical skills can comfortably handle in the time available. In the rest of this chapter we shall examine the ways in which these skills are deployed in the writing of a middle.

2   The uses of outlines

Not everybody finds it useful to have a written outline of the middle to work from; some prefer to let the lines of thought develop as they write. The trouble with outlines (as we noted briefly on p. 52) is that they tend to become lists of headings that quite neglect the critical importance of establishing the relationships of reason and meaning between those headings. Even so, they can constitute a useful summary-in-advance of the ground you propose to cover, and they provide a way of provisionally allotting the number of words, paragraphs or pages you can afford to devote to any one aspect of your answer. If, in writing your middle, you find yourself exceeding or falling short of these limits, you are then in a position to stop and ask yourself whether the outline (in effect the essay as a whole) needs to be changed to accommodate your new emphasis or whether, on the other hand, you need to revise your approach to the section you are writing to bring it back into line with your outline. Outlines are useful not because they provide you with a fixed structure for the middle, but because they give you a provisional structure that can be changed and modified as your conception of the essay gradually matures.

3   Expanding a case

In order to justify the case put forward in the introduction to your essay, it is necessary to expand on the points put forward there. This can involve you in DOING the kinds of thing we began in chapter 3 to notice other writers doing – for example defending, conceding, refuting or reconciling points of view; explaining, defining, describing or comparing various phenomena; and either generalising from evidence to an interpretation or making a generalisation stand up by recourse to particular facts, illustrations, and so on. In chapter 9 we shall be looking in more detail at how to do some of these tasks and at some of the writing problems that arise when we try to perform them successfully. In the remainder of this chapter we shall examine the most basic ways of expanding a case.

We shall do this by glancing at typical comments tutors write in the margins of essay middles and then examining how to respond to them. One of the most common – and most general – of these marginal comments is 'Needs expansion' or 'Expand on this'. What is the tutor who writes this on your essay asking you to do?

Most commonly you are being asked to do one or more of these three things:

- EXTEND your answer by considering arguments or evidence you have omitted;

- ELABORATE the point by CLARIFYING its meaning or significance, by EXEMPLIFYING it or by SUBSTANTIATING it with evidence;

- ENHANCE the value of a piece of information to your answer by explaining its circumstances, how or why it came to be, how it should be QUALIFIED, and so on.

You must first of all be aware that there is something of a conflict between the demands of extending your answer and those of elaborating and enhancing any part of it. This is a conflict between overall breadth of treatment and the depth with which you deal with any given point. There is no formula for reconciling these demands. One can only say that the common temptation to skate across the surface of a subject in the desire to be comprehensive should be resisted. Remember that an extensive array of information or a great variety of examples does not in itself constitute a justification of your case: you must often exclude material of marginal importance or relevance in order to make room for arguments and evidence which underpin your major points.

3.1   Extending your answer

Even so, the middle of an essay needs to be as comprehensive in its treatment of the subject as you can make it within the restrictions imposed by the word limit. Comprehensiveness (or breadth) comes, in the first instance, from sufficiently wide reading and, in the second, from your ability to pull the threads of your reading together. If the scope of an essay topic appears to be extremely broad (e.g. Shakespeare's tragedies, Europe of the Middle Ages, peasant societies, Western capitalism, the Third World, the symphonies of Haydn), you must read widely enough to get a general overview, while accepting the impossibility of doing justice to all this material in the body of one essay. Hence it is necessary to select just those points, cases, examples, facts, etc., sufficient to justify your case.

> Typical marginal criticisms: What about . . . ?, Yes, but you neglect to mention . . . , Not all . . . are like this, An alternative consideration is . . .

Comments such as these draw your attention to the fact that you have not read as widely as you should, or that in your reading you have either missed or ignored material the tutor considers important to your case. To guard against this kind of criticism (at least to a degree, since it is not possible always to pre-empt it), you can keep asking yourself these questions as you write:

- What more do I need to examine to establish this point?

  Useful linking terms: and, furthermore.

- What exceptions might there be to what I have said?

  Useful linking terms: but, except for.

- What reasonable alternatives are there to my account?

  Useful linking terms: or, alternatively, instead.

We shall examine how this works with an example. This essay topic comes from a geography course on problems of development in the Third World:

> Why is it that, despite many well-intentioned efforts, the rural poor in many developing countries are becoming relatively worse off?

So that we can see the case to be justified in the middle, here is an introduction to the essay.

> There are many reasons why the position of the poor in large numbers of developing countries has not improved in line with the efforts to alleviate their plight. In the first instance, many of the projects conducted by international aid agencies and others have been too limited in scope, timescale and sophistication for them to have taken proper root. Secondly, the governments of recipient countries are often as much part of the problem as of the solution. Many governments and their administrative agencies are either ineffective or corrupt, and they are self-serving inasmuch as they respond more to their own interests as a 'clientele class' of international aid and finance than to the needs of the poor. As we shall see, insufficient (or in some cases too much)

> government investment in the agricultural economy, rural infrastructure and education means that even in countries where the overall economy may be improving the gains do not 'trickle down' to where they are needed. Important as these problems are, however, what is fundamentally wrong is that developing countries are hostage to a whole set of regulatory and financial conditions imposed by international donor countries, financial institutions and others, whose interests are ultimately inimical to those of the rural poor.

This introduction outlines the main issues to be considered in the body of the essay. It will need to be demonstrated precisely how and to what extent the three limitations (scope, timescale, sophistication) mentioned in the second sentence have frustrated these aid projects. Similarly, the problems with government and with international finance announced in the rest of the paragraph will all have to be covered.

Here is a paragraph which takes up the issues of scope, timescale and sophistication:

> The first set of problems we need to examine is that too much aid has been conceived narrowly in terms of 'projects' which are limited in their aims, and are restricted to technical matters such as irrigation, the introduction of agricultural machinery or building transport networks. These projects are initiated in isolation from other problems, are made to fit short, predetermined time frames, and are designed to show particular outputs or 'results' within a specified budget in order to satisfy the donor agencies' demand for accountability (Brinkerhoff 1991: 2; Dichter 2003: 291–2). This has been shown in Tamil Nadu in India, where irrigation pump-sets have enabled wealthier owners of large landholdings successfully to increase their yields, thus satisfying demands for accountability. But these landowners use a disproportionate share of the available water with the result that poorer farmers have less access and cannot share in these benefits (Griffin and Ghose 1984: 265).

Let us now apply our three questions to this argument.

- *What more needs to be examined?*
  One example (Tamil Nadu) doesn't sufficiently constitute a case. Find and mention briefly (with reference to sources) examples of similar things happening elsewhere in developing countries.

- *What exceptions might there be?*
  The first sentence might be an over-generalisation. How much is 'too much'? Are all approaches to development so narrowly conceived? Are there significant exceptions? Are there counterexamples to the Tamil Nadu case?

- *What alternative accounts might there be?*
  Are there alternatives to the narrow 'project' approach which might be more successful?

By doing some more reading we can extend the argument to remedy these omissions. But in order to build up an adequate case, the paragraphs below focus on irrigation and dispense with agricultural machinery and transport networks, which were mentioned in the draft paragraph above:

The first set of problems we need to examine is that, especially in the earlier years of international aid from the 1960s to the 1980s, a great many projects were conceived with aims that were limited to providing technical solutions to individual problems such as the provision of irrigation infrastructure, which we shall take as a case in point. These projects are initiated in isolation from other problems, are made to fit relatively short, predetermined time frames, and are designed to show particular outputs or 'results' within a specified budget in order to satisfy the donor agencies' demand for accountability (Brinkerhoff 1991: 2; Dichter 2003: 291–2). It is often the case that any benefits that do flow from these projects are not to the poor. In Indonesia the benefits of water control and irrigation schemes were not extended to smallholders because wealthier farmers would not allow their land to be crossed by small tertiary canals (Hardjono 1983: 49). In Tamil Nadu, India, influential farmers with access to money for buying modern pump-sets deprived poor peasants of much of their share of the scarce water (Griffin and Ghose 1984: 265).There might have been an exception in Bangladesh. But the undoubted success of small irrigation schemes for the poor in that country did not stop international aid agencies putting most support into large water control schemes during the 1970s. The result was that richer farmers profited to the extent that they could buy up the land of the poor (Hossein and Jones 1983: 164, 169–70), while the aid agencies could still claim a success because of the increase in production.

It should not be thought, however, that subsequent recognition of these problems has brought about major improvements. As late as the year 2000 an irrigation project in Usangu, Tanzania, funded by the African Development Bank, was still replacing traditional weirs with large concrete ones on the upper Great Ruaha river. This meant that the farmers in this vicinity could draw ever more water for irrigation, while the farmers further downstream were finding there was no water for them in the dry season (Thomas *et al.* 2005: 202). Brinkerhoff (1991: 2) argues that these limited 'projects' should be and are being replaced by much more integrated 'programs' which take account of many more variables and which are much more flexible. Such an exception can be found in Korea and Taiwan, for example. It has long been known that irrigation schemes introduced in these two countries were successful, but only because they were introduced after major reforms in land tenure (Douglass 1983: 193–7; Black 1999: 97–8). Besley and Cord (2007: 18–19) also specify clearly defined property rights as a necessary condition for successful development. But there are many other variables besides property rights which need to go into the mix, creating even more problems: the more variables the more complex the situation becomes, and the less control the program managers can exert to realise their aims.

3.2   Elaborating a point

Whereas extending a case involves you in searching out new material, elaboration demands that you bring out the particular implications of any general point you have already made. When we are not sure where we are going, we often take refuge in vague or unsubstantiated generalisations. 'Do we know this?', 'You haven't established this', 'More elaboration needed here', 'Too general' – these are the kinds of blanket comment that direct attention to the need for elaboration.

A request for elaboration forces you to clarify, substantiate or exemplify your generalisations:

- CLARIFYING a statement: make the meaning of an idea or concept more precise; or spell out a statement's significance for the point of view you are putting forward.

  Common linking terms: viz., that is to say, namely.

  Common marginal criticisms: Define this, What does this mean?, Too vague, Explain key concepts.

- SUBSTANTIATING a generalisation: refer to or quote specific evidence.

  Common linking terms: i.e., in particular, indeed.

  Common marginal criticisms: Be more precise, Demonstrate this, Give evidence, Substantiate, Be specific.

- ILLUSTRATING a general point in such a way as to make its meaning clear and its application concrete.

  Common linking terms: for example, for instance, inter alia.

  Common marginal criticisms: Illustrate this, Give examples.

The last sentence in the example above contains two generalisations. The 'many other variables which need to go into the mix' need to be clarified. Also the general statement 'the more variables the more complex the situation becomes' needs to be both clarified and substantiated or illustrated. When you find yourself making general or abstract statements like these – usually at the beginning or, as in our example, at the end of a paragraph – ask yourself the question 'In what does . . . consist?' Then proceed to answer it in what follows.

This is necessary not so much because the reader might not understand the meaning of what we have said but because the success of the argument that follows depends heavily on what they signify. Let us attempt to answer our two questions in a paragraph each.

The variables involved in any development program I shall distinguish as micro-variables and macro-variables. The former consist in the physical, economic and social needs of the locality or region in which the program is taking place; the latter in the economic, social and political priorities of regional and central governments as well as of international donor agencies. I shall here focus on the first of these. As early as 1959 it had become clear to those who set up the Comilla project in what was then East Pakistan that piecemeal introduction of the schemes and techniques discussed above was not working (Harrison 1980: 83). Fertiliser and new seed were of little use to a farmer who had no access to credit, little knowledge of how to use these innovations or little incentive to risk new techniques alone. The Comilla project organised co-operatives and coordinated government assistance, education, public health, the provision of credit, the introduction of new farming techniques and so on. This approach later came to be known as 'integrated rural development' (IRD), which tries to take all the relevant physical, economic and social factors into account and to integrate their introduction into a designated locality. Particular emphasis is placed on the participation of all the people (what is now called 'ownership') and on finding local solutions consistent with both traditional customs and national development priorities (Lea and Chaudhri 1983: 13).

      Lea and Chaudhri acknowledge that there have been some IRD success stories and they attempt to isolate the ingredients for success (p. 17). But more often than not such 'integrated' programs have not lived up to expectations. Harrison (1980: 84) thinks this is because 'integrated rural development . . . is not integrated enough'. But this is to miss the crucial point: there are just too many factors which interact in ways we do not sufficiently understand and may never understand, with the result that there are limits on what can be 'integrated'. The 'dilemma of complexity', as Dichter (2003: 290) calls it, means that not only are each of these variables complex in themselves and become even more so when combined, they also begin to alter in unpredictable ways as they interact during the life of a development program. For example, there is evidence that a clear correlation between education and economic growth cannot be established and they are therefore difficult to integrate. The benefits of education will depend upon many variables such as whether the setting is urban or rural, whether the economic base is low, medium or high, whether or not there are opportunities for technological development, whether or not education programs are driven by narrow political, religious or other agendas, and so on. Each of these variables can change over time and produce contradictory outcomes (Leys 1996: 39–40; Lindauer and Pritchett 2002: 19–21). If this is the case with just one factor – education – the difficulties compound greatly when we start adding more.

Notice how these two paragraphs are constructed. The first takes up the idea of variables and sub-divides them into two types, micro and macro. Each of these terms is briefly CLARIFIED (or DEFINED) in the second sentence. Then, having told us that the immediate focus will be on the first of these, the micro-variables of the physical, economic and social circumstances of a development program, the rest of the paragraph is taken up with a case study of IRD. This case study SUBSTANTIATES the general point about the number of variables that need to be controlled, which was made in the final sentence of the paragraph about the link between successful irrigation programs and land-tenure reform on p. 122 above. The case study does this by spelling out even more specifically just how many different factors there are.

Having told us that the success rate of IRD is very patchy (and REJECTING Harrison's interpretation of the problem), the second paragraph then takes up the general issue of complexity that had been flagged earlier – how difficult it is to understand and control the *interactions* between variables. Dichter's abstract term 'dilemma of complexity' is introduced and then immediately CLARIFIED. The remainder of the paragraph is a concrete EXEMPLIFICATION of the complex nature of these interactions.

In each of these two paragraphs we have been able both to clarify and either to substantiate or to exemplify. When terms to be clarified are more complex than they are here (or there are more of them), you might need to separate clarifying and substantiating into succeeding paragraphs, the structure of which is fundamentally the same as that of each of the paragraphs above. At a further extreme, you might need to take a few paragraphs just to clarify the meaning and significance of some complex terms and devote a paragraph each to the detailed examination of just one piece of substantiating evidence at a time. You will see, then, that the 'shape' of a piece of writing viewed in terms of its paragraphs can contract or expand according to the demands of the content (and your word limit), while its basic structure is preserved intact.

A final point about EXEMPLIFICATION. Exemplifying can be performed in order to achieve some of the requirements of either clarification or substantiation. It is a characteristic of the kind of essay topic that we are dealing with here that exemplification can't easily be separated from substantiation: the experience of some Third World countries which constitutes the evidence to support our argument is intended simultaneously to exemplify what one would find in the Third World as a whole. The selection of such 'examples' or 'cases' is always fraught with the danger that we are taking as typical what might on another analysis turn out not to be so typical as we had thought. (The examples used above tend to be biased towards South and South-East Asia.) Parallel situations in other disciplines are the lines of a long poem selected for analysis, the paintings chosen from the work of a prolific artist, the particular deserts examined as examples of arid environments, the people selected as informants in a linguistic survey or an oral-history project. Except for certain statistical sampling techniques used in some social sciences, there are no sure-fire ways to ensure your examples are wholly representative. This means that you need to be on the look-out for significant exceptions – as we saw above on p. 122 with respect to irrigation schemes and reform of land tenure in Korea and Taiwan. One way of getting around this problem is to choose your words carefully so that you do not make too strong a claim for the evidence you have presented. For example, in the second of the two paragraphs above I used the phrase 'there is evidence that . . . ' in order to introduce the point about the lack of a 'clear' correlation between education and economic development. Had I simply asserted that there is no correlation, despite the reference to Lindauer and Pritchett given in order to support the claim, the tutor could well comment 'Substantiate this'.

3.3   Enhancing the value of your information

Enhancing the value of your information requires you to qualify your main propositions by imposing certain restrictions on their truth or range of application. These restrictions are broadly concerned with time, place, manner or means, and various aspects of causation and condition. We have already had to take some of these on board in writing parts of the middle. In particular we have had to make a few qualifications about place: for example, countries which have coupled development programmes with effective land reform (South Korea, Taiwan) seem to have escaped some of the worst manifestations of rural poverty.

Other problems begin to surface when we ask other questions: When? How? By what means or methods? By whom? To what degree? Why? For what reason or purpose? With what effect? Under which circumstances or conditions? When were these mistakes in development schemes being made? Are they still being made? There are other questions that come to mind: Who made the mistakes (central government, local officials, governments of developed countries, aid agencies, transnational corporations)? For what reasons did they attempt to solve development problems in the way they did? Do they now seem bad reasons only with the benefit of hindsight? Were the means they used inadequate to carry out their intentions? Were alternative means available? Under which conditions (social, cultural, political, economic, managerial, etc.) does it seem that some development projects fared worse than others in trying to alleviate rural poverty?

To raise questions such as these and to integrate your answers to at least some of them into the body of your essay is to make it more valuable in an important way. A well-qualified answer is a better answer because its propositions can be tested for their value more precisely. This means that, in the present case, if we want to understand why development programmes are not working as well as we hoped, we should have more variables to examine for their effect on what actually happens. For example, the successful implementation of irrigation schemes in Korea and Taiwan we have mentioned might not be able to happen in another place at another time not only because of the failure to reform land tenure but because it depends on co-operative principles which a rigidly stratified society might find very difficult to accommodate, or because local officials are corrupt, or because interest rates and energy costs have risen, or because of some combination of these and other conditions. This remains the case even though, as our sample paragraph above (pp. 124–5) has argued, the complexity of the interactions between variables makes it unlikely that we could provide a definitive answer. What we can do by such an approach is either to *eliminate* certain possibilities or at least to argue that some of them have less effect than is often thought. This makes for a much more tightly argued essay.

If your writing grinds to a halt or if you find that you are repeating yourself (especially in the conclusions to paragraphs), it might well be that you have not been asking yourself the kinds of question which lead to useful qualifications and which enhance the value of your information. In addition, when you have drafted a section of your middle, it is a good idea to read back over it asking these questions of the statements you have made. Often a gap can be filled just by inserting a few words (e.g. a date, a few places, a name) or a qualifying phrase which indicates the means, reason, purpose, cause, result, extent or degree. In these ways you can use the kinds of question exemplified above to help you compose, to check over what you have written and to pre-empt those criticisms appearing in the margin of your essay when the tutor returns it.

Let us work on the draft of a paragraph which would come towards the end of the middle. For the purposes of illustration we shall skip that bit of the argument in the draft introduction to the essay (pp. 119–20 above) which deals with the part played by ineffective and corrupt governments. Here we shall take up the last of the arguments set out in that introduction, namely that developing countries often have little room for manoeuvre when faced with international pressures from donor countries, financial institutions and so on.

> We come now to the last and most important set of reasons why development programs have often disappointed the hopes of the rural poor. This is that, for the most part, developing countries who are trying to help the poor are caught in a web of international policies, financial agreements and practices from which they can hardly escape. Most finance for development ultimately comes from the governments of major donor countries and from international financial institutions. How this money is used is therefore very greatly influenced by the politics and economic ideologies of these organisations. Where there is conflict between development priorities of the recipient country and the interests of the donors, it is to be expected that the latter will prevail.

Which questions can we ask of this? First, in the second sentence we have listed 'international policies, financial agreements and practices'. *Which* ones? *When* were they made or when did they come into play? The next sentence refers to governments of donor countries and international financial institutions, but we must ask in particular *which* governments and *which* financial institutions are the important ones for the sake of the argument. The fourth sentence raises questions about *how greatly* politics and economic ideologies influence the use of money, and *which kinds* of politics and economic ideologies? The final sentence introduces a condition ('*where* there is conflict') that will need to be specified further; and finally we might need to ask *how* and *why* the interests of donors prevail.

> When we speak of international policies towards development we must first single out those of the United States, which since the late 1990s has been by far the biggest and most powerful donor of Official Development Assistance (ODA) in absolute dollar terms despite its permanent position since 1989 near the bottom of the international donor tables as a

provider of aid expressed as a percentage of Gross National Income (OECD Development Co-operative Directorate 2007: Table 4). Because of its voting power in the forums of the multilateral financial institutions, particularly the International Monetary Fund (IMF) and World Bank, the USA more than any other country has protected its own political, security and economic interests in international trade and investment, in effect using them as an instrument of American foreign and trade policy (Black 1999: 79–80). Third World governments therefore have to acquiesce in these policies if they are to maintain access to development finance. Until the end of the Cold War in 1989 this meant being seen to be hard on communist or other left-wing movements. More recently, with the rise of neo-liberal economic and trade policies which insist on the privatising of government enterprises and the free flow of capital, the IMF succeeded in, as Black (1999: 80) expresses it, 'leveraging policy changes [in recipient countries] punishing to the poor and crippling of government authority and capacity to respond to public need'. One spectacular example of this was the financial 'meltdown' in South-East Asia during the mid 1990s, when governments, at the instigation of the IMF, lifted controls and welcomed masses of speculative international capital, little of which reached useful programs for the poor. In 1997 this capital suddenly got nervous and took flight. It was a disaster for the countries concerned, particularly Thailand, where the meltdown began, putting them even further at the mercy of the IMF (Sussangkarn 1998). But it did little more than rattle a few windows in New York and Washington.

Expansion necessarily involves writing at greater length than we did in our first drafts on any particular issue. What this compels is a reassessment of the space and prominence given to any one of those issues if we are to keep within the word limit. In coping with the requirements of extending, elaborating and enhancing our main points or propositions, we are faced simultaneously with having to reduce the number of issues we can cover adequately. This can be done by combining a few relatively particular topics into a more general one, and by choosing one or two of the particulars to examine in some detail as examples or case studies. For example, the OECD publishes aid statistics under a number of general headings, one of which is 'Social and administrative infrastructure'. This comprises a number of more particular sub-categories: education, health, water supply and sanitation, government and civil society, other social infrastructure. Similarly, the general category 'Production' includes agriculture, industry/mining, trade/tourism. In deciding where to place the emphases in your essay (again depending on the wording of the topic and the word limit) you may wish to cover all or most of the general categories, illustrating each with one sector such as education and agriculture, or you may choose to focus on 'Production' and analyse all three of the sub-categories in detail. Striking a balance between extending an answer and elaborating and enhancing the parts of it is one of the arts of writing. In creating any work of art, we cannot make final judgements about the parts until we have developed some sense of the whole. This is why everything in your middle (as well as your introduction) must be regarded as a provisional draft until you have finished this part of the essay.

3.4 A note on the use of sources

The sources used above are the following:

Black, J. K. (1999) *Development in Theory and Practice*, 2nd edn. Oxford: Westview Press.

Besley, T. and Cord, L. J. (eds.) (2007) *Delivering on the Promise of Pro-Poor Growth: Insights and Lessons from Country Experiences*. Basingstoke, Hants: Palgrave Macmillan/World Bank.

Brinkerhoff, D. W. (1991) *Improving Development Program Performance: Guidelines for Managers*. Boulder, CO, and London: Lynne Rienner Publishers.

Dichter, T. W. (2003) *Despite Good Intentions: Why Development Assistance in the Third World Has Failed*. Boston, MA: University of Massachusetts Press.

Harrison, P. (1980) *The Third World Tomorrow*. Harmondsworth: Penguin.

Hodder, B. W. (1973) *Economic Development in the Tropics*, 2nd edn. London: Methuen.

Lea, D. A. M. and Chaudhri, D. P. (eds.) (1983) *Rural Development and the State*. London and New York: Methuen.

Leys, C. (1996) *The Rise and Fall of Development Theory*. London: James Currey.

Lindauer, D. L. and Pritchett, L. (2002) 'What's the big idea? The third generation of policies for economic growth'. *Economia* 3:1, 1–39.

OECD Development Co-operative Directorate (2007) Statistical Annex from the 2006 Development Co-operation Report, Table 4. http://www.oecd.org/dataoecd/52/9/1893143.xls. Accessed 16/10/2007.

Sussangkarn, C. (1998) 'Thailand's debt crisis and economic outlook'. Paper presented to ISEAS 1998 Regional Economic Forum, Singapore. http://www.nectec.or.th/bureaux/tfri/mep_fore.htm. Accessed 25/09/2007.

Thomas, J., King, G. and Kayetta, S. (2005) 'People, perspectives and reality: Usangu myths and other stories, Tanzania' in S. Bass, H. Reid, D. Satterthwaite and P. Steel (eds.) (2005) *Reducing Poverty and Sustaining the Environment*. London: Earthscan Publications.

Wilber, C. K. (ed.) (1984) *The Political Economy of Development and Underdevelopment*, 3rd edn. New York: Random House.

The references in the passages above to Douglass, to Hardjono and to Hossein and Jones are all to papers in the book edited by Lea and Chaudhri. The references to Griffin and Ghose are to a paper in the Wilber book of readings.

If you compare the use of sources in our very first draft paragraphs with that in our expansions, you will see that one can extract a great deal more from the references immediately at hand than might at first seem possible. The poet and critic T. S. Eliot once observed that Shakespeare had learned far more about history from the single volume of Plutarch's Lives than most people could from the whole history collection of the British Library. The ability to

ELABORATE and ENHANCE your points by writing in some depth depends not just on reading more widely in the search for facts but also on reading the sources at hand in more depth.

4 Summary

Drafting the middle of the essay is a test of a number of things:

- First it is a test of how well you have drafted your introduction and of the usefulness of any outline of issues to be covered you have made.

- Secondly, it is a test of your ability to conceptualise the material in such a way that breadth of coverage is balanced against the need to elaborate and enhance.

- Thirdly, it is a test of how well you are able to use the common experience of grinding to a halt to rethink where a line of argument is taking you or to ask new and relevant questions about how to enhance the points you have already made.

- Finally, it is a test of your willingness not to be wholly imprisoned by the draft of your introduction or by the draft of any part of the middle, and of your readiness to change the emphasis in your answer. Only rarely should you feel the need to change the fundamental thrust of your answer and to re-write from the beginning. If this does happen, remember that the new assurance with which you write will compensate magnificently for the extra labour.

All these tests are ones you should try to set for yourself. The comments of other students and your tutors are (or can be) invaluable aids in helping you to recognise where something needs to be extended, elaborated or enhanced. But writing and re-writing the middle remains most importantly the opportunity to test out for yourself the argument of the draft introduction with which you began.

Endings

[In the Epilogue] you must make the audience well-disposed towards yourself...

Aristotle

> Unlike introductions, there are no widely practised styles of conclusion in the humanities and social sciences as a whole. But it is possible to tease out certain tendencies to which you can become alert. This chapter tells you what they are and how to handle them, concluding with a set of illustrative variations:
>
> - RECAPITULATING the main outlines of your argument
>
> - changing the mood of your writing from the vigorous argument of the introduction and middle to one of a more modest SUGGESTING, an acknowledgement that you are taking part in an ongoing conversation about the subject matter of your essay
>
> - reflecting on what you think your treatment of the topic has achieved and what IMPLICATIONS might flow from your treatment.

1   Recapitulation

If we present our conclusions at the beginning of the essay, how do we 'conclude' it?

There is an element of truth in the old preacher's advice to a young cleric beginning on a career of writing sermons: 'First you tell them what you're going to tell them, then you tell them, and last you tell them what you told them.' Recapitulating your arguments and emphasising the most important aspects of them is just one function of an ending. Such recapitulation should aim, as Aristotle advises, to refresh your readers' memories and make your points 'easily understood'. By choosing the words in which you express your recapitulation with care, you can simultaneously indicate which of the issues you have raised or arguments you have used are the most important. In any recapitulation there will inevitably be a degree of repetition, even of some of the very words and phrases used in the introduction or middle. But the ending should nevertheless avoid being simply a re-writing – a mere repetition – of the introduction.

Now, there are various ways in which this can be achieved. First of all, it is important to be aware that recapitulation is itself not a necessary constituent of an ending at all. There is no uniformly observed rule (Aristotle or the old preacher notwithstanding) which says the ending must contain a systematic review. If you are confident that your exposition in the introduction and the middle has been clear, you may prefer to end on a note of paradox, aphorism, larger generalisation or particular concrete instance which sums up the issues you have been discussing in an oblique manner. Essays in literature and the fine arts often end this way. Indeed, unlike introductions (various styles of which we recommended in chapter 4), endings have no really necessary constituents at all. Recapitulation and the other features of endings discussed below are all optional. All we can say with any confidence is that your essay must have some kind of ending which is distinguishable from the middle. It is the ending that provides a sense of 'closure' and unity to the composition as a whole.

Another general point to bear in mind is that, though styles of endings are optional, the choice may not be wholly free. Some disciplines may tend to favour or frown upon certain kinds of ending. Some kinds of essay topic or subject matter may prompt the choice of one kind of ending over another. For example, in those disciplines or subjects of the social sciences which lend themselves to experimental, survey or participant research, it is frequently proper to conclude by summing up the present state of knowledge and to suggest what further research needs to be done. This may be out of place in an essay which focuses on the interpretation of somebody's writings – say a novelist, a political scientist or a theoretical sociologist. I have made no attempt in what follows to give you systematic advice about the appropriateness of varying endings to different disciplines, subject matters or types of essay topic. You will be able to pick up hints about this by looking at conclusions in the secondary sources you read for your essays. What I shall do here is to point out some of the things to look for.

2   Mood: suggestion and implication

Where you do use your ending to recapitulate your main points or arguments, it can be saved from being a mere repetition – slightly reworded – of the introduction by a change in your mood. One of the opportunities an ending provides to you is the chance to reflect upon what you have written. The dominant mood of an introduction is stating or asserting. That of the middle is justifying. Both need to be vigorous and closely focused on the essay topic itself. Your ending, by contrast, can afford to relax a little, even sometimes to go so far as to admit that your argument has not solved all the problems raised by the question. The focus may shift from the topic itself to your own discussion of the topic.

One of the words often found in the conclusions to academic papers is 'suggest'. For example, 'I have tried to suggest that the distinction commonly drawn between "social democracy" and "democratic socialism" tends to distract our attention from the very fundamental characteristics they have in common.' In thus summing up a major concern of the essay, the writer has adopted a new mood to his thesis. There is here a certain modesty or tentativeness about what the essay has achieved – a recognition that one is contributing to a process of learning and discussion larger than oneself. This, broadly speaking, is a helpful attitude to adopt (even, perhaps, when your essay has been a vigorous refutation of some opponent's views) for, having thus put yourself in this mood, you might be led to cast your eye afresh over your own arguments or over their overall importance in your field of study.

You may sometimes feel that you lack confidence in your arguments anyway, so 'suggesting' might come quite naturally. But there is a danger here, a danger just as present even to experienced academic writers. This is that modest SUGGESTION can become ritualised or formulaic and so lose the kind of sincerity that may be necessary to its success. A fault to be found sometimes in the closing paragraphs of papers in academic journals is a degree of diffidence so great that the reader may come to doubt the seriousness of the whole piece of work. W. G. Runciman, an eminent sociologist who has written lots of very good things, begins the conclusion to one of his essays thus:

> **This rapid and rather cavalier survey of a complex topic cannot suggest more than a very tentative general conclusion. But if my argument is at all well founded, it suggests that . . .**

The back-pedalling here is so furious, over-generalised and drawn out that I begin to suspect either a false modesty or that the author himself suspects his argument cannot withstand much serious scrutiny.

One way of tackling this problem in your own writing is to make an attempt to separate those aspects of your thesis or argument about which you feel quite confident from those which are rather more tentative. Your conclusion can then draw attention to this distinction in a purposeful way. Something of this comes through in the extract below. The authors might not be doing justice to themselves, and in summing up their paper they could have expressed the distinction between solid gain and tentative suggestion more clearly. It is, however, genuine. This conclusion comes from a paper in linguistics by R. N. Campbell and R. J. Wales which has argued that the way in which grammarians have treated comparison (or comparative structures) has been too superficial to explain issues of meaning and logic:

> Clearly, much of what we have suggested is speculative. In particular, our grammatical suggestions require extensive justification which it is not possible to provide here. It may therefore turn out that some or all of our proposals are ill-founded. Our main purpose has been to re-open discussion of comparative structures with a view to revising the older type of analysis, which we believe to have been unsatisfactory in that it assigned superficial status to the linguistic expression of what we believe to be a fundamental linguistic, logical and intellectual operation.

In effect, the authors are saying, we cannot be sure that we have got the details of the grammar right, but we are sure, nevertheless, that the general approach to analysis we have taken is the most fruitful one. (A 'nevertheless' to begin the fourth sentence would have been helpful to the reader.)

You will see from this extract that the authors have done something else besides suggesting and recapitulating. In the second and third sentences they have also raised the matter of the relation between their paper and the further study of this topic: their own grammatical proposals require 'extensive justification'. This is an example of another characteristic feature of conclusions, a feature I am inclined to think is the most important.

This is that a conclusion will often look at the IMPLICATIONS of the work carried out in the essay. 'Implication', like 'suggest', is a commonly recurring word in conclusions to academic papers. Implications can be expressed in a variety of ways, some being particularly favoured in certain disciplines. When we ask ourselves a question about implications, we must add the corollary 'Implications for what?' Here are some of the favourite answers:

- the implications for the further study of the subject (PROPOSING);

- the implications for our assessment of present or past approaches to the subject (REVALUING);

- the implications of my narrowly focused, empirical work for more general, more theoretical, or different but related issues (GENERALISING, EXTRAPOLATING);

- the implications of my general or more theoretical work for providing a context for particular, empirical questions (CONTEXTUALISING);

- the implications of my analysis for solutions to practical or applied problems (RECOMMENDING, APPLYING);

- the implications of my analysis of some present or contemporary issue for the prediction of what might happen in the future (PREDICTING).

All of these require you to stand back from the immediate details of your answer: to look backwards, forwards, or more generally around you, and to establish a context in which your answer can be placed.

An indication of the implications of your work may also be thought of as an evaluation of its significance. Any such evaluation is subject to dangers similar to the ones surrounding 'suggesting'. In this case, by contrast, the danger seems to lie in overvaluing the implications or significance of your work. Not a few academic papers conclude with rather large claims which may be little more than thinly veiled appeals for research funds or for other researchers to jump on the bandwagon. Such self-aggrandisement needs to be resisted.

You as a student may not yet have had the chance to develop a broader perspective on your work. Discussing its implications will therefore be quite difficult. It is not, however, impossible if you keep two things in mind (and these two things apply equally to the handling of 'suggestions'). First, avoid the very large and general claim (e.g. 'This essay demonstrates conclusively for the very first time that . . . '), and concentrate on the particular issues raised in your essay as a starting point. Secondly, do not ignore the needs of a conclusion until you find them staring you in the face. If putting forward implications is important, then you must be looking out for these wider significances when you are doing your reading and note-taking, as well as when you are writing your middle. A well-written and carefully thought-out conclusion which reflects upon what you have managed to achieve in the essay will fulfil Aristotle's prescription for an epilogue which heads up this chapter: 'make the audience well-disposed towards yourself . . . '.

3   Variations on a theme

We conclude with a few examples of ways in which one essay might be brought to an end. On the optional constituents discussed above – recapitulating, suggesting, and discussing implications – we shall conduct a few variations.

So that you can see what is being varied a trifle more clearly, I shall first present the introduction of the essay. (Considerations of space preclude the presentation of the middle.) The different endings refer back to this introduction. The topic comes from cultural studies:

> Fredric Jameson describes postmodernism as 'the cultural logic of late capitalism'. Do you agree?

Introduction

If by 'cultural logic' Fredric Jameson means that postmodern culture is in some kind of lockstep with the economics of late capitalism, that somehow postmodernism can be logically derived from late capitalism, then the correspondences between the commonly identified features of postmodernism and the features of late capitalism are too indeterminate for his diagnosis to be sustained. The two most fundamental characteristics of late capitalism (as Jameson and most others agree) are, on the one hand, the development by transnational companies of global production systems and a global marketplace, and on the other the almost instantaneous movement around the world of speculative finance. The effect of this is to make the products of capital and the outcomes of the financial markets increasingly homogeneous and economic decision-making ever more centralised.

Yet if there is one thing that cultural theorists of postmodernism seem to agree upon, it is on a whole constellation of developments which emphasise decentralisation – 'decentring' of the individual self and social organisation, difference, 'otherness', 'localism', fragmentation, collage and pastiche. Moreover, since capitalism is itself one of those 'totalising narratives' that postmodernism seeks to deconstruct, there seems to be a problem with the idea that the latter is the direct outcome of the former. To be sure, we shall see that there are many instances of correspondence between late capitalism and postmodern culture. This is particularly the case in the development of a consumerism in which value is determined less by people's wants or needs and more by what a commodity, a service or a cultural form such as a painting can be exchanged for, or, indeed, what it signifies in terms of social status. Nevertheless, these correspondences arise at a more superficial level than Jameson's description would have us believe.

Our first conclusion gives almost all of its space to a fairly detailed RECAPITULATION. It finishes with a brief but strong restatement of the answer given in the introduction.

1

I have suggested that even a loosely 'logical' interpretation of the relationship between postmodernism and late capitalism does not account for the disparities between the localising and fragmenting proclivities of the former and the globalising and universalising forces of the latter. For all its new-found flexibility in production processes, labour processes and its ability to respond quickly to niche markets and changes in fashion, late capitalism does what capitalism has always done. This is to exert a homogenising influence on both the products it makes and the consumers to whom it markets them. As we have seen, those features of present-day Western culture which are described to be postmodern – fragmentation or decentring of individual and social identities, collage in art and architecture, pastiche in advertising, the pursuit of the 'different' and exotic, the deconstruction of the old grand narratives into ever more relativised texts, and so on – all these may be 'real' enough as cultural observations. And certain aspects of them can indeed be traced to forces in late capitalism. But for the most part these aspects are relatively superficial, as superficial indeed as the very 'surfaces' that much of postmodernism loves to play with. Playing with surfaces is nothing new, as our brief examination of pre-capitalist Baroque and rococo

> architecture has tried to show. To change the metaphor, what late
> capitalism has done is to create an impression – a mirage – that it has
> changed culture fundamentally. Jameson has in large measure been
> taken in by that mirage.

In our second conclusion there is rather less recapitulation, the second half of the paragraph going on to pose a rhetorical question about the disparity between capitalism's need for certainty and postmodernism's emphasis on uncertainty. The paragraph concludes not by trying to supply a definitive answer to this question – because that would be to start off on another essay topic – but by PROPOSING where the study of this subject needs to concentrate its attention if the disparity is to be resolved.

2

In suggesting that the relations between late capitalism and postmodern culture are less 'logical' and more contingent and circumstantial than Jameson and many others believe, I have tried to show that the enormous variety in the goods and services produced for mass consumption is more apparent than real. We have seen how manufacturers and service providers increasingly cater for a wide variety of individual needs and tastes, but that for the most part these variations are little more than the icing on a fairly homogeneous cake. The modular design and production techniques developed by late capitalism simply create a pastiche of the same or similar elements in slightly differing combinations. If this is the case at the relatively superficial level of consumer goods and services, the much larger claim that late capitalism has directly brought about a fundamental shift in culture as a whole is even harder to sustain. Capital and its advocates insist on the need for a climate of 'certainty' in which to make its investment plans. Theorists of postmodernism, by contrast, argue persuasively that one of the defining cultural features of the present age is uncertainty. How is this gap to be explained in terms of the cultural logic of capital? Capitalism has always based itself on productive efficiency in order for a firm to survive in a competitive marketplace, and efficiency tolerates uncertainty and variability only at the margins. What needs to be done in the study of the relations between culture and capitalism is to work out where these margins are, and not to mistake the postmodern window-dressing for what is actually on capitalism's shop floor.

Our third looks at a different set of IMPLICATIONS. The adequacy of Jameson's position, and that of others who argue a similar case, is questioned in terms of the Marxist assumptions that lie beneath it. That is to say it GENERALISES the argument from one about post-modernism and late capitalism to one about the broader (perhaps more theoretical) relations between culture and economics. This conclusion finishes by making a PREDICTION which will test the soundness of my answer, slightly softened by being couched in a conditional 'if'.

3

In arguing, as I have done, that the bonds between late capitalism and postmodern culture are not nearly so tight as Jameson and most writers on this subject believe, we must ask in conclusion what it is that accounts for this near-unanimity of belief. Of those whom we have canvassed, only Jean Baudrillard presents a very different interpretation – one which I find even harder to accept. My argument has turned on drawing a distinction between postmodern surfaces and appearances on the one hand and the fundamentals of capitalist production and marketing on the other. Baudrillard sees only the first side of this dichotomy, and glories in it: 'seduction' rather than capitalist productive power drives postmodern cultural life in a society dominated by the image or 'simulacrum'. Now it is significant that Jameson and most others write from a Marxist standpoint. This does not mean that they all interpret the connection between late capitalism and postmodern culture in exactly the same way, and nor does it mean that they accept that version of Marxism which says that the cultural 'superstructure' is wholly and inflexibly determined by a material, economic base – any more than I have done. Even so, we have seen how David Harvey nevertheless holds to the Jamesonian view that cultural life lies '*within* the embrace of this capitalist logic' (my italics). My own attempt to examine the relationship hinges upon positing a certain un-Marxist disjunction or lack of overlap between cultural life and the economics of capitalist production: the 'dialectic' can be interpreted to a significant extent as one *between* the economic and the cultural. If postmodernism turns out to be a transient cultural phase which will fall away when the surfaces and appearances are recognised for what they are, while capitalism roars on regardless in its usual manner, then I think my interpretation stands up. Only time will tell.

Using the information you will have gleaned from the paragraphs above, you could try, if you wish, to write another ending to this essay.

Part III

Language

7

You, your language and your material

How can we know the dancer from the dance?

W. B. Yeats

The quality of your thought and argument (Parts I and II of this book) and the quality of your language are intimately connected. Your ability to articulate your ideas well might vary from one discipline you are studying to another, or you might have trouble with material that becomes progressively more complex.

   The next three chapters on language alert you to some common confusions of thought and understanding which often end up as confusing language – and which your word-processing program's grammar check is mostly incapable of helping you with. This chapter treats:

- subjective and objective: how and how not to use 'I' and 'we'

- how to avoid the pitfalls of confusing yourself with what you are writing about: avoiding dangling modifiers, using and abusing the passive voice, and disentangling the knotty connections between time and the tenses you use

- how to keep as clear as possible the distinction between what you are doing with your text and what the writers of your sources have done

- how to decide where and when to quote the language of your sources

> • how to handle certain common words of enquiry whose uses generate a lot of heated controversy.

One of the main themes in this book has been that an essay is *your* best answer to a question. If the essay is to be *your* answer, rather than *the* answer or *an* answer or *someone else's* answer, it is necessary to start paying close attention to some of the problems that arise in your use of language as you strive to establish a relationship with the material you have to mould. In this chapter we shall study a few of these problems. The first is an old bugbear – whether one should use 'I' in an academic essay. But there are others (set out in the box above) which can just as easily arise if you are uncertain about your position as a scholar and writer.

1   Subjective and objective: the uses of 'I' and 'we'

There is much confusion, not just in students' minds but in tutors' too, on whether 'I' and 'we' may be used in academic writing. Some tutors encourage you to be direct in your writing and to use 'I'. Others perpetuate an old myth that if you use 'I' your writing is too 'subjective'. You will probably find that the two words 'subjective' and 'objective' are very commonly flung about in your university or college as a shorthand to distinguish the unreliable and idiosyncratic opinions of individuals from the tried and tested truths of science or scholarship.

    Preferences are obvious examples of subjectivity. For example, 'I like Picasso prints in my bathroom' states no more than an individual idiosyncrasy. A statement like this is often confused with ones that can look rather similar: 'I think Machiavelli's reputation as an amoral rogue is thoroughly undeserved'; or 'I conclude that the texture of the language in Arundhati Roy's novel *The God of Small Things* is wholly appropriate to the world she creates.' Now, whether or not these two statements are subjective has absolutely nothing to do with the use of 'I'. It depends entirely on whether these judgements have been justified (or are to be justified) in the piece of language of which they form the conclusion. You can see that the presence or absence of justification is not affected if you take out the introductory phrases 'I think...' and 'I conclude that...'. Judgements, as we have seen, should be personal. Whether or not they are also objective depends on argument and evidence, not on whether you introduce them with an 'I'. Similarly, a purely subjective opinion or preference is not made objective by changing 'I' to 'we'.

The fact that 'I' can be, and is, used in academic writing is not to say, nevertheless, that every judgement you make should be flagged by 'I think', 'I believe', 'it seems to me' or some equivalent expression. The reason for this should by now be quite straightforward. This is that, since your essay should by definition be an account of your own justified judgements and beliefs, nothing is to be gained by continually making this explicit. 'I' is best used sparingly and reserved for a few typical situations:

1 When you need to make it clear to the reader that a judgement is your own and not to be confused with that of an author whose judgements you have been reporting or discussing; or when you want to emphasise where you stand with respect to other work, for example whether you want to agree, concede, rebut, question, reformulate, reconcile, etc. (see chapter 3, section 4):

> Unlike some critics who think the texture of the language in Arundhati Roy's *The God of Small Things* draws too much attention to itself, I find it scintillating in a manner wholly appropriate to the world she creates.
>
> While conceding to most commentators that the Ninth Symphony is a work of grandeur, I question whether Beethoven avoided parodying himself.

2 When you wish to emphasise your own degree of confidence in the outcome of your reasoning:

> Given the unreliability of some of this evidence, I think it impossible to draw any firm conclusion.
>
> This [evidence] suggests to me that in making the changes he did Michelangelo was just as concerned to preserve his reputation for being

> different from other architects as to correct any supposed shortcomings in Bramante's design for St Peter's Basilica.

3 When you want to announce to your reader how you propose to proceed or what modes of analysis you are engaging in:

> I shall try to demonstrate that . . .
>
> I have defined poverty in relative terms.
>
> Before describing what happened, I shall explain the background to these events.

'We' has two common uses, neither of which, as we saw above, should be to pretend that a personal judgement is a generally accepted 'objective' judgement. The legitimate uses of 'we' are these:

1 When you wish to report a conclusion that your reading has actually shown you to be generally accepted. 'We' in this usage includes 'I' the writer, 'you' the reader and 'they', other scholars (i.e. it means 'we all'). The verbs most commonly used with 'we' in this way are 'know' and 'believe':

> We know that as early as 1942 the Allies had plenty of information on what was happening to Jews in the concentration camps.
>
> We believe that the short-term memory capacity of the brain is 7 ± 2 units or 'chunks' of information.

2 When you the writer wish to guide the reader through what you propose to do or what you have already done in your essay. In this usage, 'we' includes 'I' and 'you' (the reader) but excludes others. It is most frequently used with verbs of observation, perception and analysis (e.g. see, observe, inspect, analyse, examine, find):

> **When we come to examine whether the Allies in World War II deliberately ignored the plight of the Jews, we shall find the evidence is not conclusive.**
>
> **When we analyse the second stanza of the poem, we discover that the rhyme scheme has become even more complex.**
>
> **We have seen in *Heart of Darkness* how Marlow's narrative distorts the sequence of the events as they must actually have happened to him. Now we must ask what structural implications Conrad's experimenting with time has for this novel.**

3 When an essay or article is written collaboratively by more than one author, in which case 'we' will be employed for those uses of 'I' set out above. Since most of your essays or papers will be written alone, you shouldn't often have need for this use of 'we'.

Acquiring confidence in your use of 'I' and 'we' should help you to define more clearly for yourself your relationship with the material, with other scholars' judgements on it and with your reader. It should, in addition, help you to avoid some of the pitfalls in structuring sentences and clarifying meanings that await those who try to write in a spuriously objective style. To these pitfalls we now turn.

2   Confusing yourself with your material

2.1   Dangling modifiers

It might seem quite improbable that you would confuse yourself with what you are writing about. But people often structure their sentences in such a way that this seems to be happening. Let us re-write a few of the examples above using structures that are quite common:

> **When examining whether the Allies deliberately ignored the plight of the Jews the evidence is not conclusive.**
>
> **Unlike some detractors who think the texture of the language in Arundhati Roy's *The God of Small Things* draws too much attention to itself, it is scintillating in a manner wholly appropriate to the world she creates.**
>
> **Before describing what happened, the background to these events must be understood.**
>
> **Examining the second stanza of the poem, the rhyme scheme is even more complex.**

These sentences exemplify what are sometimes called 'dangling modifiers'. The first part of each sentence is said to 'modify' the main proposition, which is contained in the second part of the sentence. These modifying phrases 'dangle' because, as you will see, the nature of the subject has changed in the transition from the modifying phrase to the main proposition. In each of the cases above this has been caused by the writer's failure to distinguish between what he or she does (examine, judge, describe) and what is being talked about (evidence, some detractors, background, rhyme scheme). Put another way, the structure of these sentences makes it appear that the evidence is doing the examining, the texture of the language in Roy's novel is unlike the detractors, the background is describing what happened and the rhyme scheme is examining the poem. While you will recognise these to be absurdities, you might be tempted to say that what is intended is quite clear. In fact, it isn't always clear what the writer intended and, in any case, we should always strive not only to mean what we say but also to say what we mean.

The third example illustrates these problems quite well, for there is a double slip here which has been caused by the writer not having clarified the distinction between self and material. The use of the verb 'understand' (in place of the 'explain' used in the earlier version of this sentence on p. 150 above) implies that the writer must be doing the understanding as well as the describing. Actually, the writer probably means that it is the reader and writer together who must understand the background to the events ('understand' is a verb which, in academic writing, is more typically found with 'we' than 'I' as its subject). This sentence has muddled up writer, reader and object of enquiry.

As soon as you begin to use the language of enquiry (in these cases verbs like 'examine', 'describe' and 'understand'), take care that you use 'I' or 'we' appropriately. The other recourse is to make no reference at all to what you do, for example:

> The evidence that the Allies deliberately ignored the plight of the Jews is not conclusive.
>
> The rhyme scheme of the second stanza is even more complex.

But if you wholly eschew the language of enquiry it becomes impossible for you to make statements of disagreement and analytical intention. The second and third examples on p. 152 above are at least trying to do this, however unsuccessfully. Hence it is necessary to learn to feel comfortable about using such language. As you practise such usages in your writing, scrutinise them carefully to ensure that you have not confused the processes that properly belong to the writer (I), to the writer and reader (we), and to the matter being written about (it).

2.2   Passives

Similar care is needed when you use the passive voice of a verb instead of the active voice. In the active voice, the person or phenomenon performing the action is made quite explicit:

> I have defined poverty in relative terms.
>
> When we examine whether the Allies deliberately ignored the plight of the Jews, we find the evidence to be inconclusive.

In these sentences 'I' and 'we' are performing the respective actions of defining and examining, the active voice making this quite clear. If, on the other hand, we write these sentences in the passive voice, the subjects disappear and a vagueness of meaning can creep in:

> **Poverty has been defined in relative terms.**
>
> **When the evidence that the Allies deliberately ignored the plight of the Jews is examined, it is found to be inconclusive.**

In these sentences the questions begged are '*Who* has defined poverty in this way?' and '*Who* examined the evidence and thinks it inconclusive?' It is no longer quite clear whether the writer is simply reporting what other scholars have done or whether the writer is affirming his or her own judgement. Your tutor will probably assume the first of these interpretations, and will immediately demand that you EXPAND on these statements by giving references to sources, and by suggesting that there are alternative definitions of poverty you have ignored or that not all scholars think the evidence inconclusive (see chapter 5).

Using the active voice forces you to decide quite definitely whether you are giving your own judgement, reporting that of just some scholars or reporting what is a generally accepted judgement. However, if it *is* your own judgement that is being made here, the passive voice can be kept just so long as you make this position clear in some other way. A reference to your own essay text is one such way:

> **Poverty has been defined *above* in relative terms.**
>
> **When the evidence that the Allies deliberately ignored the plight of the Jews *comes to be* examined *below*, it will be shown to be inconclusive.**

These statements are now announcements to the reader about what you have done or what you will do in your text, a function of language very different from the delivering of a judgement. They will not therefore attract a request to EXPAND.

Some books on writing counsel their readers always to avoid the passive voice. This is ridiculous. What you must do when you use the passive is to ensure that you have not begged a significant question about the identity of the actor. This is particularly important when the distinction between what you are saying and what others have said is at stake.

2.3   Time and tense

A third source of confusion between oneself and one's material is the failure to realise that, very often, we as writers and scholars may inhabit a slightly different universe of time from some of the things we write about. Consequently, there are certain conventions about the use of tenses – especially past and present – in academic writing which are not intuitively obvious. You will probably be quite familiar with the straightforward convention which decrees that events which happened in the past are written about in the past tense. (So in history essays we will write that 'Napoleon *retreated* from Moscow in disarray' rather than adopt the style of some television documentaries. In the latter, narrators – in the manner of sports commentators – will tell us 'Napoleon *retreats* from Moscow in disarray' as we watch some painting or re-enactment of this event.) But problems begin to arise when we draw distinctions between reporting or describing past events on the one hand (what Napoleon did) and interpreting them on the other (what I believe or argue Napoleon did). They also arise when we are dealing with certain kinds of material – in particular, texts written in the past or societies studied by anthropologists at some time in the past.

Look at the use of tenses in this extract from George H. Sabine's *A History of Political Theory* (1963: 16). In this passage Sabine is discussing the view of the eighteenth-century English statesman Edmund Burke that the rights of man are founded not so much in nature as in the conventions established by a civilised society:

> It is true that [Burke] never denied the reality of natural rights. Like Hume he admitted that the social contract may be true merely as a bit of hypothetical history, and much more than Hume he was convinced that some of the conventions of society are inviolable. Just what these immovable principles are he never tried to say – property, religion, and the main outlines of the political constitution would probably have been among them – but he certainly believed in their reality. However, again like Hume, he believed that they were purely conventional. That is to say, they arise not from anything belonging to nature or to the human species at large, but solely from the habitual and prescriptive arrangements that make a body of men into a civil society.

Sabine uses the past tense to report *that* Burke did or believed certain things (e.g. 'denied', 'admitted', 'was convinced', 'tried', 'believed'). These are treated as (past) events in Burke's mental life. But when Sabine wishes to emphasise either his own point of view ('it is true') or the ideas themselves, which are just as present to Sabine as he writes as they were to Burke and his contemporaries when Burke wrote about them, he shifts to what is called the 'universal' present tense. (Sabine slips up once: 'he believed that they *were* purely conventional'.) The activity of Burke's thinking is a past event in history; what he thought about is still 'present' to the modern reader in Burke's texts.

Hence it is usual to use the present tense to write about what you find in texts no matter when they were written. If you are a literature student, in particular, you need to remember this convention, since most of your writing is about what is found in texts. You might write that Milton *believed* so and so, but that in *Paradise Lost* he *says* such and such.

There is a problem with yet another dimension of time that you must keep in mind as you write about literature. This is that you should be careful about the time dimension in which you operate while you read a work and the space–time sequence of words on the printed page. That is to say, you should avoid making statements like this:

> When reading the poem, as we noticed the mood changing between lines 6 and 8 so did the diction.

This use of tenses might suggest that the diction of the poem changed as we were reading the poem and noticing the mood changing. What has been confused here is a report about 'our' reading processes (a psychological and historical event) and a report about what is on the printed page (a literary phenomenon). The diction, like the mood, changes between lines 6 and 8, not between the time we began to read line 6 and the time we finished line 8. So the best recourse is probably to change the tenses in this example from the past into the present. It used to be thought that it is better to omit any reference to the private activity of reading a text and to concentrate on the conclusions your reading has brought you to. But more recently it has been realised that the experience of 'reading as a woman', 'reading as an exile', 'reading as an ex-colonised person' or, for example, reading an Arabic text as an (ethnic) European suggests that one willy-nilly brings one's own feelings and experiences to a text in the act of reading itself. What is important is that you try to become aware of a problem with time like this one, and to bring yourself to the text and your writing about it with some appreciation of the possible pitfalls.

If you are a student of sociology, anthropology or another social science which requires the reporting of field-work in which you have engaged, there are other quite tricky problems in the use of tenses which are bound up in changing views of how these disciplines conceive themselves. It was once the generally held convention that when you are reporting particular events you observed, interviews you conducted or other such observational activities of your own, the past tense is appropriate. But the moment you begin to generalise about these observations, to describe the behaviour of groups or institutions, you should move into what is called the 'ethnographic present tense', a conventional tense which locates the writer and the subject matter in the same time frame. Under this convention, even if there is good cause to believe that, as you write, aspects of the social structure you are writing about have changed significantly (not uncommon in anthropology), the present tense is maintained.

Notice how in this extract about the Nuer people in southern Sudan, E. E. Evans-Pritchard (in Radcliffe-Brown and Forde 1950: 361–2) moves from the present tense, in which he makes general statements or interpretations, to the past tense, in which he reports a particular experience of his own which illustrates his general point:

> **Nevertheless, in spite of their many contacts with one another and of their concerted action in their relations with other villages, there may be rivalries between different parts of a single village . . . *Wa pekda*, 'I go to my end (of the village)', often indicates, besides direction, a particular loyalty within the wider village. As an example of this feeling I mention an experience in the village of Nyueny, which is referred to again later. I gave spears to two youths who often visited me from the other end of the village than that where I had pitched my tent, and a man at our end protested to me in private . . .**

Much of the research on which Evans-Pritchard bases his essay was carried out in the 1930s and 1940s, and it is very likely that certain aspects of Nuer social organisation had changed between then and the time he was writing around 1950, as the editors of this volume acknowledge (1950: 84–5). Nevertheless, Evans-Pritchard sticks resolutely to the present tense in his generalised descriptions.

How different is Sharon E. Hutchinson (1996: 42–3), writing about the Nuer some forty-five years later. She takes Evans-Pritchard and others severely to task:

> **. . . it is difficult to determine how much of the fluidity in values I perceived among the Nuer was the product of more than fifty years of tumultuous history and how much was the product of shifting rhetorical styles and theoretical interests within the discipline of anthropology as a whole. [Many more recent anthropologists] and other critics of 'ethnography' have all expressed profound reservations about the ways cultures were defined and described by Evans-Pritchard . . . and other key figures within the discipline . . . especially . . . of the ways many of**

these authors tended to mask the inherently reflexive, historical nature of field research with a rhetorical aura of timeless objectivity.

So Hutchinson decides to correct this 'rhetorical aura of timeless objectivity' by writing in the past tense to emphasise how she found the Nuer at the time she was doing her own field research. For example (pp. 83–4):

I should, perhaps, first check the assumption that money and cattle were wholly interchangeable. Not all money was good, I was told, for buying cattle. There was something called *yiou cieth* (the 'money of shit') that allegedly could not be invested fruitfully in cattle... *yiou cieth* was quite literally money people earned in local towns collecting and dumping the waste of household bucket latrines.

The use of tense, then, can be closely bound up with changing theoretical and other attitudes in the disciplines you are studying, attitudes which may be fiercely contested among your tutors. It is therefore advisable to check with your tutors when you are in doubt.

Switching between present and past tenses (even within the same sentence) is common in academic writing – as the Sabine extract above illustrates. What is important is that you make these switches in a principled way, for example to signal a shift between your own interpretations and your reports of events, and that you be consistent. Checking consistency in your use of tense is one of the jobs that must be carried out when revising your drafts.

2.4   Your own text and others' texts

Another confusion that can easily arise is one between what you write and what the authors of your sources have written. You need to manipulate your language with some care when you are writing about the sources you are using if you are to avoid running together what is in those texts with what is in your own, or (to put it another way) to avoid running together what the authors of the sources do with what you do.

Note, first, that a quotation is most often something that you have performed. A quotation is not something written by the source you are using. Hence, rather than write,

> This quotation *by* Evans-Pritchard shows that loyalty among the Nuer does not extend to the whole village,

you should write,

> This quotation *from* Evans-Pritchard shows that . . .

The difference between 'by' and 'from' distinguishes between who is responsible for the action of quoting and the person affected by the action. You (the writer) are the person who is actually quoting, whereas Evans-Pritchard is merely being used by you as a source you are drawing *from*. If you find yourself vacillating between 'by' and 'from' as you write, try to sort out the position in terms such as these.

Here is a similar problem:

> The Commission's activity broadened to encompass other aspects of urban renewal, as outlined by Coleman (1970) in section 3.1 above.

The best way to get this to say what, apparently, was intended is to make it quite explicit who wrote section 3.1 above by using 'I' or 'we' and also to make it clear who is doing the outlining – I (the writer) or Coleman. For example:

> In section 3.1 above I outlined Coleman's (1970) account of how the Commission's activity broadened to encompass other aspects of urban renewal.

or

In section 3.1 above we examined Coleman's (1970) outline of how the Commission's activity broadened to encompass other aspects of urban renewal.

Finally, take care to avoid this kind of misleading statement:

The poem is reminiscent of a happier time which the two lovers in it have associated with the park.

Ask yourself who is doing the reminiscing – the poem (or the lovers 'in it'), or the writer of the sentence? If we say 'The poem is reminiscent', it is the writer of the sentence who is doing the reminiscing. If, on the other hand, we say 'The poem reminisces', it is quite clearly the poem. The writer of this sentence clearly intends the second meaning, since he is not concerned with his own memories of the park but with those of the poet himself and of the lovers who are in the park.

Since much academic writing engages in the self-conscious analysis of what the writer says about what other writers have said, it is very easy to blur the distinction between self and other by an unwise choice of word or structure. But if you are clear in your own mind what it is *you* are doing, and if you resist the temptation to hide behind the texts of your sources, you should have little difficulty avoiding the kinds of confusion exemplified above.

3   Quoting – and not quoting

Whether you should quote from other sources in your essays, and when you should do it, are questions particularly relevant to the success with which you establish a satisfactory relationship between your language and your material. Tutors in the humanities and social sciences are not impressed by scissors-and-paste essays which consist largely of quotations stitched together by a few linking sentences and paragraphs. (Even less are they impressed by blocks of text down-loaded directly into an essay from the internet. Never do this, unless the material is primary evidence you wish to discuss.) Here is one tutor's comment on an essay that has quoted too much: 'You quote fairly extensively from different secondary sources but you allow what they say to govern the drift of your essay to the point where you can't hold a consistent line of your own.' If you quote excessively, you are allowing the words of somebody else to choke off your own chances of coming to understand and interpret the material. Your essay cannot then be your own best answer.

You might most frequently be tempted to quote when you feel you have not sufficiently understood the meaning of your material and cannot find words of your own to express the idea. When this happens you should try to adopt the approach to reading and note-taking set out in chapter 3, particularly that in the section 'Interpreting a difficult text'. Your aim, as we saw there (pp. 87–8), is to create a 'compound' from elements of your own language and that of the sources you are using.

When it comes to presenting straightforward facts or general, uncontroversial information, there is rarely if ever any justification for quoting from your sources. DESCRIBING things, events and sit-uations you will probably have practised more than any other kind of writing. So even though you might at times find it difficult to work out how best to describe coherently some complex set of events and the relationships between them, you should nevertheless resist the temptation to quote one more or less randomly chosen author's account.

The best justification for quoting is the presentation of such primary data or evidence as you then go on to analyse, for example experimental results, the answers to survey questions, a table of raw figures or statistics, lines from a literary work, a statement from some primary historical document. Quoting is a way of putting before your reader the object to be discussed, just as you might get out a family photograph to point to when some discussion about it takes place.

The views and interpretations of the writers of secondary sources may be used in much the same way. We quote them not to save us the bother of rendering their ideas in our own words, or merely to appeal to the authority of the author. Rather, we quote so that we can say to our reader: 'This is what so-and-so says. What does she mean? How well does the evidence support her view? I agree (or disagree) with her point of view because . . . ', and so on. It is probably true to say that academic authors quote the views of others when they want to challenge that view more often than when they want to accede to it.

Finally, quotations may also be used if an author has expressed a point particularly clearly, succinctly or elegantly. I have done this at the beginning of the chapters in this book. It is also commonly found in introductions and conclusions to essays. If your own cultural background is one that places great value on quoting classical authorities, such enhancement of your own writing can be a good idea, so long as the quotation is apt. But its value to an academic essay lies in its sparing use. To indulge yourself too often in the quoting of others' great thoughts is to run the risk of never learning to formulate your own.

4 Some verbs of enquiry: how to use them

We have already met many of the verbs you will use to express your own and other scholars' processes of enquiry (e.g. know, believe, analyse, see, observe, examine, find, show, describe, explain, define). For the most part the distinctions in meaning between these words do not cause us a great deal of trouble; we get into trouble with them – as we have seen – when we combine them with other elements in a sentence. There are, nevertheless, some verbs of enquiry whose meanings and uses often do cause considerable difficulty, partly because they are used fairly loosely in non-academic writing and speech. Below is a gloss on the uses of those that cause most difficulty.

Uninterested/disinterested

These words are not, strictly speaking, verbs, but let that pass. 'Disinterested' has recently colonised that part of the map of meaning once occupied by 'uninterested', but in the process has been losing what was once its own distinct identity. The traditional distinction between these words probably oversimplifies the relations between self and subject matter; it will nevertheless be passionately adhered to by many of your tutors.

'Uninterested' was once reserved to express one's lack of interest in enquiring into a subject at all. You will probably have studied some subject, found it not interesting to you and given it away at the first opportunity. To say that you are uninterested, therefore, is merely to state a subjective or idiosyncratic aversion, that you are 'indifferent' or 'bored' (useful alternatives suggested by Pam Peters in *The Cambridge Guide to English Usage* (Cambridge: Cambridge University Press, 2004, p. 158), a point of view which is of no relevance to academic enquiry. To express your disinterest, on the other hand, is said to affirm a detachment which says that you are ready to make your judgements only on the evidence and arguments available and to change your mind if necessary. This is probably too large an ask, since – as we have constantly seen in this book – complete detachment from the *outcomes* of your enquiries is neither necessary nor possible. If you are so utterly detached, then why were you interested in the subject in the first place? That the boundaries between the meanings of these two words have become fuzzier than used to be thought does not, however, provide an argument for ignoring the distinction altogether.

Imply/infer

This is another distinction to whose preservation many of your tutors will be passionately devoted. For the most part it is a useful one, even though there are times when it can quite legitimately be blurred, and even though (as *The Oxford English Dictionary* shows) such scholars as John Milton in the seventeenth century and James Mill in the nineteenth have ignored it.

You, as a scholar, can both imply and infer. If you imply something you imply it *to* your reader, and your reader infers it *from* your text. If, on the other hand, you infer, your inference is made either from a text you are reading or from data you are examining. If your inference is a legitimate one, then it might be said that the text or the author of the text implied what you say it did. Inferring, therefore, is a function of someone's reading and interpreting of texts and evidence; implying is a function of writing. You might use either word in the appropriate way to make much the same point:

> Sabine's account of Burke implies [to me] that, rather than rejecting natural rights, Burke completely absorbed them into his notion of the conventional rights embodied in a 'civil society'.
>
> I infer from Sabine's account of Burke that . . .

Feel

Treat 'feel' with some caution. It is often used by students in such a way that the 'feeling' cannot be justified in any public way. In writing about the arts (literature, music, painting, sculpture, etc.), 'feel' is used and can be used because only the most hard-nosed of academics would deny that the arts do arouse in us an emotive response. But try not to use it merely as an affective substitute for 'think'.

Speculate, conjecture

Speculation and conjecture are often coupled with 'mere' by people of a wholly practical or empirical turn of mind. Speculation is a perfectly legitimate academic activity, as necessary as imagination, even to the most methodologically precise and experimental of disciplines. Speculating and conjecturing are not the exclusive preserve of mystics and poets, but may be engaged in whenever knowledge is sought. Chapter 2 of this book is largely about how to speculate. *The Oxford English Dictionary* quotes Dickens's *Our Mutual Friend* to convey the opprobrium attached to speculation: 'His knowledge of its affairs was mostly speculative and all wrong.' Coleridge, at times a speculative thinker himself, puts the other side of the case: 'A certain number of speculative minds is necessary to a cultivated state of society.' The utilitarian J. S. Mill includes his treatise *Representative*

Government in the category 'speculations concerning forms of government', declaring that 'speculative thought is one of the chief elements of social power'. The charge to avoid is not 'mere speculation' but 'idle speculation'.

Imagine

Most worthwhile knowledge is achieved by what the scientist Jacob Bronowski has called 'a creative leap of the imagination' rather than by a set of discovery procedures. What was necessary for Einstein is necessary for us. The ability to imagine 'possible worlds' is a necessary accomplishment in many disciplines: for example, by trying to imagine what is not the case, what could not be the case, or what might be the case, we are led to appreciate more clearly what is the case. Even historians – with their traditional distaste for historical 'ifs' – have tried to assess the economic significance of the spread of the railroads in nineteenth-century America by imagining what the economy would have been like *without* them. Like speculations and conjectures, only vacant and idle imaginings are to be rejected.

Wish, hope

No attitude to one's material can be founded only on wishes or hopes. Consequently, these verbs will more commonly be used in combination with others conveying a sense of certainty or assertion, for example 'I hope to demonstrate that . . . ', 'I wish to acknowledge that . . . '.

8

Analytical language 1: sentences

The world was made before the English language, and seemingly upon a different design.

Robert Louis Stevenson

This chapter first reviews the sentence *structures* which underlie the preferred formal style of academic writing:

- the functions of REFERRING and PREDICATING in simple sentences: why these functions are important to academic writing, and when it is possible to bend the rules

- how conjunctions, sentence adverbials and punctuation are used to build successful complex sentences out of simple ones.

Then we look at the *meanings* of the sentence's parts – participants, processes and circumstances – and the nature of the relations between them, so as to avoid the danger of:

- putting together in the same sentence human or non-human participants with incompatible processes which don't 'make sense'

- turning what are really processes into abstract participants in such a way that your language either obscures the identity of the participants or confuses abstract participants with concrete processes

- failing to preserve a distinction between what we can say about words and texts and what we can say about the material world which we enquire into.

1   Discrimination and confusion

The quotation from Robert Louis Stevenson above expresses one writer's rueful admission that there is nothing easy or natural about getting the English language (or any other, for that matter) to constitute adequately what the world is like. The language has to be pushed and coaxed, stretched and compressed, filed and hammered to get it to match the reality you are trying to make sense of. It is common to talk about 'polishing' your language – like a diamond – as if that is all you have to do. But before that the diamond has to be mined and cut. This is the hardest part. As T. S. Eliot says:

> Words strain,
> Crack and sometimes break, under the burden,
> Under the tension, slip, slide, perish . . .
>
> ('Burnt Norton' in *Four Quartets*)

When they do these things we easily become confused and, hence, what we are writing about becomes confused and not always easily understood by a reader.

Though this chapter is about English grammar, you will not find in the pages that follow a comprehensive guide to the grammar of English. It takes a whole book to do that. What you will find are just a few pointers designed to help you to recognise and to pre-empt some of the confusions that might creep into your own academic writing.

Some of these confusions, you might find, only become a problem when you are writing academic essays and papers. It is sometimes the case that students discover they cannot consistently write grammatical sentences only when they begin a university or college course. Others find problems begin to arise only in the second or third year of their course. If either of these things happens to you, the cause is probably the extra demands placed on your understanding by more complex, more subtle or more abstract ideas. You might need to give your language a chance to catch up with your growing understanding. Structuring sentences, which, early in the year, can be causing you many problems, could well begin to right itself as you become clearer about what it is you are trying to say. Even so, by studying the pointers to sentence structures and processes contained in this chapter, you can make yourself aware of some of the pitfalls to look out for.

Yet other students find that their ability to structure sentences collapses in just one or two of the subjects they are studying. If you find your English expression is praised by the geography tutor and severely criticised by the tutor in sociology or in history, it might well be that you are finding it harder to make sense of the ideas or methods of enquiry practised in sociology or history. It is also the case that disciplines vary somewhat in the kinds of distinction they make use of. It is therefore quite easy to write confused sentences until the nature of the relevant distinctions is pointed out to you. We cannot here cover all the sources of grammatical confusion that might arise in the humanities and social sciences. There is, however, something you can do for yourself. If a tutor writes 'Confused' – and no more – in the margin of your essay, make a special effort to have the precise nature of the confusion explained to you. It is important to you, and it doesn't do the tutor any harm to have to articulate the problem.

2   Elements of sentence structure

2.1   Referring and predicating

The first distinction you must be able to draw is the one that underlies the structure of most of the sentences you will write. Academic language (perhaps more than other kinds) engages in making statements or propositions. Propositions and the declarative sentences (or statements) based on them have two main parts: (a) a NOMINAL (naming) expression which REFERS to some object, idea or entity in the world; and (b) a VERBAL expression which PREDICATES of these nominals some action, process, situation or relation. That is to say, something we want to write about is identified by giving it a name (referring), and then we go on to say something about it (predicating). Making sense of the world demands that some statement about it combines these nominal referring expressions and predicating verbals. This structure is represented in Figure 5.

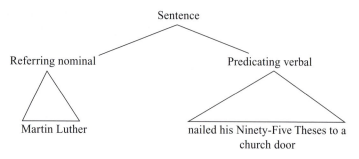

Figure 5

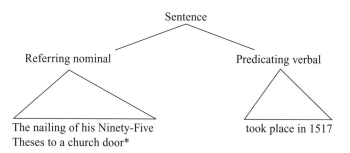

Figure 6

Now, nominals and verbals are not easily distinguished according to the kinds of entities they express. Both include non-physical entities such as states, situations, actions, events, processes, relations, and so on. Rather, it is the *functions* of referring and predicating that distinguish them. An action, for example, that might be a verbal predicator in one sentence (as in Figure 5) may, with some slight but important grammatical changes, become part of a nominal referring expression in another (see Figure 6). The underlying structure therefore remains the same. The fact that we have incorporated the verbal of the first sentence into the nominal of the second requires us to find a new predicating verbal ('took place in 1517') with which to complete the structure.

The predicating verbal usually needs to contain what is called a 'finite verb' (e.g. nailed, took place), as opposed to a 'non-finite verb' (e.g. nailing, to nail, taking place, to take place). The term 'finite' here

---

* Notice that, even when the referring nominal is an extended one like this, there is no need for a comma between the nominal and the verbal.

means 'limited' or 'restricted'. Perhaps the easiest way to recognise whether a verb is finite is to see whether it is limited in respect of its *tense* – past, present or future. The non-finite (infinitive) form with 'to' (e.g. to nail) is tenseless. In this sentence 'to nail' is part of the nominal referring expression and has nothing to do with the predicate:

> **To nail the Ninety-Five Theses on the Wittenberg Chapel door was a calculated political act.**

Like the 'to' infinitive the '-ing' form of the verb (e.g. nailing) is non-finite unless it is preceded by certain auxiliary verbs that do carry tense. These auxiliaries are forms of the verb 'be' (am, is, are, was, were), the verb 'have' (has, have, had) and the so-called modal verbs (e.g. shall–should, will–would, can–could, may–might, must, ought). In Figure 6 there is no tense in the 'nailing' of the referring nominal, whilst 'took place' in the predicating verbal is in the past tense. It is the absence of a predicating verbal carrying tense in the second 'sentence' below which makes it unacceptable in formal academic English:

> **In 1517 Martin Luther performed a calculated political act. Nailing his Ninety-Five Theses to the Chapel door in Wittenberg.**

To be able to discriminate between these two major constituents of a simple declarative sentence – the referring nominal and the predicating verbal with its finite verb marked for tense – is absolutely necessary if you are to follow some of the complications and exceptions introduced below. It is also necessary if you are to avoid the kinds of common confusion we shall examine later in this chapter. The reason for this is simply that many of the choices of vocabulary and grammatical structure you make in the referring nominal determine the choices available to you in the predicate (or vice versa). If these choices do not match, your writing becomes ungrammatical and confused.

2.2   Sentences without finite verbs

We saw above an example of a piece of language which cannot be called a sentence because it lacks a predicating verbal. Here is another:

> **Luther did not think the papacy or an ecclesiastical elite could determine faith. Faith being dispersed throughout the community of the faithful.**

It can easily be fixed, either by incorporating the fragment into the first sentence,

> **Luther did not think the papacy or an ecclesiastical elite could determine faith, faith being dispersed throughout the community of the faithful.**

or by simply changing the non-finite 'being dispersed' to the finite 'is dispersed':

> **Luther did not think the papacy or an ecclesiastical elite could determine faith. Faith (he thought) is dispersed throughout the community of the faithful.**

There are, nevertheless, certain conditions under which the finite verb, or even the referring nominal, can be dispensed with. The first condition is that the finite form can be recovered from a verb in the preceding sentence either by repeating it or by using a substitute. Examples of substitutes are 'do' for an action, 'happen' for an event and 'be' for a state or situation. To repeat the verb or to use a substitute leads not only to unnecessary redundancy but also to the insertion of rather meaningless nominals to complete the syntactic structure:

> **The edict of Emperor Charles V which put Luther under a ban of the Holy Roman Empire never led him to advocate the separation of Church and State. Quite the contrary. Luther continued to maintain fiercely the**

> mediaeval doctrine that Church and State are one and that princes are the guardians of the Church.

The second of these sentences is wholly grammatical because the omitted verb 'did' standing in for 'advocate' is recoverable from the first sentence. To add in the verb would, further, have required one of those relatively meaningless words like 'action' or 'case' which add nothing of substance to the idea being expressed:

> His action was quite the contrary.
>
> Quite the contrary was the case.

An illustration of how substitute verbs can be recoverable from the preceding sentence is this:

> Did Luther seek to avoid a confrontation with the Emperor Charles V? Nothing of the sort. He worked hard to bring it about.

'Nothing of the sort' could be expanded to 'He did nothing of the sort' or, perhaps, 'Nothing of the sort took place.' The verbless sentence is more effective than either of these. The examples of verbless sentences above illustrate the second condition that such sentences should fulfil in academic writing: they are best used as a transitional comment summing up the writer's attitude to what has gone before or to what follows.

You will find many examples of sentences without finite verbs in novels, journalism and popular writing. (They are discussed by Ernest Gowers under the entry 'Verbless sentences' in the second edition of Fowler's *Modern English Usage* (Oxford: Clarendon Press, 1965, p. 674).) Most of these are not appropriate to academic writing. The style of certain detective novels, for example, in which particular prominence is given to circumstances of place and time is feeble in academic prose:

> Luther declared his opposition to the sale of indulgences. In his
> Ninety-Five Theses. In Wittenberg. On the Chapel door.

This kind of writing is at odds with what an academic essay should probably be emphasising – the main proposition, contained in the first sentence, rather than the circumstances of time and place.

2.3   Conjoining clauses into complex sentences

Conjunctions and sentence adverbials

A sentence which consists of a single nominal, referring expression and a predicating verbal expression is also said to constitute a single 'main clause'. A main clause asserts the principal proposition of a sentence. We can add further propositions to a sentence by adding to the main clause or embedding within it various other kinds of clause. It is the function of these clauses to EXTEND, ELABORATE and ENHANCE the main proposition, very much in the way we saw these processes operating in chapter 5, section 3. That is to say, they have these functions: to add on new information; to provide exceptions and alternatives; to clarify, substantiate and exemplify the main proposition; or to enhance it by imposing such circumstantial restrictions as time, place, manner, means, cause, condition and concession on its truth and range of application. You can probably handle many of the structural problems posed by these compound and complex sentences. There are, however, a few which do commonly cause difficulty. To these we now turn.

The first general point to keep in mind is that certain kinds of word must normally be employed when you want to attach extra clauses to the main clause. The most common of these are called 'conjunctions' since they conjoin clauses. Examples are 'and', 'but', 'or', 'whereas', 'because', 'so that', 'if' and 'although'. Conjunctions are to be distinguished from another class of words whose meanings are similar but whose grammatical use is quite different. These latter (called 'sentence adverbials' or 'linking terms') do not join together clauses in the same sentence; rather, they provide the links of thought and meaning between quite separate sentences. Examples are 'furthermore', 'on the other hand', 'by contrast', 'alternatively', 'for this reason', 'therefore' and 'however'. Whether we choose to write longer sentences whose clauses are joined by conjunctions or shorter sentences linked by sentence adverbials is usually a matter of style and emphasis (see chapter 10).

What we cannot usually do is to join clauses by means of sentence adverbs or link sentences by means of conjunctions or the relative pronoun 'which'. (The exceptions to this rule are the coordinating conjunctions 'and', 'or' and 'but', which may be used to begin a new sentence.) However common it may be in journalism and elsewhere – in particular the 'because', and 'which' sentences in the first two examples below – this kind of language will be regarded with disfavour by many of your tutors:

Martin Luther nailed his Ninety-Five Theses to the Chapel door in Wittenberg. Because he wanted to make a political statement that would draw the Elector of Saxony's support.

In nailing his Theses to the Chapel door in Wittenberg, Luther wanted to enlist the Elector of Saxony's support. Which, for the most part, is what he eventually achieved.

Luther wanted to secure the Elector of Saxony's support for his Theses, therefore he nailed them to the Chapel door in Wittenberg.

Luther was successful in gaining the Elector's support, however, he overestimated the latter's ability to protect him.

The Elector of Saxony supported Luther. Whereas most of the rulers of German states succumbed to the pressure of the Emperor Charles V.

Punctuation: colons and semi-colons

There are two important qualifications to this. Both involve using those punctuation marks, the semi-colon (;) and colon (:), that you might feel unsure about. Sentence adverbials, as in the third and fourth examples above, can be used to conjoin clauses into a single complex sentence if that join is made with a semi-colon in place of the comma. The semi-colon is the super-glue which can hold together almost any pair of statements whose subject matter is related; it can even be used if the nature of that relation is not made explicit by a sentence adverbial (as this sentence illustrates).

The colon, by contrast, indicates a relation of a certain kind: one between a general and a particular statement. In the sentence below the first statement mentions 'a calculated political act'; the second specifies the particular nature of that act:

> In 1517 Luther performed a calculated political act: he nailed his Ninety-Five Theses to the Chapel door in Wittenberg.

You are probably familiar with this use of the colon in slightly different contexts: when in your lecture notes you make a general heading, to be followed by more specific statements; or when in an essay you make a general statement and follow it with a quotation to make your point concrete and particular. To sum up, you can use the colon when ELABORATING a point, as we saw in chapter 5 (pp. 123–7), namely to CLARIFY, to SUBSTANTIATE and to EXEMPLIFY.

There is a kind of complex sentence structurally somewhat different from those we have looked at, but which expresses a relationship similar to that signalled by the colon. In this structure the main clause consists – as usual – of a nominal referring expression and a predicating verb ('Luther argued' in the example below). The verb expresses perception (observe, see, hear, etc.). An extra clause is added to this main clause by using 'that', and so is informally called a 'that' clause:

> At the Diet of Worms in 1521 Luther argued that only Scripture and reason could be used to prove him wrong.

The connection with the use of the colon should be quite obvious. The 'that' clause specifies what Luther argued, a paraphrase of what he actually said:

> Luther argued: 'it is impossible for me to recant unless I am proved wrong by the testimony of Scripture or by evident reasoning'.

Notice one thing about the punctuation of this structure. In modern English there is no comma either before or after the 'that'. Do not write: 'Luther argued, that only Scripture . . .'; or 'Luther argued that, only Scripture . . .'.

We are not now going to look any further into the purely formal structures of declarative sentences. Despite the various qualifications we have noticed above, it remains the case, first, that the fundamental structure of any sentence you write needs to reflect those complementary functions of referring and predicating. You can help yourself make this distinction if you can also learn to distinguish between a finite verb – which specifies the tense of your statement – and a non-finite form of the verb. Once you are clear about this, you can in very particular circumstances modify your sentence structures by deleting certain elements. And then, secondly, you can complicate simple sentences by adding further clauses with the aid of conjunctions, semi-colons and colons. To be able to manage these things will not guarantee that you will always write well-structured, grammatical sentences. But it will help to underpin your ability to avoid certain other sources of confusion in their design. These last are perhaps more obviously connected with structuring meanings. So to potential confusions of meaning in structuring our sentences we now turn.

3   Participants, processes and circumstances

We have learned to distinguish the functions of referring and predicating when we construct our sentences. We shall now look at the sentence and the clause from a slightly different point of view – the combining and manipulating of their elements to express how the world we write about is ordered or how it might be ordered.

We make sense of the world, both to ourselves and to our readers, by exploring the various PROCESSES that go on in it – actions, events, situations, perceptions, relations of various kinds, and so on. We also seek to identify the various phenomena that take part in these processes. The phenomena most closely studied in the humanities and social sciences are people – the abstract ideas, the social structures and institutions, the works of art and the languages they create, as well as aspects of the natural world in which they live. These phenomena we shall call PARTICIPANTS in the various kinds of process mentioned above. For example, dogs (participants) bark (an action); politicians get elected (an event); people own houses (a relationship of possession between two participants, people and houses); and scholarship is difficult (a relationship which ascribes a characteristic to the participant).

In addition, participants engage in these processes in certain restricted CIRCUMSTANCES of time, place, manner, means, condition, concession, causation, intention, etc., which often need to be made explicit. So, dogs bark *when* they are alarmed; politicians *in* ideal democracies get elected *by* appealing successfully to the electorate; people own houses *if* they can afford to *and if* government allows the private holding of dwellings; scholarship remains difficult *despite* the assistance of modern information technology.

Now, it is from our study of the world and its representation in language that we learn how to combine various participants with various processes and circumstances in ways that make sense. We should not ordinarily write that scholarship gets elected by painting landscapes, that dogs own houses in order to abolish equilibrium, or that houses own people under a kilogram of kinship ties. Statements like these look like nonsense, the nonsense arising from the coupling of incompatible participants, processes and circumstances. On the other hand, we might well write that politicians both bark at and bite each other, that a dog's obeyed in office, and that these dogs control the House by means of their whips. Since language slips and slides about (as it does in these last examples) the line between sense and nonsense can be quite fuzzy and difficult to clarify, especially when you are embarking on the study of some subject quite new to you.

What we shall do now is examine some of the commoner problems that arise when we confuse some of the processes, participants and circumstances studied in the humanities and social sciences. We need to do this in particular because *you cannot rely on the grammar check in your word-processing program to alert you to these problems. It simply won't pick them up.*

3.1 Clarifying participants, human and non-human

It might seem unlikely that you would say things of human participants that can only properly be said of non-humans, or vice versa. Yet this is routinely done. At times it is quite acceptable. We use metaphor: 'A *dog's* obeyed in office.' We use metonymy, personification and other devices by which an inanimate object can substitute for a human or human institution: 'The power of the English *crown* was whittled away in the century following the 1688 revolution'; '*1688* saw the beginnings of constitutional monarchy.' These ways of expressing the world come so naturally to us that we would think absurdly literal anyone who pointed out, for example, that the year 1688 can actually 'see' nothing at all.

Similarly, there are some processes which allow the participant which carries them out to be either human or non-human, but upon which there are restrictions on the kind of participant that may be affected by the process. The first of these participants (the one who 'does') we can call the 'actor'. The second we can call the 'affected':

> With his discovery of the mathematical laws of perspective, Brunelleschi opened the door to modern realist painting.
>
> The door to modern realist painting opened with Brunelleschi's discovery of the mathematical laws of perspective.

In the first sentence the non-human door is the participant affected by the process of opening, and Brunelleschi is the actor. In the second sentence, the door has become the actor in this process of opening.

'Open' is one of the verbs which allow this switch of human and non-human actor to take place.

In most processes, by contrast, it is quite unacceptable to substitute the non-human for the human actor. Discovery is one such process: Brunelleschi might be either the actor who discovers or the affected who is discovered; but the laws of perspective cannot do the discovering. Discovery, like all those processes of perceiving and enquiring that figure so centrally in academic writing, is generally attributed only to intelligent, sentient minds.

The student who wrote the sentence below has quite confused the participants and processes involved in the study of history:

> **Documentary evidence unearths the reasons behind events in searching for better historical explanations.**

What kind of participant engages in the processes of unearthing and searching for things in academic activities of the kind being written about here? The answer will be the enquirer, in this case the historian, who is not mentioned. This sentence says it is the documentary evidence. (You will notice an example here of a dangling modifier, 'in searching . . .', discussed in the previous chapter.) Moreover, it is the documentary evidence which is the participant affected by the unearthing, rather than the reasons. That is to say, the documentary evidence is what is 'unearthed'; the reasons why we should explain events in one way rather than another are provided by the historian. That, at any rate, is one of the uses of the word 'reason' by historians. Perhaps the writer half had in mind yet another participant not mentioned at all: the historical figures who had their reasons for initiating the events being enquired into.

So what have become lost in this sentence are the distinctions between quite a number of things:

- human participants performing an action, that is the historical enquirer unearthing documents and searching for better explanations;

- non-human participants on which the action is performed, that is the documents unearthed;

- both human (the people) and non-human (the events) participants which constitute the subject matter of the documents;

- the reasons given by historians to justify their explanations;

- the reasons given by historical figures for the events they took part in.

Here are a few attempts to get into the writer's mind and work out what she was trying to say:

> **Historians seek better explanations of events by unearthing documents which provide new evidence about the reasons historical figures gave for their actions.**
>
> **Historians use documentary evidence the better to justify their explanations of historical events.**
>
> **Documents contain evidence of the reasons for events which historians need when searching for better historical explanations.**

There are other possibilities. Notice, first, that they mean different things. Hence, if you suspect that you have written a sentence which seems to have confused a number of different participants and processes, you must do your best to work out which of the various meanings you really intend. Your answer will depend largely on the context in which the sentence arises – what you have already written so far. In our example, the writer should probably have looked back through her paragraph to decide – in the first instance – whether she was writing about (human) historians, about (inanimate) documents or, indeed, about the evidence contained in the documents. Once the topic or theme of the passage of writing is identified from options such as these, it may be made the nominal referring expression in the main clause of the sentence, and the rest of the options in meaning and structure can then be selected to fit in with that starting point.

3.2   Concrete and abstract

Processes expressed in abstract nouns

We have hitherto tended to assume that the processes in which our participants take part are usually expressed in the form of finite and non-finite verbs. That is not the whole story. There are many processes which are expressed in referring nouns or in nominals which have been formed from verbs. Most of them are quite easy to recognise. Sometimes there is no change or little change in the form of the word (e.g. study–study, rise–rise, believe–belief, grow–growth). More often '-ing', '-ation' (or '-tion'), '-ment', '-al' or '-age' is affixed to the end of the verb to make the nominal (e.g. thinking, organisation, adoption, arrangement, dismissal, wastage). These are formed from the verbs 'think', 'organise', 'adopt', 'arrange', 'dismiss' and 'waste'. Now, these nouns refer to processes, just as verbs express processes. And like verbs, a participant is associated with them, even if it isn't expressed explicitly in the sentence. Somebody or something performs the study, the growth, the thinking, the organisation, the adoption, and so on.

If we employ the abstract style of writing (especially common in sociological and political writing as well as in much recent linguistics and literary studies), we get sentences littered with abstract nominalisations of processes:

> The utilisation of the concept of underdevelopment requires firstly a recognition that it is based on the concept of a dialectical relationship between the development of the First World and the underdevelopment of the Third World.

One of the reasons why this kind of writing is difficult for many people to follow is that rarely are the participants ever made explicit. In this statement it is we (the enquirers) who do the utilising and the recognising, whilst the developing and underdeveloping is the responsibility of an undefined abstraction. It is easy to be tempted by the books you read into imitating this kind of language. But it is a language quite difficult to control, even for the experts. The sentence above can be made to bring the participants to the surface, for example:

> **If we are to use the concept of underdevelopment, we must first recognise that it is based on a dialectical relationship between how capitalism has developed the First World and how this necessarily entails that the Third World remains underdeveloped.**

Now, there is nothing ungrammatical about the original version of this statement. It is, simply, harder to understand until you have become practised in 'translating' this kind of language into a version somewhat like that immediately above.

But this mode of thinking can cause another kind of problem. If you are not practised in the handling of processes that have been nominalised and made abstract, it is very easy to make grammatical mistakes:

> **Salisbury considers that the Pacific islanders gained from the introduction to steel tools.**

'Introduction', you will recognise, expresses a nominalised process of the kind we have been discussing. You will see that there is something funny about the phrase 'the introduction to steel tools'. Now, if you ask the question 'Who introduced steel tools and to whom were they introduced?', you find that there are two participants involved, not just the one made explicit in the sentence: the unidentified participant is (presumably) the Western trader; and the second the Pacific islander. Which of these two participants does the writer wish to concentrate on? To choose the one or the other requires a different sentence structure. Notice the switch in the prepositions 'of' and 'to':

> **Salisbury considers that the Pacific islanders gained from *the* [traders']**
> **introduction *of* steel tools.**

or

> **Salisbury considers that the Pacific islanders gained from *their***
> **introduction [by traders] *to* steel tools.**

A similar mistake has been made by the writer of this sentence:

> **Hyndman had the belief of respect of social order.**

The participants associated with 'belief' and 'respect' are quite different – Hyndman (a nineteenth-century English socialist writer) and socialists. And, like the previous example, this one contains a mistake with a preposition ('to' in the earlier one, 'of' in this). The best way to make this sentence both clear and grammatical is to use verbs to represent the processes, a change which makes the participants quite clear:

> **Hyndman believed that socialists should respect social order.**

Alternatively, the second participant (socialists) may remain implicit if we change the structure in other ways:

> **Hyndman believed *in* respect *for* social order.**

From these examples a useful warning emerges. When you are reading back over the sentences you have written, look out for the structure 'the' + abstract noun, where the noun refers to a process. Always satisfy yourself that the participant associated with each process is quite clear from the context, that it has not changed in mid-sentence, and that you have not made a mistake with any preposition you have used. If you are in doubt, try re-writing the sentence in such a way that the processes are expressed as verbs rather than as abstract nouns.

Noun–verb agreement

If the noun you use to refer to a participant is abstract, then the process must be represented by a verb which is compatible with an abstract noun. In this sentence the major participant, architecture, is abstract:

> The architecture of the Indus valley was built with a strong sense of form and mass.

One builds buildings, not architecture. So we must decide whether it is the abstract or the concrete we wish to write about:

> The architecture of the Indus valley displays a strong sense of form and mass.

or

> The buildings of the Indus valley were constructed with a strong sense of form and mass.

Similarly, one cannot in certain contexts 'use' landscapes. One can use land or one can change landscapes:

> There have been changes in the use of landscape in the city of Moorabbin.

'Landscape' (as it is used in geography – unlike one of its uses in art) is abstract; 'land' is concrete. So we might say either:

> There have been changes in the use of land in the city of Moorabbin.

or

> There have been changes in the landscape in the city of Moorabbin.

Abstract processes are easy to confuse with concrete participants:

> These differing interest groups were brought to a head by the question of compensation for the loss of land.

What are 'differing interest groups'? We might say:

> The differences between these interest groups were brought to a head by the question of compensation for the loss of land.

or

> These differing interest groups clashed over the question of compensation for loss of land.

Differences can be brought to a head; or interest groups can clash.

It is not easy to lay down general rules about what is abstract and what is concrete, or about which nouns can be coupled with which verbs. The borderlines between abstract and concrete nouns can be difficult to discern and may vary with the discipline being studied. If you are in doubt, it is probably safer to err on the side of concreteness in your choice of both participants and processes. In any case, check with a good dictionary, in particular a specialist dictionary in the relevant discipline.

3.3   Texts, words and things

The function of quotation marks and italics

What can be said about phenomena in the world cannot necessarily be said about the texts which deal with them or about the words in those texts. Nor, conversely, can some statements about words or about texts be couched in language designed to talk about other kinds of phenomenon. By omitting inverted commas around the first word, this sentence, for example, does not discriminate sufficiently between the word and the phenomenon it refers to:

> **Ambivalence consists of four syllables.**

The result is both nonsensical and untrue.

If you are a student of literature, in particular, you must constantly decide whether what you want to say is about the words in the texts or about the phenomena these words represent. For example, in Conrad's novel *Heart of Darkness*, the word 'darkness' is used a great deal with varying shades of meaning. Anybody writing about this novel must take care to distinguish between Conrad's deployment of the word in his text and the ideas of mystery, the unconscious, lack of understanding, sin, the jungle, absence of civilisation, and so on, which it conjures up.

Similarly, the convention of italicising the names of texts must be followed if you are to avoid writing sentences like this one, in which it is not immediately clear whether the participant is Hamlet the character or *Hamlet* the play:

> **The central dramatic question posed by Hamlet is not 'Why did Hamlet seek revenge?' but 'Why didn't Hamlet avenge his father?'**

It is the play, not the character, which poses the 'dramatic question', a question which Hamlet himself cannot answer since he is only one part of the drama. Hamlet poses questions of a somewhat different kind – for example 'Am I a coward?' (II, ii, 606) – which might constitute just part of the evidence you could call on in your own answer to the larger dramatic question posed by the play as a whole. You will see, then, that the italicising of titles and the enclosing within quotation marks of quotations and references to words is more than just another inexplicable convention of academic writing. It marks the difference between two separable categories of experience.

It is not just literature students who must deal with texts and the differences between words and things. The texts of both primary and secondary sources in any discipline constitute verbal evidence with which your own analytical writing must deal. It is therefore important that you think carefully before assuming that there is no distinction to be made between what a source is talking about and the words in which the idea is couched. To help you appreciate this distinction and to use it in your writing, it is often valuable to compare the accounts of the same thing given by different authors. You will remember that in chapter 3 we conducted such an exercise on three different accounts of the opening to Kant's *Critique of Pure Reason*.

Object-language and meta-language

Finally, there is a large vocabulary of terms especially characteristic of academic writing which is used to refer to the participants and processes of academic enquiry itself – what is often called a 'meta-language'. These terms have already been made much use of in this book, so you will be familiar with many of them. They include all those terms which express what academic authors and enquirers DO, introduced in earlier chapters, for example:

> proposing, acceding, conceding, refuting, dismissing, reconciling, describing, comparing, defining, explaining, theorising, justifying, evaluating, extending, elaborating, enhancing, generalising, particularising.

Then, there are many other nouns and nominals associated with these activities, for example:

> fact, evidence, data, idea, concept, conjecture, thesis, hypothesis, theory, opinion, belief, judgement, observations, findings, result, explanation, reason, argument, conclusion.

To be able to combine terms such as these into grammatical sentences is a skill that does not always come easily, and often takes time. (For this reason you should pay careful attention to how they are used in the books you read.) But there is something you must try to avoid from the very start – notwithstanding the claim by many post-structuralist theorists that there is 'nothing beyond the text'. This is the confusing of these meta-linguistic terms with the object or objects of your enquiry which do exist or may exist in the 'real world':

> This fact has a marked effect on ground temperatures.

Facts belong to the world of enquiry and thought. Such things do not normally (except perhaps in the rarefied world of quantum physics) affect natural phenomena like ground temperatures. This should be quite easy to see. Here is a somewhat more difficult one:

> Pluralists argue that power is widely dispersed throughout society. This is very idealistic. In the real world this argument contains many loopholes due to the complicated structure of the economic and political system. However, there are situations in today's political climate where this line of reasoning does exist.

The argument doesn't contain loopholes in the real world, but in the 'meta-world' of arguments. Similarly, the pluralist line of reasoning doesn't so much 'exist' in today's political climate; rather, it can be *applied* to account for that climate. What we must do is to reconstruct these sentences in such a way that the relationship between arguments and the 'real world' of politics is made more secure. If you get into the kind of situation that has troubled the writer of this passage, you might decide, on the one hand, to focus more particularly on what happens in the world:

> **Pluralists argue that power is widely dispersed throughout society. This argument is very idealistic and contains many loopholes. In the real world power is very unevenly distributed owing to the complicated structure of the economic and political system. However, there are situations in which we do find power to be well dispersed.**

Alternatively, you might decide to focus on the qualities of the argument:

> **Pluralists argue that political power is widely dispersed throughout society. This argument is very idealistic and contains many loopholes in that it oversimplifies the complexities of power distribution to be found in actual economic and political systems. However, it does give an accurate account of some parts of the system.**

What you should aim for is to separate out as well as you can words and structures appropriate to argument from those appropriate to the object or phenomenon the argument is about.

3.4   Singular and plural

Perhaps unlike some of the problems we have examined in this chapter, you probably have no difficulty discriminating between singular and plural. The rule is simple enough: in most instances nominals in the singular must be followed by verbals in the singular, and plurals by plurals. Nevertheless, for some reason many students fail to make their nominals and verbals agree in number often enough to make it seem as though this constitutes a problem; and even very competent writers can slip up if they do not check over their sentences carefully. You might find that you make mistakes with number when you are labouring mightily over other aspects of your meaning. So if you have found a passage particularly difficult to write, it is a good idea to check back over it just to make sure you haven't made slips with singulars and plurals.

It is easy to make a mistake when the referring nominal is separated from the verb by lots of other words:

> The *relations* between line, form, space, tone and colour to be found in a picture *is* very complex.

Secondly, take especial care if your singular nominal is of the kind which refers not to one specific individual but to any member of that class of individuals – the so-called 'generic' reference. In the sentence below 'The social worker' refers generically to any social worker and all social workers, not to a single identified individual. The writer of this sentence has therefore had this in mind rather than the needs of number agreement:

> The social worker do not compromise their own standards and values to suit any occasion.

It is likely that the desire to avoid language which specifies the sex of the social worker is also implicated in the error here, as you will see from the 'their'. 'Their' cannot be substituted for 'his' or 'her' without your checking back through the sentence to ensure that everything agrees.

Thirdly, if a singular referring nominal is followed immediately by an 'of' phrase with plural nominals, it is easy to be distracted by these plurals when you come to assign number to the verb. This is probably because the plurals are most immediately in one's mind:

> The *frequency* of exercises in the old composition manuals *suggest* that number agreement can be a problem for many writers.

It is not the exercises that suggest, but their frequency that suggests.

Finally, there is a smallish group of nouns (called nouns of multitude) which, when used in the singular, may be followed by a verb in the plural. An army, committee, government, community, peer group, party, tribe, fraternity or jury – to take some common examples – may be viewed either as a collection of many independent individuals or as a single united whole. If the former meaning is to be emphasised, the verb is plural, whereas the singular verb emphasises the corporate action or responsibility of the group:

> **The jury have decided on their verdict.**
>
> **The jury has found him guilty.**
>
> **The European Union, who have always had their disagreements on agricultural policy, do accept the need for continually revising the funding formulae.**
>
> **The European Union does not hesitate to appeal to the World Trade Organization over dumping by the USA and others.**

This chapter has been concerned principally with helping you to get the main elements of your sentences to cohere with one another in a unified structure. A structure of any kind, if it is to be a good one, must always be looked at as a whole. If you are uncertain about, or wish to change, any of the elements in a structure you are building, you must always look beyond the bothersome element itself. You need to consider the effects which the various options open to you at one point in the sentence will have on the design of the whole. This means looking at your sentences much in the way you look at a picture: not just a succession of individual bits linked into a chain, but as an arrangement of forms and ideas.

If you feel that one of your sentences is getting into a dreadful mess and you cannot sort it out, perhaps the best thing to do *first* is to look carefully at the referring nominal which constitutes the actor in the main clause. Debate with yourself whether this is really what you are trying to write about. You might have used a word which refers to an abstract, non-human participant when really what you want is a concrete, human one. Ask whether you are focusing rather on what someone has said or written about the subject than on the subject matter itself (so far as you can disentangle them). Indeed, ask whether you can clarify in your mind what the participant is at all, because if that is vague, the chances are the rest of the sentence has nothing to hang on to. And so on. Falling between two stools (abstract/concrete, human/non-human, singular/plural, etc.) is a very common cause of injuries to sentences. It helps greatly if you can recognise the stools and decide which one to aim for.

9

Analytical language 2: rhetorical strategies

Who, or why, or which, or what,
Is the Akond of Swat?

Edward Lear

This chapter takes up some themes in chapters 3 and 5, relating them to other aspects of your language, particularly (but not only) at the level of the paragraph and beyond. These aspects are especially important in academic analysis and argumentation. It shows you

- how to subordinate descriptive writing to analysis by getting away from merely paraphrasing your sources

- how to understand the dynamics of defining and how to see your writing of definitions as another important mode of analysis

- how to construct COMPARE AND CONTRAST arguments not by listing 'similarities and differences' but by finding appropriate criteria according to which you will make your *judgements* about value.

1   Analysing versus describing

In your writing there will be a place for description. You will need to describe such objects of your attention as a painting, the kinship system of a particular society, the land forms of a stretch of country, a chain of historical events, and so on. You will also from time to time need to describe what the authors of your sources have said about the subject matter you are enquiring into. But in modern academic writing, it is generally true to say, description by itself is not enough. It must be used to serve the purposes of analysis – of reflecting upon the significance of the information, the data, the evidence and the arguments that you assemble in your attempt to answer the question raised by your topic. We have noted in an earlier chapter that one of the more common remarks tutors make on an essay is that it is 'Too descriptive' or that it 'Needs more analysis'. How can these criticisms be met?

We have already seen how important it is for your essay to establish a case and argue for it. This is the first and most important condition to be met if your writing is to be analytical. But it is not the only one. In chapter 5 we examined the ways in which the case can be expanded. Not only might you need more information, but you also need to consider exceptions and alternatives, clarify the meaning of statements and substantiate your generalisations. You need, furthermore, to enhance the value of your information by asking and answering a whole variety of questions, like: When? Where? Who? By whom? For whom? By what means or methods? To what degree? For what reason or purpose? With what effect? Under which conditions? The application of these strategies was exemplified by the passages on rural poverty in the Third World in chapter 5. It is by expanding on your descriptive information in these ways that your writing can begin to become analytic.

Thirdly, analytical writing is of a piece with the analytical quality of your reading. In chapter 3 we saw how asking questions about what writers of your books are DOING (and not doing) makes it possible to analyse and interpret their words. If we pay attention only to the 'content' of Thomas Glick's paragraph (11) about the *dhimma* contract in mediaeval Spain (p. 75 above), we will be tempted to produce a purely descriptive account – a paraphrase – of what Glick is writing about:

When al-Andalus was under Moorish occupation, the Muslim rulers followed the Qu'ranic injunction known as the *dhimma* contract that said all descendants of the Abrahamic tradition (Muslims, Christians and Jews) should be tolerated and not discriminated against. In practice the contract enabled all three groups to interact with each other in the normal course of living in a fairly relaxed manner. Later, when the Christians became the dominant majority in Spain, they also tried to continue this tradition. But because it was enacted only in civil rather than religious law, it became a pale shadow of what had once existed and did not put down solid universal foundations either in the body politic or in the people themselves (Glick 1992: 6–7).

Alternatively, by attending to what Glick is DOING (and, in this case, *not* doing – see the concluding sentence in the paragraph below) as well as to what he is SAYING, we can begin to display some of the features of analytical writing:

Thomas Glick (1992: 6–7) REJECTS the claim by Elena Lourie that the Christian rulers of late mediaeval Spain implemented a policy towards the minority Muslims and Jews which was a 'mirror image' of the earlier Moorish Qu'ranic law of the *dhimma* contract. He ARGUES that there was a quite fundamental difference. This he does by DESCRIBING the relations between Muslims, Christians and Jews under the Moors as being emotionally less 'supercharged' in the course of daily living than he IMPLIES it later became under the Christians. He EXPLAINS this by pointing to a significant difference in the foundations of *dhimma* in both the body politic and society as a whole under the Muslim and Christian regimes. While CONCEDING that the Christian rulers tried to follow the *dhimma* contract, he FINDS that, because it was implemented merely in civil rather than religious law, it did not put down solid universal foundations, and was prey to the ever-changing demands of day-to-day political and administrative expediency. Such a CONCLUSION is entirely plausible; but Glick himself SUPPLIES LITTLE EVIDENCE for the

> differences in 'emotional supercharging' he notes, for which we must look elsewhere.

Clearly, 'looking elsewhere' for the evidence will be the subject of the next paragraph.

Finally, your ability to write analytical prose will depend on how well you bring to bear on your material certain *criteria* of analysis and evaluation. Criteria are more or less conventional standards that we apply to the evidence and arguments presented to us by our sources. In principle, there is nothing particularly special about this. When you go shopping you routinely apply such general criteria as price, quality and appropriateness to your needs to help you analyse the wares on offer. In addition, you will have further, more specific criteria, the choice of which depends on the nature of the article you are seeking. Examples might be design, durability, compatibility with articles you already possess, adaptability to a variety of likely uses, authenticity of the manufacturer's label appearing on the item, and so on. You might also apply certain political and moral criteria: you might exclude items made in certain countries, in 'sweat-shop' factory conditions, or manufactured in part from wild-animal skins. Many of the criteria that inform academic analysis are not dissimilar from some of these.

Here are some of the more general criteria that are commonly applied:

- What is the *relevance* of this material to the issue under discussion?

- How *reliable* is this evidence for the particular point being made?

- How *valid* is this evidence or argument?

- How *plausible* is the argument?

- How *compatible* is the evidence or argument with what we already know?

- How *consistent* are the individual parts with each other and with what we know about the whole?

- Is this explanation sufficiently *comprehensive* to take into account the evidence we have? Is it so comprehensive (or vague) that it is not *testable* by observation or evidence?

- What are the *implications* of this for other things we know to be important? How *significant* is it?

The questions in which the terms in italics appear above are not the only ones that can be asked. Learning the meanings of the criteria and learning how to phrase suitable questions around them takes time and study. Although the criteria above are widely used, their meanings can be rather unstable. In particular, they can mean different things to different disciplines, and different things to different schools of thought within those disciplines. For example, in psychology 'valid' can mean something like 'this test does measure what it purports to measure'; in logic it means 'this argument is well formed'.

Here is a paragraph which takes up one of Glick's points. It makes explicit use of some of the general criteria listed above as well as a few more specific ones:

In rejecting Elena Lourie's claim that *dhimma* under the late mediaeval Christian rulers of Spain was a 'mirror image' of that under the Moors, Glick (1992: 6–7) makes do with very *generalised assertions*, the *reliability* of which needs to be *tested* against evidence he does not himself provide. He tells us that, in ordinary everyday life, relations between the Muslim majority, Christians and Jews during the earlier period were 'less supercharged emotionally' than they later became under the Christians. What we need to ask is how such an *elusive quality* as this could be pinned down. Presumably, it could only be *inferred indirectly* from a relative absence of recorded incidents of friction between the three communities. Such evidence might be found, for example, by comparing court records for the two periods. But even then we should have to question how *valid* such records might be as an

> indication of the overall temper of relations between whole communities,
> as opposed to that between particular individuals engaged in litigation
> who just happen to be members of differing communities.

You will notice that description has largely disappeared from the paragraph above. Readers of this paragraph not immediately familiar with the Glick text must therefore rely on the few hints given. An allusive analytical style like this, when unrelieved and unsupported by some concrete description, can become unreasonable in its demands upon any but the very knowledgeable reader, as you will probably have found when wading through some of your books. Do not, therefore, be afraid to include descriptive passages in your writing. Only take care that they are designed to make your analyses clearer and more telling.

2 Defining

2.1 The dynamics of definition

Defining is a rather more complicated business than our usual experience with even a good dictionary leads us to suspect. A long time ago, Humpty Dumpty thought he could rule the roost. In Lewis Carroll's *Through the Looking Glass*, Humpty Dumpty told Alice: 'When *I* use a word . . . it means just what I choose it to mean . . . The question is . . . which is to be master – that's all'. It soon became clear that no one person could be the master; but certain academic communities decided that they should and could all agree communally on what a word should mean – and then impose that definition. In his *Introduction to Logical Theory* (London: Methuen, 1963, p. 9) the logician P. F. Strawson tells us that defining is a process by which 'we can deliberately fix the boundaries of some words in relation to those of other words'. In using the word 'deliberately' Strawson is following the advice of Humpty Dumpty, with the proviso that it is now 'we' rather than 'I'. Others have since realised that defining is not as simple as allowing some scholars clubbing together to establish a received definition or to 'fix' boundaries. It works for some disciplines, particularly in the natural sciences when a technical term is pre-defined by the rules of a formal system. In the humanities and social sciences the propensity of a word to equivocate, for its boundaries to be 'fuzzy', is increasingly being conceded.

What does one do, for example, with a word like 'sanction'? Used as a noun it often (not always) refers to a PROHIBITION:

> **The United Nations has imposed economic sanctions on country X.**

Used as a verb, it usually means quite the opposite – a PERMISSION:

> **The United Nations sanctions the use of military force under certain circumstances.**

It is therefore quite easy to get in a mental whirl if we combine elements of these two sentences:

> **The United Nations sanctions the use of economic sanctions against country X.**

Many post-structuralist writers have followed the example of the French philosopher Jacques Derrida in thus 'deconstructing' the definitions of terms used in the humanities and social sciences, demonstrating how the opposite meaning of a word is often implicit in its ordinarily accepted meaning. He does this with words as ordinary and hitherto uncontroversial to many humanities and social science disciplines as 'speech', 'structure', 'centre' (remember this one from our example in chapter 6 on Fredric Jameson's views concerning late capitalism and postmodernism, pp. 140–1) and 'context'. More conventionally, Raymond Williams's classic *Keywords: A Vocabulary of Culture and Society* (London: Fontana, 1976, 1983) gives an excellent insight into the shifting sands of meaning in many of those words with which you will constantly have to deal.

Clearly, we cannot do without attempts to define; but, equally clearly, we cannot define something in any old way that happens to suit our immediate purpose. One of the functions of analytical writing is to decide which meanings can be given to words and concepts that might prove important to a particular field of study. This is why (as we saw in chapter 2, pp. 38–9) desk dictionary definitions of such words are not usually very helpful. You will find pages, not infrequently whole books, given over to an attempt to define difficult terms like 'justice', 'knowledge', 'class' or 'culture'. The result is that we do not have fixed and unchanging notions about the right or wrong meanings of such words, but rather *conceptions* or *theories* of justice, knowledge, class and culture, theories which are strenuously debated.

In defining some term, therefore, you will need to search out its boundaries or limits, however 'fuzzy' they turn out to be. How is this done? First you will need to decide on the *criteria* you will use in order to delimit where those boundaries will be. In this way, as you will see, defining things is just another kind of analysis. As with other kinds of analysis, you will need to learn the kinds of criteria each discipline you study applies to the definition of terms.

There is one fundamental distinction, however, which is common to all our attempts to define. This is the distinction between criteria that do make possible the searching out of boundaries and those that do not. These are called 'defining' and 'non-defining' criteria. (The distinction is important for certain aspects of your sentence structure and punctuation, as we shall see.) How do we define a motor car in order to delimit a boundary between it and other similar objects – a bus, a minibus? Is the vehicle sometimes known as a 'people carrier' or 'people mover' a car? Criteria like the number of wheels or the size of engine are quickly eliminated as non-defining since they do not help us to delimit the boundary. We might then start to argue about the number of seats, the proportion of passenger space to luggage space within certain (to be defined) limits, or other more subtle criteria.

An old problem in linguistics concerns the definition of a word. Here is a popular or folk definition:

> A word is a sequence of letters which is separated from another by a space.

This definition has two fairly characteristic parts:

- The first clause assigns the phenomenon to be defined to a *class* or *category* of phenomena to which it belongs and which has other members – 'a sequence of letters'. (There will be other phenomena which are members of the class 'sequence of letters' but which are not words.)

- The 'which' clause assigns a defining *criterion* which distinguishes a word from the other possible members of the class. The criterion in this example is the presence of a space that separates the sequences.

Now, were you to be writing about this definition, you could look to the questions of whether it assigns a word to the right or the best class, and whether the defining criterion is adequate. The definition above assigns a word to a class of written or orthographic phenomena ('letters'). Against this, you might wish to argue that, irrespective of whether languages are written down, they all have words. Therefore a word is better assigned to the class of phonological phenomena (sounds). Moreover, the term 'sequence' is too vague, since any sequence is implied. The sequence of sounds must be *structured* (a new defining criterion) according to certain rules of word formation. These rules will become the substance of a new set of defining criteria to replace the one with which you began ('separated by a space'), a criterion that is no longer appropriate to sounds. This is the point at which your evolving definition will have to draw on the general kinds of criteria to be found in the discipline of linguistics: you would now have to become technical and to develop defining criteria by drawing on observations from phonetics and phonology, morphology (the forms of roots and inflexions in words), syntax (sentence structure) and semantics (meaning). Considerable space might need to be given to the elaboration of each of these issues. In this way a simple one-line definition grows into a major section of an essay or a whole essay itself.

The paragraphs below illustrate the beginnings of how this might be done. The first takes up the form of the definition and systematically builds upon the two major parts – the class membership statement and the ascription of defining characteristics. The second and third paragraphs introduce a discussion of the kinds of criteria that have been used. The suggestion by one linguist that a boundary be drawn around 'word' to distinguish it from a 'lexeme' is questioned, the more comprehensive definition being preferred.

The popular definition of a word as 'a sequence of letters separated from another by a space' is deficient in many fundamental respects. In assuming that a word is an orthographical object, this definition neglects the primacy of sound in language: we speak of 'words' even in languages which have not been written down; and illiterate people who have never seen a page of print have no trouble identifying the words in their language.

But this does not mean that a word can be defined as 'a sequence of sounds separated from another by a pause'. In the first place, the sequence must be a structured one, since all languages have phonological rules according to which sounds can be combined with one another. Secondly, the idea that there are 'pauses' between words in spoken language greatly oversimplifies and misrepresents the phonetic facts. Finally, although a word is basically a phonological entity, it cannot be defined on criteria of sound alone. To define a word adequately it is necessary also to see it in three more ways: as a structured combination of morphological units; as an element in the syntactic structure of sentences (words form grammatical classes such as noun, verb and adjective); and as an element of language which carries meaning. Such a comprehensive approach results in this common definition: 'A word may be defined as the union of a particular meaning with a particular structured complex of sounds capable of a particular grammatical employment.'

> By contrast, many attempts at defining the word have tended to concentrate on one or two of these criteria. Some linguists particularly exclude semantic properties of the word from its defining characteristics. Lyons (1968: 197–200), for example, defines a word purely grammatically, distinguishing it from a 'lexeme', which has properties of meaning. But there is, I believe, no good reason to exclude semantic or phonological criteria. A word is best viewed as a complex linguistic 'cluster concept', whose meaning can vary according to the context in which it is being used.

What we have here is not so much a definition as the opening to a discussion of what needs to be considered in order to arrive at a definition. Each of the points raised above would need to be elaborated in the ways you will now be familiar with. This discussion could conclude (though it might not have to, depending on the wording of the essay topic) with your own attempt at a definition.

You will have noticed that the discussion above introduces the question of whether a word should be distinguished in some fundamental way from a lexeme. Some essay topics will ask you quite explicitly to make such distinctions. As an example, here is a topic from anthropology:

> What is the difference between trade and exchange? Illustrate your answer with ethnographic examples.

The problem posed by a topic such as this is fundamentally the same as that we have just examined in connection with the word. You will, however, have to COMPARE the characteristics of trade and exchange in order to arrive at a conclusion about which of them *best* distinguishes the one from the other. When you read the literature you will no doubt find that trade and exchange are not mutually exclusive terms but have certain overlapping characteristics in common – the non-defining characteristics (in the Euler circles in chapter 2, p. 45, these are $A \times B$ in Figure 3.2). Alternatively, you might find that trade is a subclass of the more general class exchange (A in

Figure 3.1). You might conclude that, although there is evidence that trade cannot be distinguished from exchange on simple economic grounds (both involve agreeing on a price), exchange always involves certain distinguishing characteristics – a particular type of reciprocal obligation between groups, a particular type of ceremony, or something else. Your task will be to work out which of the various criteria suggested in your books best defines the difference and to separate from these the criteria which do not help you to delimit the boundaries.

2.2   Defining and non-defining relative clauses

Ascribing defining and non-defining characteristics to phenomena is one of the most common actions you perform when writing, even when you are not consciously setting out to define a term or a concept. Almost every time you use an adjective before a noun you are raising the issue of whether that adjective assigns a defining or a non-defining characteristic to the phenomenon denoted by the noun. Look at this sentence:

> **Jacqueline Rose's recent book on Zionism aroused considerable controversy.**

'Recent' is potentially ambiguous. If this word represents a defining characteristic, then the statement implies that Rose has written previous books on Zionism which were not controversial:

> **Rose's recent book on Zionism [unlike her earlier ones] aroused considerable controversy.**

The phrase 'on Zionism', which comes after the noun, is similarly ambiguous. If 'recent' is interpreted to be defining in the sentence above, 'on Zionism' is non-defining. But what if Rose has recently written books on other subjects?

> **Rose's recent book on Zionism [unlike her earlier book on psychoanalysis] aroused considerable controversy.**

'Recent' in this sentence is non-defining and 'on Zionism' is defining. Unless some clarifying phrase, like those between brackets in the sentences above, is added in, the only rigorous way to determine whether or not 'recent' and 'on Zionism' are defining is by looking up Rose's publishing history. If the point you are making is at all important, and if the context of this sentence doesn't resolve the potential ambiguity, you should save your reader this trouble by adding a clarifying comment.

Phrases like 'on Zionism' that come after the noun are sometimes called 'relatives'. Often, we write whole clauses that come after the noun, clauses which are typically introduced by 'who', 'whom', 'which' or 'that'. (This last sentence has two of them.) Like the relative phrase 'on Zionism', these clauses can be either defining or non-defining relatives (also known as 'restrictive' and 'non-restrictive' relatives). It is possible for you to indicate whether you intend your relative clause to ascribe a defining or a non-defining characteristic to the noun by two simple techniques.

The first lies in your choice of 'which' or 'that'. (With 'who' or 'whom' it is not possible to make this distinction.) If you want your relative clause to define the noun, it is usually possible to use either 'that' or 'which' to introduce it, and often possible to omit them entirely:

> **The book that Rose recently wrote about Zionism was very controversial.**
>
> **The book which Rose recently wrote about Zionism was very controversial.**
>
> **The book Rose recently wrote about Zionism was very controversial.**

If, on the other hand, your relative clause is not intended to define the noun, you will not be able to use 'that'. In addition you must call on the second of the two distinguishing techniques, the comma (which is all that distinguishes defining and non-defining clauses beginning with 'who' or 'whom'):

> **Rose's recent book, *which* was about Zionism, was very controversial.**

The 'which' clause bracketed by commas is an indication that the characteristic it ascribes to the book is not to be regarded as defining. The particular book in question will have been defined sufficiently by some preceding statement.

Finally, in journalistic and other popular writing, 'which' clauses are often found as stand-alone sentence fragments:

> **Rose recently published an extremely controversial book about Zionism. Which was a very courageous thing to do.**

The 'which' clause refers not to a term to be defined but to the whole action of publishing a controversial book about Zionism. It is thus neither defining nor non-defining, but rather a comment ('which' can be replaced by 'this', as most academic writers would prefer). See also p. 175 above.

3   Comparing and contrasting

3.1   The dynamics of comparison

To compare and contrast is a very common requirement of the essay topics you are set. In addition, it is often necessary to engage in comparing and contrasting when you are dealing with topics worded in other ways. This kind of writing can be quite difficult to handle if you are unclear about the nature and purpose of comparison. The first thing to keep in mind is that it is fundamentally no different from the kind of analysis we have already learned about in this book. In particular, comparing and contrasting is hardly to be distinguished at all from defining.

If you ask yourself what the purpose of comparing two things could conceivably be, you will see that the answer can best be expressed in terms of defining the boundaries of one with respect to the other. For example, the topic we looked at above as an exercise in definition – 'What is the difference between trade and exchange?' – could equally have been worded 'Compare and contrast the notions of trade and exchange'. In order to carry out a comparison, we must therefore make use of those *criteria* about which we have had much to say in this chapter. We can only compare two things with respect to certain specified qualities or criteria. So the main difficulty in comparing and contrasting lies in finding them. It is this, rather than hunting about for 'similarities and differences', that you should concentrate on.

The shopping analogy we used earlier might help you see this. Compiling a list of the similarities and differences between brands does not of itself help you decide unless you order these characteristics according to some set of criteria – price, quality, durability, compatibility with what you already own, design, and so on. You must then WEIGHT or RANK these criteria according to some set of PRIORITIES you have established. Even if 'price is no object', some other criteria will be. You are also likely to find that each product has some features which are quite absent in the others. Listing these miscellaneous differences is of little help to your decision-making unless you have some means of assessing their importance. You cannot actually COMPARE or CONTRAST the quality of the four-speaker stereo system fitted as standard in one motor car with that of the air-conditioning unit fitted to its competitor. All you can do is to rank these features with respect to what you think important in a car. That ranking will be affected by quite other criteria.

It is for these reasons that listing a set of descriptive characteristics on one side of a page and another set for the contrasting phenomenon on the other side is by itself insufficient as a method of preparing your comparative essay. Let us take a topic from sociology:

> Compare the functionalist and Marxist perspectives on the institution of the family.

One common way of preparing an essay on a topic like this is to make a heading 'Functionalist perspectives' and another 'Marxist perspectives', and then list the perspectives under each heading. But a better way might be first to work out which institutional features of the family need to be explained, for example its status as an economic unit, its function as an institution to care for and to socialise children, its position as a microcosm of the gender and political hierarchy in society, its role in reproducing the attitudes and beliefs of a society. Having worked these out, you can then set down the functionalist and Marxist approaches to each one. You should then be in a position to decide on which criterion or set of criteria fundamentally unifies or separates (as the case may be) these two perspectives on the family.

In the attempt at an opening to an essay on this topic below, the defining criteria suggested are inequality, exploitation, conflict versus consensus and change versus stability:

> Marxists and functionalists both view the traditional family as a key unit of industrial capitalism, which it helps to maintain and reproduce. In drawing attention to the essentially exploitative nature of the relation between capital and labour, Marxists emphasise the conflict between them. Out of this conflict will come change. Functionalists, on the other hand, stress the mechanisms by which consensus and stability in society are attained, even in the face of inequality and a certain degree of exploitation (or alienation). For the functionalist society is first and foremost a system. Although there will be tensions and even contradictions in this system, all its parts are constantly being modified in order to preserve the essential stability of the system as a whole. The differences boil down to the relative emphases on change and stability. These fundamental differences of viewpoint about society are reproduced in the Marxist and functionalist analyses of the family.

> To the Marxist the internal structure of the family as an economic unit reflects the division of labour and the domination of labour by capital to be found in the economy as a whole. And, like the worker in a factory, the family unit is exploited by the requirements of capitalistic production. The family also serves to perpetuate the class divisions of society through the inheritance of property. The functionalist, by contrast, sees the division of labour and economic power as a necessary adjustment to economic reality and social stability, and argues that the distribution of economic power in both the family itself and the society as a whole is much more fluid than the Marxist admits. Because the notions of inequality and exploitation are found in both theories, they do not clearly distinguish them. For the functionalist, inequality and the exploitation of the family by capital is not complete, and is offset by other economic benefits which began to accrue when production moved out of the home. The Marxist emphasises the way in which the multiplication of small family units offers an enormous captive market for the products of capitalist manufacturing.
>
> The family is, however, more than an economic unit of society. Similar differences between Marxists and functionalists can be seen in other facets of the family institution: the socialisation of children, the gender and other distributions of political power, and the reproduction of social and cultural values. As we examine each in turn, we shall see how the differences between Marxists and functionalists on inequality and exploitation are really differences of degree. Their perspectives on conflict and consensus and on change and stability in the family are, by contrast, quite different in kind.

You will see that this piece of writing is organised on the basis of the defining criteria (inequality, exploitation, conflict, etc.) and the characteristics of the family itself. Doing it this way means that one is continually moving back and forth between what the two perspectives have to say with respect to these things. This movement is signalled by such words and phrases as 'by contrast', 'on the other hand' and 'more . . . than'.

Now, this is not the only way to organise a comparative piece. It is certainly possible to set up the essay as a whole in this fashion:

1. Marxist perspectives

　　Economic issues

　　Socialisation of children

　　Gender distribution of power

　　Other aspects of power distribution

　　Reproduction of social and cultural values

2. Functionalist perspectives

　　Economic issues

　　Socialisation of children

　　Gender distribution of political power

　　Other aspects of power distribution

　　Reproduction of social and cultural values

3. Conclusion (synthesis)

This traditional schema for a comparative essay is still to be found and can be made to work quite well. But unless you can operate it with skill, it does have considerable dangers. You are very likely to be tempted into writing two 'mini-essays' (one on each perspective) rather than a well-integrated comparison. If this does happen, it is almost impossible to write a conclusion which effectively synthesises the critical issues. What tends to get lost is that fundamental constituent of any good essay, the case for which you are arguing. In addition, you will see such a schema makes it easier to shirk the hunt for the defining criteria on which your comparative analysis should be based.

　　In sum, approach an essay or part of an essay which demands comparison in the same analytical spirit which you will devote to any other kind of writing. As you expand on the fundamental points you want to make, you will find that not only a sentence or two but a whole paragraph or a series of paragraphs will be needed to explain one of the phenomena to be compared. The special demand of comparison is that for each of these paragraphs (or part of a paragraph) an answering one is required to take up the very same issues. This continuous antiphonal structure, in which the one explanation is immediately answered by the other, is the best means of ensuring that everything you say remains relevant to the question and advances the argument.

3.2   Comparative structures

Comparing and contrasting can only be carried out on what we perceive to be like phenomena. You cannot compare the population distribution of hunters and gatherers in Namibia with the arrangement of colours in an Australian Aboriginal landscape painting, unless, by some feat of ingenuity, you can find some quality in common between the two – which is, of course, not impossible. There needs always, as we have just seen, to be an 'answering' – a parallelism – between the two or more things to be compared.

This means that when you structure your sentences you must take special care that you do compare like with like. You cannot, for example, compare Marxism with functionalists, because one is a doctrine or theory and the other a group of people:

> **Marxism emphasises change whereas functionalists stress the grounds of social stability.**

You need to decide for each sentence whether to write about the theory or about the adherents of the theory:

> **Marxism emphasises change whereas functionalism stresses the grounds of social stability.**

or

> **Marxists emphasise change whereas functionalists stress the grounds of social stability.**

When writing comparative statements, always check them out to ensure that this parallelism is maintained. One of the most common mistakes of this kind is to compare two incompatible objects:

> Marx's arguments lose nothing in comparison with his detractors.

Marx can be compared with his detractors, or his arguments with his detractors' arguments. Hence you might write:

> Marx's arguments lose nothing when compared with those of his detractors.

or

> Marx's arguments lose nothing when compared with his detractors'.

Similarly, take care that you do not compare an action with an object:

> Marx in his early works placed great emphasis on the concept of alienation, like Weber.

Rather, you might write:

> Marx in his early works placed great emphasis on the concept of alienation, as did Weber.

We cannot exemplify all the unhappy combinations of people, objects, actions, activities, situations, states and relations that are easily mis-compared. Since it is very easy to confuse these things when you first set down a comparative structure, take care to check them as you write. You will remember from chapter 8 (p. 193) that falling between two stools is a common cause of injuries to sentences. Since comparison, by its very nature, demands a parallelism between like and like, your sentence structure needs to reflect this.

A final word about the preposition to use with 'compare'. When Shakespeare wrote in Sonnet 18 'Shall I compare thee to a summer's day?', he was assuming that the summer's day is a conventional standard or criterion *to* which his loved one was superior. Most of your academic writing is not like this. You will be comparing the qualities of one thing *with* those of another, weighing them as in a scale. You might make a summary judgement in a situation where Marx is being set up as the conventional standard:

> **Compared *to* Marx, Weber made a more subtle and lasting contribution to the understanding of society.**

Where, on the other hand, you are being asked to weigh the relative merits of Marx and Weber according to criteria you yourself have to establish in your essay, you will be comparing Marx *with* Weber. To compare one thing to another is to accept a conventional criterion; to compare one thing with another is to question and discuss the very criteria on which your judgement is to be made. This latter is one of the fundamental demands of good academic writing.

Cohesion and texture

. . . to combine textural appeal with an appropriate scheme of textual cohesion, in such a way that one supports the other, is a fundamental stylistic task. The text, however, has primacy; plot is more important than diction, though diction may be involved in plot.

Walter Nash

This chapter shows how to use the resources of English to connect with your reader on almost a subconscious level. For you, though, it needs to be as conscious as possible. It is like the musical 'language' available to a song-writer, to reinforce the lyrics or the 'plot'. You will find out how to

- deploy the words and structures in order to achieve a sense of depth and resonance among the different parts of your essay, with the cultural background from which you write, and with the stylistic traditions of your various disciplines

- make the most fruitful use of the time you have set aside to revise your text in order to improve its cohesion and texture – to bring out those resonances which will make your writing really stand out.

1   Determinants of cohesion and texture

A coherent essay depends in the first instance, as we have seen in many preceding chapters, on the careful formulation of the case to be argued. If your answer to the question posed is conceived as a 'golden thread' that runs right through the piece of writing, it is in the answer itself and its various implications that the beginnings of coherence lie. But once you have decided on your answer, you cannot assume that there is some natural order of thought that produces in your essay a coherence that is above and beyond the details of the words you use. It is in your disposition of grammatical structures and in your choice and deployment of those words that you bring your text together. To work at this is to produce *cohesion* and *texture* in your writing.

Text consists in your attempts to bring all the elements of your writing together into a unified whole. The language makes provision for this, such that the connections between words and between structures can be made more or less explicit to your readers in various ways and to varying degrees. The rudiments of this process we have already examined. In this chapter we shall look much more closely at the ways in which the details of your language can make the difference between a text which satisfies the minimal requirements of coherence and one which draws as many of its elements as you can manage into that unified whole.

These features of cohesion and texture are not superficial. Although some of them play about the surfaces of words and structures – reflecting, refracting and intensifying relationships of meaning – together they give an added depth to what you have to write. To attend to these things in your writing is not to seek after a 'style' quite separate from your thought. To do so is rather to use the resources of the language to find out for yourself what the main streams of your thought really are. (This is why, in order to emphasise the contrast between the ideas of the last two sentences, not only did I need the sentence link 'rather', I also had to ensure that both sentences started with the same infinitive structure 'To . . . '.) Certainly, much of this operates in the subconscious of both the writer and the reader. If, by attending consciously to some of the techniques of writing set out in this chapter you can make them part of yourself, your tutor will be grateful – even if he or she cannot say exactly why.

Although, as we have said, some of your textual effects will be subconscious, it is in the conscious revision of your text that you will be able to rework some of its major deficiencies into a better unified whole. (This is one reason for leaving sufficient time for revision.) The main things you need to attend to in this revision are these: sentence adverbials, referring expressions, coordinating structures and vocabulary.

1.1 Sentence adverbials (linking terms)

Signal to yourself and your reader where you are going and what you are DOING. Most of the signals you need to send have been covered in chapters 3, 5 and 8. The basic sets of signals are the sentence adverbials and other linking terms (e.g. firstly, furthermore, in particular, consequently, in other words, alternatively, in comparison, by contrast, similarly, admittedly, certainly, to digress, to recapitulate, to resume). These are the terms in which you point out just how you are extending, elaborating, enhancing or analysing your material and structuring your own text. About these we shall say no more.

1.2 Referring expressions

Referring expressions are used to help clarify what goes with what in your text. A subject or participant introduced at one point in the text becomes the fulcrum on which both earlier and later references to it will turn. Referring expressions include:

- the definite article 'the';

- the pronouns 'it', 'he', 'she', 'they', 'him', 'her', 'them';

- the demonstratives 'this', 'that', 'these', 'those';

- the quantifiers 'some', 'many', 'much', 'all', 'none', 'each', 'any', etc.;

- other terms: 'such', 'so', 'the very . . . ', 'the same . . . ', 'previously', 'the former', 'the latter' (note the double 't' in the spelling of this word), 'here' and (at a more distant remove in your text) 'there', 'earlier' and 'above'.

All these words refer *backwards* in your text to participants you have announced earlier. What you must take pains to ensure is that the *particular* word, phrase or statement to which they refer is crystal clear. Confusion sets in if your reader cannot work out quickly and precisely what an 'it', a 'this' or an 'each' refers to. If there is doubt, it is better to repeat the word or phrase itself.

Similarly, there are words and phrases which refer *forwards* in your text (e.g. below, as we shall see, thus, the following, to be discussed). In addition, the colon (:) is a punctuation mark that refers forwards.

1.3   Coordinating structures

When you are building up stretches of text, cast your eye back to see whether you have used your grammatical structures to achieve cohesion. Constructing a piece of writing has much in common with constructing anything else. The parts to be joined together – in this case grammatical structures – have to be sufficiently alike in shape at the place where they meet to fit securely. A nut and a bolt are quite different objects; but their threads need to match.

Two very common structures can be troublesome. With number, it is quite easy to slip inadvertently from singular to plural; and with tense, present and past are easily pushed into an unhappy union. (We noticed a slip of tense in the passage by Sabine on Edmund Burke's conception of natural rights, on p. 156 above.) If you do find yourself switching number or tense about too often, this lack of cohesion might have quite deep-seated causes. These causes are examined in chapter 7, section 2.3, and chapter 8, section 3.4.

Coordination is typically performed by 'and', 'in addition', 'or', 'but' and their equivalents, as well as by other devices. When you bring two ideas together in this way, check that the two structures on either side of the join are parallel. The first sentence of this paragraph is a case in point. Two sets of terms are coordinated by 'as well as'. Both these sets of terms are dominated by the word 'performed'. In order to secure the join, the 'by' in the first set is repeated in the second. Now, it is perfectly acceptable in short simple coordinations to omit the second of these binding elements:

> **Coordination is typically performed by coordinate conjunctions, (by) certain adverbials and (by) other devices.**

But academic prose is in part characterised by the complexity of the elements to be coordinated – in sentences, in paragraphs and over a whole essay. It therefore becomes extremely important to develop a consistency of structure and to draw attention to that consistency by preserving the structural parallels and repeating the motifs that make them apparent. The architecture of prose is in this respect similar to that of a building or a piece of music.

In order to give you some idea of what can happen when structural coordination is neglected, I shall re-write the three sentences immediately above in an uncoordinated way. Un-parallel forms are italicised and omissions indicated with a caret:

> **But academic prose is in part characterised by the complexity of elements to be coordinated – in sentences, Λ paragraphs and Λ a whole essay. It therefore becomes extremely important to develop a consistency of structure and *drawing* attention to that consistency by preserving the structural parallels and *repeat* the motifs that make them apparent. The architecture of prose is in this respect similar to Λ a building or Λ piece of music.**

One situation in which you should always check the consistency of your structures is when you are making a list. Here is a list in which the items are not parallel:

> **There are four features of cohesion to be attended to virtually simultaneously:**
>
> - **sentence adverbials;**
> - **ensuring that referring expressions do in fact refer to the terms intended;**
> - **keep your coordinate structures grammatically parallel;**
> - **vocabulary should be chosen with an eye to other words used in the text.**

Not one of the items in this list is parallel with another. In sorting out which structure to use and repeat, go back to your introductory statement and decide what your wording demands. In the present case the list is to be of 'features to be attended to', so each must include a feature of cohesion and the kind of attention it needs:

> **There are four features of cohesion to be attended to virtually simultaneously:**
>
> - **sentence adverbials need to be carefully distributed;**
> - **referring expressions must be made to refer to the terms intended;**
> - **coordinated structures should be kept parallel;**
> - **vocabulary should be chosen with an eye to other words in the text.**

1.4   Vocabulary

A careful patterning of your vocabulary is one of the things which brings most satisfaction in the act of writing and, by greatly enhancing the texture of your prose, makes it satisfying to read. This kind of patterning – lexical cohesion – can be achieved in many different ways. We shall touch here on just two – repetition and substitution.

Whether you repeat a word or substitute a synonym for it cannot easily be considered separately, since a decision to repeat a word will be affected in part by what substitutes might be used. Inexperienced writers tend to repeat a key word either far too much or hardly at all. You might remember the kind of story you wrote as a child:

> **The dog bit the man. Then the dog ran into the barn. The man chased the dog into the barn and the dog bit the man again.**
>
> **The dog bit the man. Then he ran into the barn and he chased him and he bit him again.**

Other writers go to extraordinary lengths to avoid repetition, with comical results:

> **The dog bit the man. Then the canine ran into the barn, where he was chased by the unfortunate victim. But the cur again sank his fangs into the now doubly abused personage.**

The art of achieving lexical cohesion is to decide which words are the important ones in the thematic structure of your text and to drop them into the argument as a recurring motif – not so heavily as to make your reader think you have a very limited vocabulary, nor so lightly as to have them go quite unremarked. In *The Tempest* Shakespeare performs intricate thematic arabesques with 'Art', 'power', 'master', 'slave', 'dream', 'spirit', 'music', 'freedom', 'air', 'earth', 'sea', 'Nature' and other words which underlie the 'argument' of the play. An academic essay does not, of course, attempt the complexity of lexical patterning to be found in much literature for the reason that the former's argument tends to be more restricted in scope. Nevertheless, your prose will be much less cohesive – and your thought correspondingly less coherent – if you always choose a word in virtual isolation from the others on your page.

We shall now examine lexical cohesion as well as the other kinds of cohesion set out above in an extended example of how to revise a draft text. In carrying out such revisions it can hardly be over-emphasised that no matter how many initial changes you make to your text as you write on the computer screen, the kind of final revision exemplified here can only be performed really well with a pen or pencil on hard copy that you have printed out.

2   Revising and improving text

Here is a topic on Shakespeare's play *The Tempest*:

> 'Learning is a major theme in the play; we learn that Miranda is capable of it and Caliban not, and why this should be so; but [in Prospero] we are also given a plan of the place of learning in the dispositions of providence.' (Frank Kermode)
>
> Discuss learning and knowledge as it is portrayed in *The Tempest*.

First, I shall present an opening paragraph stripped of as many features of cohesion and texture as is possible without producing something entirely unintelligible. Then I shall set out the paragraph as it was first drafted and add a few more paragraphs to it to develop some parts of the argument. This is a moderately cohesive piece of writing. But it is capable of much improvement. The improved version is then presented.

1

In *The Tempest* reason is set against 'fury', nurture nature. The duke is not the perfect expression of the providential power of knowledge and civilisation. Caliban is not ruled solely by passion and unregenerate nature. Prospero's Art is not a humane kind of learning and the duke renounces magic at the end of the play. Caliban is not what he says – 'A devil, a born devil, on whose nature / Nurture can never stick'. Caliban does learn. At the end of the play Caliban says 'I'll be wise hereafter, / And seek for grace'. Prospero does not. If we are to look for a criterion of knowledge it will be Miranda, in whom there is nature, reason, nurture and passion. Miranda does not know very much about the world. On seeing Ferdinand Miranda says, without any hint of metaphor, that Ferdinand is a spirit, 'a thing divine'. What she displays is more important.

Did you work out the connections between reason, fury, nature, nurture, Art, magic, passion and civilisation? What is the relation between the duke and Prospero? What is the relation between

Prospero, Caliban and Miranda? Who said that Caliban is 'A devil, a born devil'? What doesn't Prospero do? How can Miranda be a criterion of knowledge if she does not know much about the world? What is it she displays that is more important than what?

If you know *The Tempest* you might be able to draw on your knowledge to answer many of these questions without too much difficulty. If you do not, you will have to hunt around in this first text fairly assiduously before clues to some of the answers become apparent. The next (extended) version should make most, but not all, of these questions much easier to answer.

2

In *The Tempest* reason is set against 'fury' and nurture against nature. But the duke Prospero is not the perfect exemplar of the providential power of reason and nurture any more than Caliban is a savage ruled solely by fury and unregenerate nature. Prospero's magical Art, despite the contrast he draws with the magic of 'the foul witch Sycorax', is not a humane kind of learning; for otherwise he would have no cause to renounce it at the end of the play. Nor is it true, as Prospero says of Caliban, that he is 'A devil, a born devil, on whose nature / Nurture can never stick'. Caliban does learn, arguably even more than Prospero, inasmuch as at the end of the play he says 'I'll be wise hereafter, / And seek for grace', which finds no echo in anything Prospero says. If we are to look for a touchstone to knowledge in *The Tempest*, it will be found in Miranda, in whom nature and nurture, reason and passion are perfectly mixed. Miranda does not 'know' very much at all about the world: on first seeing Ferdinand she thinks him, without any hint of metaphor, a spirit, 'a thing divine'. What she displays is something more important, a depth of understanding or sympathy.

Prospero's learning seems to be of two quite distinct kinds. Neither is admirable. In recounting the story of how he was dispossessed of his dukedom, he boasts to Miranda how

> *being so reputed*
> *In dignity, and for the liberal Arts*
> *Without a parallel; those being all my study,*

The government I cast upon my brother,
And to my state grew stranger, being transported
And rapt in secret studies. (I, ii, 72–7)

Prospero's studies were of the seven traditional liberal arts, and through absorption in them forfeited his power in the state. A duke cannot be a pure scholar or theoretician. These liberal studies were not the magical Art that he practised on the island (the studies were 'secret' only in the sense that they were private and recondite). This latter 'so potent Art' was studied solely for the power it bestowes on an egocentric Prospero to do violence to nature ('I have bedimm'd / The noontide sun') and to effect his revenge on other people. We notice that the volumes that Prospero prizes 'above my dukedom' become a single book (III, i, 94; V, i, 57), which he consults to further his project and which he promises to drown only when he can be sure that he will no longer have to rely on it. The book to Prospero is little more than the bottle to the drunken butler Stephano.

This is something Caliban learns. He knows better than Stephano and Trinculo that the rebellion against Prospero can only succeed if first they burn his books; for without them Prospero is 'but a sot, as I am, nor hath not / One spirit to command'. There is a clear parallel between the effect of Stephano's 'celestial liquor' on Caliban and Prospero's charms – 'the ignorant fumes that mantle / Their clearer reason' – on the usurpers he wishes to subdue. The sense of power conferred by the butt of sack is, of course, illusory; but so is that of Prospero's Art. Both turn ordinary mortals into 'masters' (a word used constantly throughout the play). But true learning is not a matter of attaining mastery over nature, over other people or even, through the use of reason, over oneself. This is the point which Gonzalo wishes to have set down 'With gold on lasting pillars':

                                        in one voyage
Did Claribel her husband find at Tunis,
And Ferdinand, her brother, found a wife
Where he himself was lost, Prospero his dukedom

> *In a poor isle, and all of us ourselves*
> *When no man was his own.* (V, i, 208–13)

Some of the answers to the questions raised with respect to (1) should now be much easier to see. It should be clear that reason and nurture are being contrasted with 'fury' and nature, and that Prospero (who is himself the duke) is not a perfect specimen of good learning any more than Caliban completely represents its absence. This draft does not, however, make it clear early on that Caliban is Prospero's slave or that Miranda is Prospero's daughter. We now know that it is Prospero who calls Caliban 'A devil, a born devil', and that the master suffers by comparison with his slave in that he does not learn enough by the end of the play to ask for grace. With respect to Miranda, it is made clearer that 'knowing' about the world is less important than another kind of learning with which this is contrasted – understanding or sympathy.

The first paragraph is built on a series of contrasts. For the most part the devices of cohesion have been sufficiently employed to clarify the main lines of these contrasts. Linking terms are there, referring expressions do their job and the contrasts are pointed up by the coordination devices of the grammar. There are a few slips on some of these counts, in both this paragraph and the two that follow: 'the' in line 2 and an omitted 'he' before 'forfeited' in line 11 of the second paragraph are two of them. But what is perhaps principally lacking is the extra dimension of cohesion produced by vocabulary. True, 'reason', 'fury', 'nature' and 'nurture' are repeated throughout. 'Expression' (line 2) and 'criterion' (line 8) are changed to 'exemplar' and 'touchstone' – modifications which might point the contrast between Prospero and Miranda a little bit better, but which are still rather lame. 'Art' is left hanging until the second paragraph. By and large this draft is pretty thin soup.

The finished text, (3) below, attempts to clean up the mistakes, repair the omissions and to point up the main themes of the argument. The chief thrust of these changes is to establish more securely the theme of mastery in learning and the connections it has with an illusory sense of power over nature and other people. Hence Prospero's schoolmastering is introduced in the second paragraph as a preparation for the argument that follows. The experimental, alchemical nature of Prospero's art is given more emphasis ('philosopher's stone' is implicitly contrasted with 'touchstone'); and the distinction between the conventional 'studies' of volumes in the liberal arts, which led to his loss of power, and the use of his 'book' as an experimental manual or handbook to regain power is made clearer. The difference between Prospero's view of knowledge as reason and the alternative view of it as understanding and sympathy is reinforced in the last sentence of the passage by the substitution of 'insight' for 'point'. ('Cool' is added in line 2 of the last paragraph to allude to some lines in *A Midsummer Night's Dream* in which Theseus asserts the limitations of reason.) There are other lexical changes too. In the first paragraph there is a stress on white, enlightened, civilised; and black, dark, ignorant, savage. The contrast between what Caliban and Prospero 'say' becomes more sharply focused in that the one 'resolves' and the other 'promises'.

There are many other changes, all designed to improve cohesion and texture, for example the adding in of new sentences to open and close the first paragraph. If you wish to plot all these changes in detail, you will find the annotated manuscript of (2) reproduced in Appendix 3.

3

In *The Tempest* Shakespeare takes up common Elizabethan and Jacobean themes of learning. Reason is set against 'fury' and nurture against nature. But these themes are not resolved by the simple triumph of reason and nurture on the one hand over nature and 'fury' (or passion) on the other. Prospero, the exiled Duke of Milan, though the dominant force in the play, is not a perfect exemplar of the providential power of reason and nurture, any more than his slave Caliban is a savage ruled solely by fury and unregenerate nature. Prospero's white magical Art, despite the contrasts he himself draws with the black magic of 'the foul witch Sycorax', is not a humane kind of learning; for otherwise he would have no cause to renounce it at the end of the play. His Art is alchemical and redolent of the philosopher's stone. Nor is it true, as Prospero says of Caliban, that the slave is 'A devil, a born devil, on whose nature / Nurture can never stick' (IV, i, 188–9). Caliban does learn, arguably even more than Prospero, inasmuch as at the end of the play he resolves 'I'll be wise hereafter, / And seek for grace'. This is a resolution which finds no echo in anything Prospero promises. Prospero is not a white, enlightened master of civilisation; Caliban is not a dark, ignorant slave of nature. Shakespeare in this play is testing and revising the conventional dichotomies of his time.

If we are to look for a touchstone to knowledge in *The Tempest*, it will be found in Prospero's daughter Miranda, in whom nature and nurture, reason and passion are perfectly mixed. Miranda's rather special kind of knowledge is not the product of Prospero's own irascible and peremptory schoolmastering: 'Dost thou attend me? . . . Thou attend'st me not . . . Dost thou hear?' (I, ii, 78ff.). Miranda is always acquiescent in this didactic tutoring. But at the end of it all, she does not actually 'know' very much about the world. On first seeing the prince Ferdinand she thinks him, without any hint of metaphor, a spirit, 'a thing divine'. The kind of learning she does display is a quality vastly more important than anything her father has actually taught her – a depth of human understanding or sympathy.

Prospero's learning seems to be of two quite distinct kinds. Neither proves to be admirable. In recounting the story of how he was dispossessed of his dukedom, he boasts to Miranda how

> *being so reputed*
> *In dignity, and for the liberal Arts*
> *Without a parallel; those being all my study,*
> *The government I cast upon my brother,*
> *And to my state grew stranger, being transported*
> *And rapt in secret studies.* (I, ii, 72–7)

Prospero's studies were in the seven conventional liberal arts, and through absorption in them he forfeited his power in the state. A duke, he now realises, cannot be a pure scholar or theoretician. The studies were 'secret' only in the sense that they were private and recondite. These liberal arts he then replaces with the less conventional magical Art that he practises on the island. This latter is a 'so potent Art' that he makes use of solely for the power it bestows on an egocentric Prospero to do violence to nature ('I have bedimm'd / The noontide sun . . . Set roaring war: to the dread rattling thunder / Have I given fire' (V, i, 41ff.)). Learning of this kind is effected solely for revenge on those who toppled him from his dukedom. We notice, too, that the volumes that he once prized 'above my dukedom' have become whittled down to a single 'book' (III, i, 94; V, i, 57), which Prospero consults as a manual to further his experimental project with nature and human beings. This handbook he promises to drown only when he can be sure that he will no longer have to rely on it. Prospero's book is Stephano's bottle.

This is something Caliban learns. He knows better than the drunken butler Stephano and the equally drunken jester Trinculo that the rebellion all three hatch against Prospero to dispossess him of the island can only succeed if first they burn the master's books. Without them, Caliban has realised, Prospero is 'but a sot, as I am, nor hath not / One spirit to command' (III, ii, 90–1). Caliban also learns by the end of the play that he was a 'thrice-double ass . . . to take this drunkard [Stephano] for a god' (V, i, 295–6). Shakespeare draws a clear parallel between the effect of Stephano's 'celestial liquor' on Caliban and the effect of Prospero's charms – 'the ignorant fumes that mantle / Their clearer reason' (V, i, 67–8) – on the usurpers the duke wishes to master. The sense of power conferred by the butt of sack is, of course, illusory; but so is that of Prospero's Art. Both turn ordinary mortals into 'masters', a word used constantly throughout the play to suggest at once authority and lack of control.

True learning is not a matter of attaining mastery over nature, over other people or even, through the use of cool reason, over oneself. True learning is the kind of understanding which comes not from any 'master' in the play but from the young Miranda and the old Counsellor Gonzalo. It is Gonzalo who wishes this insight to be set down 'With gold on lasting pillars':

> *in one voyage*
> *Did Claribel her husband find at Tunis,*
> *And Ferdinand, her brother, found a wife*
> *Where he himself was lost, Prospero his dukedom*
> *In a poor isle, and all of us ourselves*
> *When no man was his own.* (V, i, 208–13)

Conventions of academic writing

*A rule stands there like a sign-post. – Does the sign-post leave
no doubt open about the way I have to go?*

Ludwig Wittgenstein

This chapter explains how to use style guides, what you
should look for in them, and why the rules for one school
or department might differ from those of others. It covers

- how to navigate through some conventions of formal and
  informal language

- how to be wary of using the technical language of one
  discipline in another

- how and when (and when not) to use devices of layout –
  headings and sub-headings, numbered paragraphs, bullet
  points, tables and figures, and so on

- how to set out quotations

- how to attune yourself to the often minute and
  mysterious differences in the rules for setting out notes,
  references and bibliographies.

1   Academic culture

To be a student in a college or a university is not only to be a learner.
It is also to be a member of a community and a culture with customs,
myths and rituals which differentiate it in significant ways from other

communities and cultures to which you might belong – sporting clubs, churches, political parties, and so on. To be in university or college is to submit to a sometimes bewildering array of customs and expectations that can take many, many months to feel at home with. To study history or anthropology is to enter the department of history or the department of anthropology, where you are quite likely to be regarded as having begun a novitiate to the vocation of historian or anthropologist. You must therefore learn the customs and rituals of the vocation.

Most departments initiate you by providing a manual or outline of studies. In this there will often be a section called 'Essay writing' or, more candidly, 'Rules for the presentation of written work'. These are the rules you have to learn, notwithstanding the initially confusing fact that the requirements of one department might well conflict with those of another. A book like the present one can therefore give you no more than a very general overview of the matters you need to attend to, and can merely draw your attention to what to look for when you study the departmental rules. If these rules fail to give you direction on any matter – as well you might expect, given what the philosopher Wittgenstein says about rules at the head of this chapter – you might need to consult your tutor. Where you cannot be quite sure which convention to adopt, choose one you think is likely to be satisfactory and try to be *consistent* in your use of it.

These rules are conventional, but that does not necessarily make them wholly arbitrary. Some, it is true, have simply become fossilised in particular disciplines, for example the Latinisms *supra* and *infra* ('above' and 'below') of certain footnoting systems. Others, by contrast, have grown out of the need to solve particular problems of method and technique in the analysis of certain kinds of primary evidence. For example, the Harvard referencing system – in which a source is specified in the text by author's name, date of publication and page number (Smith 1998: 263) – might be quite adequate for most writing in the social sciences but useless to the historian or literary scholar. Other conventions of style, particularly with respect to punctuation, are adopted for typographical reasons: certain things are thought by some to look better on a page of print, for example NATO, BBC, NSW rather than N.A.T.O., B.B.C., N.S.W. There will often be other justifications for a convention. Your immediate task is less to worry about these justifications than to find out (sometimes by trial and error) which of these rules are quite rigidly enforced in a given department and which not.

2   A skeleton key to stylistic conventions

2.1   Formal and informal language

Academic language need not be stuffy. Even so, the colloquialisms of conversation and the informalities of advertising copy and of certain newspapers and magazines are best avoided. Good language thrives on variety and freshness, but what is fresh and acceptable in one context might be simply gauche in another. Here are a few pointers which are fairly reliable in all your academic writing.

Contracted speech forms

Contractions like 'don't', 'didn't', 'haven't', 'I'll', 'she's' and 'they're' should be kept for talking about your work with your tutor or friends. (I have used them in this book, which is less formal than an essay.)

You, we, I

Unlike a guide such as this, an academic essay does not directly address the tutor. 'You' should be kept out of an essay. Use it for a seminar, a tutorial delivery or a conversation with friends and tutors. 'We' will usually do as a substitute for the colloquial 'you'. On the uses of 'I' and 'we', see the discussion on pp. 148–51.

Abbreviations

Practice with abbreviations varies considerably. Even common ones, like NATO or MP, should be approached warily, though widely known acronyms like Unesco or Anzac which have passed into the language – indicated by the use of lower case after the initial letter – are usually acceptable. With a less well-known one (judgement on this will often depend on which part of the world you live in), the best procedure is to write the name out in full at first mention and include the abbreviation in parentheses (e.g. South East Asia Treaty Organization (SEATO)). Thereafter, you can use the abbreviation alone. This rule is sometimes applied to standard technical abbreviations (e.g. kilometres (km)) where much use has to be made of them. 'Etc.' is probably best avoided altogether, and is not improved by writing 'et cetera'. Prefer 'and so on', but use it sparingly.

2.2   Technical vocabulary

The very particular technical vocabularies appropriate to some disciplines may not travel well to others. This is sometimes because the concept is simply inappropriate to the modes of analysis in the other disciplines. Sometimes the reason is ideological or political. (The practitioners of one discipline often dislike their language being colonised by the vocabulary of another.) While you might write with impunity about 'the socialisation of the child' in any department of sociology, you must consider carefully whether to write of 'the socialisation of Jane Eyre' in an essay on Brontë's novel for your English department. If you suspect that a word or phrase has a loaded meaning in one department, or for some school of thought, test the waters in other departments before you throw it in. One way of doing this is to listen carefully to the words your lecturers use, and to drop any doubtful word into a tutorial discussion to see how it is received.

2.3   Layout

Layout concerns the disposition of your text on the page. Every reader appreciates a well-designed page. Pay attention to rules like double spacing, the numbering of pages and the width of margins. Don't go overboard with the use of the different fonts in your word-processor; and before you print out an essay, be sure that any headings or sub-headings are not left stranded at the foot of a page. Bear in mind that you want the tutor marking your essay to start out well-disposed towards the job of reading what you have written.

Headings and sub-headings

In some departments and disciplines you will be commended for laying out your essay with numbered sections, headings and sub-headings. It is sometimes done in the manner of this book; at other times a mixture of Roman numerals, Arabic numerals and letters is preferred. Some departments encourage you to use numbered sub-headings for reports or field studies but not for essays. In yet others the merest sign of a numbered paragraph, a sub-heading or even a list of numbered points (i) ... (ii) ... (iii) or bullet points within your text will be to offend certain traditions and sensibilities. Generally speaking, the younger the discipline and the more closely oriented to the social sciences the more disposed it is to use these devices of layout. Do not, even so, use them as a substitute for developing a coherent argument throughout the essay. Excessive use of numbered sub-headings will often clearly betray a scissors-and-paste piece of work.

Tables and figures

Tables and figures are a useful way of summarising information in a manner clearer and more succinct than ordinary prose. ('Figure' is the name given to any diagram or illustration other than a table or a photograph, which is called a 'plate'.) They should always be positioned as closely as possible to your discussion of them in the text, and you must always ensure that you do discuss them rather than let them 'speak for themselves': treat them as you would any primary source, as discussed in chapter 3 above (pp. 57–9). Normally tables and figures are numbered consecutively throughout the essay and referred to in your text as Table 1, Table 2, etc., and Figure 1, Figure 2, etc. Each table or figure should have, together with its number, a caption explaining what it is. Tables commonly have their numbers and captions positioned *above*, while figures have theirs *below*.

The ability to construct good tables and figures is an important skill to acquire if you are working in the social sciences. Books on methodology in the social sciences and manuals of scientific writing are the best sources of advice.

Indenting of paragraphs

Unless your matter is a long quotation or something else inset into the text, indent the first line of each paragraph. If you do not, it can be difficult for a reader to see where a new paragraph begins if the preceding one finishes at the end of a line. One way of overcoming this is to leave double your usual space between paragraphs. Indenting, however, is the more widespread practice.

2.4   Quotations

The setting-out of quotations often causes difficulty. The common conventions are these:

- If your quotation will take up more than three or four lines of your page (some style guides allow as much as 100 words), indent the whole quotation, keeping the left margin straight. An indented quotation does not need to be enclosed by quotation marks.

- If your quotation is shorter than this, you can incorporate it into your text. (Essays on poetry might occasionally prefer to indent even a one-line quotation.) In this case you must use quotation marks. The rules of whether to use single quotation marks (') or double (") may vary. Check your style guide. If you are in doubt, use single quotation marks.

- If you leave out any words in the quotation, mark this ellipsis with three dots.

- You may modify the original structure of words or insert words of your own into a quotation. You will often need to do this in order to preserve the grammatical structure of your own sentence, into which the quotation is integrated. Interpolations are also used to clarify something the quoted material leaves vague, for example by substituting a name for 'he' or 'she'. Any such modification of the author's words must be signalled by enclosing the interpolations in *square* brackets. For example, Sabine asserts: 'It is true that [Burke] never denied the reality of natural rights'.

2.5   Notes

Notes may be placed either at the bottom of the page (footnotes) or at the end of the essay (endnotes). Endnotes are usually numbered consecutively throughout the essay, and footnotes from 1 on each page. Some disciplines have strict conventions governing either or both of these. Study your style guide. There are also conventions governing where you place the identifying number in your text. The most common in the arts disciplines is to place it at the end of the appropriate sentence or after the nearest punctuation mark after your reference. You may, however, be permitted to place it somewhere else within the sentence. An alternative, now being practised in some disciplines, is to gather all references together at the end of a paragraph.

2.6   References and bibliographies

The permutations and combinations of the elements of order, punctuation and other things in references and bibliographies are almost endless. When you are doing your references, put your style guide in front of you and follow it not only to the letter but to the very comma. The structural bones of a reference are these:

- author's family name;

- author's initials or given name;

- the title of the article (where appropriate);

- the title of the book or the name of the journal;

- the volume number of the journal;

- the place of publication: usually the name of a major city is enough; smaller towns will commonly be complemented by the name of the county, province or state – take your cue from the title page or the copyright page of the work you are using;

- the name of the publisher;

- the year of publication;

- page number or numbers.

This is the skeleton. Now use it to examine any system you have in front of you by looking for the following kinds of variation:

- *Omissions.* Sometimes there are major limbs that become detached (e.g. publisher's name, page number, p. before page number).

- *Additions.* Sometimes other bones are added on (e.g. the name of the editor of a book in which an article appears, the volume *and* number of a journal).

- *Order of assembly.* Sometimes the elements are sequenced one way (e.g. first name, given name, date, title, place) and sometimes another (e.g. given name, first name, title, place, date).

- *Punctuation.* Almost every time you look at a new system you will find the bones secured at the joints by different conventions of punctuation. Look in particular at the use and disposition of parentheses, commas, colons, semi-colons, full stops, single quotation marks, double quotation marks and capital letters. You will rarely be able to predict with confidence how they operate in an unfamiliar system. The only rule that seems not to be variable is the one which says that the titles of books or other major works (not essays or journal articles) and the names of journals should be in italics.

- *Context.* In some disciplines one set of conventions might be used for references appearing in footnotes or endnotes and another for references appearing in the bibliography at the end of the same essay.

- *Citing websites.* Websites must be cited in full, including the usual http://www.appearing at the beginning. It is usually also necessary to say when you accessed the site: e.g. 'Accessed on 28/3/2008'. This is because many sites are modified from time to time or disappear entirely.

- *Ordering of entries in the bibliography.* Most humanities and social science disciplines order the bibliography or list of references alphabetically according to the author's family name in European and some other cultures. (Be aware that in some cultures quite the same distinction between 'family' and 'given' name does not apply.) Some science disciplines sequence the list by number allocated in the order in which the works are referred to in the text. Check this if one of your subjects is on the disciplinary borders.

- *Items to be included in the bibliography.* Some departments encourage you to list all your relevant reading in the bibliography; others view this practice with extreme disfavour, allowing you to list only those works you have referred to in the text of your essay. Do not 'pad' your bibliography unless you are sure this is permitted. Always ensure that any work referred to in your text is in fact included in the final list of references.

- *Title.* Some departments wish your final list to be called 'Bibliography', others 'References'. Respect this wish.

- *Annotations.* Sometimes you will be asked to annotate your bibliography – to write a few lines saying how and to what extent each item contributed to your essay, or to write a short general account of how you used your sources. Do not annotate unless specifically instructed to.

Do not expect to feel comfortable with all these conventions immediately. Since they are rites, you will have to go through a period of preparation and initiation, a period in which you might feel rather uncertain of yourself. Most tutors will give you some time to master these things. They will, even so, begin to become impatient if you do not show attention to this detail and demonstrate progress from essay to essay. The point was made in chapter 1 that you should not spend so much effort on conforming to these conventions that other aspects of your thinking, reading and writing suffer. The fact remains, nevertheless, that well-written essays tend also to get the essentials, if not all the details, of these conventions right.

Appendix 1

Writing book reviews

An essay, as we have seen, demands that you analyse arguments and evidence in order to decide on your best answer to the question raised by the topic. Fundamental to this answer is your argument and your evaluation. A book review requires you to perform the same tasks. Just as you begin your work on an essay by asking of your topic 'What is this question driving at?', so you begin work on a book review by asking 'What is this book driving at?' In everything we have had to say about reading we have stressed the importance of asking yourself constantly 'What is this author DOING?' This is the first question a book reviewer will ask. The reviewer will also ask two other questions: 'How well was it done?' and 'Was it worth doing?' Answering these questions involves assessing the book's contribution to the field of study.

If you feel diffident about your ability to give an authoritative assessment of the book's contribution to public *knowledge* in the subject, you nevertheless have a significant alternative open to you. This is to evaluate the author's contribution to your own *understanding* of the subject within the context of the other works you have read. Notice this last condition. You will not be able to assess any single work if you do not try to integrate it into what you already know.

The broad procedures to adopt in working on a book review are therefore these:

1 Try to get a provisional idea of what the author is fundamentally trying to do in the book – what his or her major *motives* are. You can establish your 'first approximations' by looking at the jacket, the preface, the introduction or introductory chapter and the table of contents – more or less in that order. (Practised reviewers

also commonly look through the bibliography at this stage.)
Write down your provisional statement.

2 Try to write down a sketch of an 'opening paragraph' to an
essay you might write on this subject, mentioning any other
books that come to mind. (You might find it better to do this
first.)

3 Go back to the book, looking again at the introductory
matter and noting which of the chapters might seem
especially interesting to you. *Read* the index in order to see
which topics are included (noting any that come to mind
which might be omitted), and assess by the entries and
density of page references the emphasis given to particular
subjects.

4 Browse through the book, concentrating on those chapters
of particular interest or on the subjects which you know
something about. As you do this, keep trying to establish
the connections between the author's general motives and
the more specific things he or she does. The kinds of thing to
look for are set out in chapter 3 of this book. Make a few
notes.

5 In the light of what you have done so far, make some
revisions to what you have written down. This revision
might well become the draft opening of your review.

6 Read the book properly from cover to cover taking notes as
you go in the manner suggested in chapter 3.

7 Draft your review as you would an essay. Use much the
same approach to the middle of the review as is set out in
chapter 5. You will need to make many fewer references to
other works, if any at all, than you would for an essay, for
you will be concentrating on a critique of the book before
you. In trying to assess how well the task has been
performed by the author of your book, you will need to
have some criteria in mind. These can be supplied by your
reading of other works and by such appropriate general and

specific criteria as are sketched out in chapter 9. While you are writing, keep the book under review beside you so that you can check your assertions.

8 If you have analysed the book in the manner suggested above, you should have been able to impose your own shape on the review. Resist the temptation to 'tell the story' according to the same sequence of ideas, chapters or events as the author uses.

9 Do not be afraid to comment on the way in which the book is written. If you found the language hard to understand, at least in part, give a few examples and try to interpret them (see chapter 3, section 7). With practice and experience you might be able to build up a way of discussing the success with which the author reconciles language with content.

10 References and a bibliography are appropriate to your review if you have made specific reference to other works in your text.

The processes of preparing a book review are set out above as stages or steps. Do not feel constrained to follow them slavishly if you find you can work better in another way – perhaps by combining some of those I have separated into one set of procedures. For example, you might well react so strongly to the author's language (either favourably or not) or to the author's treatment of a particular aspect of the subject somewhere in the middle of the book that you will choose to organise your work around that. Writing a review is the best way to make a book a part of yourself. Your review should try to reflect this.

Appendix 2

Sample analyses of essay topics

1   Film studies

One critic has said: 'Truffaut is trying to establish connections between theatre and politics, between personal relationships and political involvement, between the idealism of the few and the pragmatism of the many.'

Do you think he succeeds in his aims? What verbal and visual means does he use to establish these connections?

1.1   The meanings of terms

> Truffaut – a French film-maker.
>
> Idealism and pragmatism – check standard dictionary definitions of these terms as a start. For example, *The Concise Oxford Dictionary* has: *Idealism* – 'representation of things in ideal form'; *ideal* – 'answering to one's highest conception; . . . existing only in idea; visionary . . .'. *Pragmatism* – 'officiousness; pedantry . . . doctrine that estimates any assertion solely by its practical bearing upon human interests'.
>
> Verbal and visual means – review the course so far and references given to get an idea about the categories of (a) verbal analysis and (b) visual analysis that are appropriate. No other problems with the understanding of terms.

1.2   Relationships of meaning between terms

How many questions are being asked? There seem to be two ('Do you think . . . ?' and 'What verbal and visual means . . . ?'). How can I reduce these to one fundamental question?

The fundamental question which requires my own evaluative answer is the first. The second question can be integrated into my answer to this by considering it as a set of reasons for this answer, for example Truffaut succeeds in his aims because he uses these visual means and these verbal means to good effect.

Here is the key: the three sets of connections listed in the topic are the 'aims'. The verbal and visual categories of analysis are the 'means'. Therefore I have to establish how well Truffaut realises his aims within the means specified. There are, on the surface, two sets of terms (or variables) to be related: aims and means.

NB. There is a third variable not mentioned in the topic. Which film (or films) are to be considered? If this is not clear from the course itself, a tutor should be consulted. We will assume just one film in what follows.

1.3   The shapes of some possible answers

All

> In film X Truffaut succeeds completely in realising all three aims because he controls the verbal means (to be specified) and the visual means (to be specified) perfectly.

None

> Truffaut fails entirely. In film X he manages to establish no clear connections between any of the three issues because his verbal and visual techniques do not work.

This seems to be an unlikely answer if only because the second question – 'What verbal and visual means does he use to establish these connections?' – assumes that there has been some success. If this case is to be argued, check first with the tutor because it changes the assumptions behind the questions.

Some

The fact that there are three 'aims' and two 'means' to be related gives an extremely large set of possible shapes for an answer. Here is just one fairly obvious approach:

> **Truffaut succeeds well with respect to his first aim because he manages here to integrate both his visual and verbal techniques in order to establish the connections between theatre and politics. However, he is less successful in achieving his second and third aims because, although his visual effects work well (indicate how), the language of the film leaves unclear the precise nature of the connections between the personal and the political on the one hand, and between idealism and pragmatism on the other (indicate how).**

The various permutations on this answer should be reasonably clear. But instead of focusing on the 'aims', an alternative approach might be to organise an answer around 'means'. This would possibly be more difficult in certain respects, but is nevertheless possible. For example:

> **Truffaut is a better film-maker than he is a dramatist. Those connections that lend themselves particularly to visual images are handled better than those which rely more especially on words. The means by which he establishes the connections between more concrete things – theatre and politics, the personal and the political – work well. Idealism and pragmatism are abstractions harder to realise in visual images; and this is where Truffaut is less successful. His language never sufficiently distinguishes between what might just as well be the self-consciously expressed pragmatism of the few and the inadequately articulated idealism of the many.**

Having thought about such possibilities as these, I should need to formulate one of them and put it to the test of further reading and observation.

2   Physical geography

> Uplift and mountain building are of fundamental importance to the origin of landforms. Discuss some of the ideas proposed to account for the existence of mountains, paying particular attention to those which involve the theory of plate tectonics.
>
> Illustrate your answer where possible with reference to Australia, New Zealand and Papua New Guinea.

2.1   The meanings of terms

From John B. Whittow's *Penguin Dictionary of Physical Geography* (1984) comes this information:

> Uplift – movement of the crustal rocks *'en masse* in a vertical or radial direction' at a continental scale.
>
> Mountain building – folding, faulting and thrusting 'during which sediments are buckled and deformed'. Unlike uplift, this is tangential to the earth rather than vertical or radial.
>
> Plate tectonics – the theory, developed in the 1960s, that the earth's crust is constructed of seven major and twelve smaller plates, which are moved about by large-scale thermal convection currents.

2.2   Relationships of meaning between terms

Can uplift and mountain building be considered synonymous for the purposes of this essay? Probably not – see definitions above.

Establish what other 'ideas' besides the plate tectonics theory try to account for mountain building.

Relate the theories ('ideas') to the evidence from Australia, New Zealand and Papua New Guinea. Relate it also to some evidence not from this region. Which idea (or combination of ideas) does this evidence give strongest support to?

2.3   The shapes of some possible answers

All

> Of the various ideas put forward to account for the existence of mountains, plate tectonics has no rival. The evidence from the study of both uplift and mountain building in Australia, New Zealand and Papua New Guinea gives complete support to that from elsewhere in confirming the plate tectonic hypothesis. The reasons are . . .

None

> The evidence from the study of both uplift and mountain building in Australia, New Zealand and Papua New Guinea, like that from elsewhere, offers no support to the ideas of plate tectonics. The things that this theory cannot explain are . . . It is other ideas, namely . . . , that can explain these phenomena.

Some

There are five fairly clear variables to be considered in thinking of possible shapes for a discussion of this topic – plate tectonic theory; other theories; uplift and mountain building; the evidence from Australia, New Zealand and Papua New Guinea (this is a complex variable which it might be possible to break down into a number of 'subvariables', since the geological information on these three countries might not all point to the same conclusions); evidence from other parts of the world. Therefore, like the topic from film studies considered above, there will be many ways in which the variables can, in principle, be combined. Here is just one example of a possible shape for the answer:

Of the ? main theories which attempt to account for uplift and mountain building, plate tectonics is well supported by much of the evidence from Australia, New Zealand and Papua New Guinea. Better than any other idea, plate tectonics explains folding and faulting in mountain formation. However, there are certain significant features of uplift in parts of this region (particularly . . .) which p.t. can account for no better than – and, in certain instances, not quite as well as – the older ideas of . . . There appears to be uplift in other parts of the world which similarly poses difficulties for the p.t. theory. The problem is therefore how to reconcile the inconsistencies between p.t. and other ideas using the evidence on uplift we now have.

3   Media studies

'Audiences are not just a product of technology, but also of social life' (McQuail). Discuss this statement with reference to the ways in which the concepts of audience have changed over time in relation both to technologies and to social institutions.

3.1   The meanings of terms

The three major terms – audiences, technology and social life – are in ordinary everyday use and may not seem problematic. However, the very fact that an issue has been raised about them (i.e. that they are part of an essay topic) alerts us to the likelihood that that there may be more to these terms than meets the eye. With respect to audiences this is confirmed in the second sentence of the topic, which refers to 'concepts of audience' (notice the abstract 'audience' as opposed to the concrete 'audiences' in the quotation from McQuail). We shall therefore have to go looking for differing concepts or theories of audience which, the topic tells us, 'have changed over time'. Similarly, we shall have to be on the lookout for a range of different technologies (plural) which might affect differing conceptions of audience, as well as for differing social institutions.

3.2   Relationships of meaning between terms

The major relationship between the terms which the topic asks us to discuss is that changing concepts of audience are a *product* of both technologies (which presumably have themselves changed over time) and social life and institutions, i.e. technologies and social institutions are in some sense *causes* of changes in the concepts of audience. We are also asked to discuss *the ways* in which the changes have occurred – a 'how' question. This means we shall have to make a judgement about which are the important ways and which the less important. There may also be the issue, contained in McQuail's proposition, of the *relative importance* of technology and social life as causes of these changes in concepts of audience: perhaps the implication is that over time social institutions have become more important than technologies as drivers of change in the concept of audience. This, in such an early stage of our analysis, can be no more than a hypothesis which will need to be tested by our reading.

3.3   The shapes of some possible answers

All

> Changes in the concept of audience can be ascribed wholly to social life and institutions and not at all to technology because of the particular nature of these changes.

None

> Changes in the concept of audience owe nothing to social life and institutions and everything to technology because of the particular nature of these changes.

Given the thrust of the McQuail quotation and the explicit instruction in the rest of the topic, both of these shapes of possible answers seem to go quite beyond the intent of the topic. The topic clearly asks us to accept that both are involved. As with the film studies topic above, should you wish to challenge this, first consult your tutor.

Some

Some concepts of audience (which ones?) have been driven by technology, and some are the product of changes in social life (which ones?).

> The significant changes in the concept of audience in chronological order are . . . The earliest of these were driven more by technological innovations such as . . . , in that these technologies had first to create the modern sense of audience, and social life followed in its footsteps. However, aspects of this social life themselves became institutionalised, and as time went on the dynamics of these institutions began themselves to change our concepts of audience and new technologies were then developed to exploit this.

The decision here has been to try out the idea that the earlier concepts of audience were technology driven, while the more recent ones are the outcome of the realisation that social life and institutions have more effect than previously thought. With a bit of preliminary reading we can put some flesh on this shape, modifying it where necessary. For example:

> The most significant change in the concept of audience was the move from regarding it as a uniform mass, entirely passive in its reception of media productions, to one in which it is conceived as individualist and very active in its response to and demand for media which satisfy its own needs and expectations. The first modern media technologies – radio, cinema and early television – worked on what is widely called the

'hypodermic syringe' model, in which passive audiences were 'injected' with what media producers thought they needed or wanted, the technologies themselves being a one-way transmission device to create a compliant culture. Audiences were seen only in quantitative terms. Early changes to this model, particularly the 'two-step flow' which emphasised the assistance of opinion leaders in moulding audiences, were still basically of this type. But the media culture thus engendered began to take on a life of its own and assert itself as part of the institutionalisation of an individualist culture in social life from the 1960s and 1970s onwards. Concepts of audiences became qualitative, emphasising that not only do individuals exercise choice (the 'uses and gratifications' concept of audience) but also that audiences themselves greatly influence the message and how it is delivered (the 'obstinate audience' concept). It is this that drives the most recent media technologies rather than the reverse.

Remember that the proposals above are not intended to be final answers to the questions contained in these essay topics. They are merely possible shapes for an answer. Where I have lacked the information or an insight into what to say, I have simply left blanks. Where I have filled in these blanks, as in the example immediately above on concepts of audience, I have merely taken a partly informed stab at a possible answer. It might well turn out after further reflection and reading that what I have said about concepts of audience is rather naïve. (I suspect this answer is indeed naïve because something tells me that there are probably more complex interactions between audiences, technology and social life than this proposal allows: the seamless chronological transition from the one to the other seems a bit simplistic.) But, unless I had done this, I would not have had anything of some substance, however inadequate, to begin working on.

Appendix 3

A revised manuscript

INSERT ①

~~In The Tempest~~ Reason is set against 'fury' and nurture against nature. /INSERT ② ~~But the duket~~ Prospero, *the exiled Duke of Milan, though the dominant force in the play,* is not *a* ~~the~~ perfect exemplar of the providential power of reason and nurture, any more than *his slave* Caliban is a savage ruled solely by fury and unregenerate nature. Prospero's *white* magical Art, despite the contrasts he *himself* draws with the *black* magic of 'the foul witch Sycorax', is not a humane kind of learning; for otherwise he would have no cause to renounce it at the end of the play. *His Art is alchemical and redolent of the philosopher's stone.* Nor is it true, as Prospero says of Caliban, that ~~he~~ *the slave* is 'A devil, a born devil, on whose nature / Nurture can never stick'. *(IV, i, 188-9)* Caliban does learn, arguably even more than Prospero, inasmuch as at the end of the play he

~~says~~ *resolves* 'I'll be wise hereafter,/ And seek for grace'/⊙ INSERT③

This is a resolution / which finds no echo in anything Prospero ~~says~~ *promises*./ If we

are to look for a touchstone to knowledge in The

Tempest, it will be found in/ *Prospero's daughter* Miranda, in whom nature

and nurture, reason and passion are perfectly mixed.

INSERT④ *But at the end of it all, she* / ~~Miranda~~ does not/ *actually* know very much ~~at all~~ about the

world/ *⊙* on first seeing/ *the prince* Ferdinand she thinks him,

without any hint of metaphor, a spirit, 'a thing

divine'. *The kind of learning* ~~What~~ she/ displays *does* is ~~something~~ / *a quality* more *vastly*

than anything her father *has actually taught her* — *human* important// a depth of/ understanding or sympathy.

Prospero's learning seems to be of two quite

distinct kinds. Neither *proves to be* ~~is~~ admirable. In recounting

the story of how he was dispossessed of his dukedom,

he boasts to Miranda how

being so reputed

In dignity, and for the liberal Arts

Without a parallel; those being all my study,

The government I cast upon my brother,

And to my state grew stranger, being transported

And rapt in secret studies. (I,ii,72—7)

Prospero's studies were ~~of~~ *in* the seven ~~traditional~~ *Conventional*

liberal arts, and through absorption in them/ *he* forfeited

his power in the state. A duke, *he now realises,* cannot be a pure

scholar or theoretician. These liberal ~~studies~~ ~~were~~ *arts he then replaces with the*

less conventional ~~not the~~ magical Art that he practised*s* on the island.

(*T*he studies were 'secret' only in the sense that they

were private and recondite). / This latter/ *is a* 'so potent

that he makes use of Art' ~~was studied~~ solely for the power it bestowes on

an egocentric Prospero to do violence to nature ('I

INSERT ⑤ (V,i,4ff.)') ⊙ *Learning of this kind is*

have bedimm'd / The noontide sun// ~~and to effect his~~

effected solely for *those who toppled him from his dukedom*

/revenge on ~~other people~~ We notice, *too,* that the volumes

that ~~Prospero~~ *he once* prizes*d* 'above my dukedom' *have* become *whittled down to* a

single 'book' (III,i,94;V,i,57), which ~~he~~ *Prospero* consults/ *as a manual* to

further his/ *experimental* project *with nature and human beings. This handbook* ~~and which~~ he promises to drown

only when he can be sure that he will no longer have

to rely on it. ~~The book to~~ Prospero's *book is Stephano's* ~~is little more~~

~~than the~~ bottle. ~~to the drunken butler Stephano~~

This is something Caliban learns. He knows better
than /Stephano and/ Trinculo that the rebellion /against
[the drunken butler, the equally drunken jester] [all three hatch]
Prospero/ can only succeed if first they burn ~~this~~
[to dispossess him of the island] [the master's]
books/. ~~For~~ Without them, /Prospero is 'but a sot, as I
[W] [Caliban has realised,]
am, nor hath not / One spirit to command'. ~~There is~~ a
[INSERT⑥] [(III, ii, 90-1) Shakespeare draws]
clear parallel between the effect of Stephano's
'celestial liquor' on Caliban and/ Prospero's charms -
[the effect of]
'the ignorant fumes that mantle / Their clearer
reason'/ - on the usurpers ~~he~~ wishes to ~~subdue~~. The
[(V, i, 67-8)] [the duke] [master]
sense of power conferred by the butt of sack is, of

course, illusory; but so is that of Prospero's Art.

Both turn ordinary mortals into 'masters', /a word used
constantly throughout the play// ~~But~~ True learning is
[to suggest at once authority and lack of control]
not a matter of attaining mastery over nature, over
other people or even, through the use of/ reason, over
[cool]
oneself./ ~~This is the point which Gonzalo wishes~~ to
[INSERT⑦ It is Gonzalo who wishes this] [insight]
~~have~~ set down 'With gold on lasting pillars';
[be]

                    in one voyage

Did Claribel her husband find at Tunis,

And Ferdinand, her brother, found a wife

Where he himself was lost, Prospero his dukedom

In a poor isle, and all of us ourselves

When no man was his own. (V,i, 208—13)

Index

Note. Entries in small capitals are used to indicate language functions.